GIFFORD PINCHOT

Bull Moose Progressive

Men and Movements Series

Library of Congress Cataloging in Publication Data

Fausold, Martin L
   Gifford Pinchot.

   (Men and movements series)
   Reprint of the ed. published by Syracuse University
Press, Syracuse, N. Y.
   Bibliography: p.
   1. Pinchot, Gifford, 1865-1946.   I. Series: Men
and movements (Syracuse)
[E664.P62F3 1973]   329'.0092'4 [B]   73-7672
ISBN 0-8371-6943-7

GIFFORD PINCHOT
Bull Moose Progressive

Martin L. Fausold

GREENWOOD PRESS, PUBLISHERS
WESTPORT, CONNECTICUT

This work has been published with the
assistance of a Ford Foundation Grant.

THE author wishes to thank the following publishers for
their kind permission to quote from works held in copyright:

University of Wisconsin Press—Quotations reprinted
with permission of the copyright owners, the Regents of
the University of Wisconsin, from Robert M. La Follette,
*La Follette's Autobiography: A Personal Narrative of
Political Experiences* (Madison, Wis.: Robert M. La Follette Company, 1913).

Viking Press, Inc.—Quotations reprinted from Alpheus
T. Mason, *Bureaucracy Convicts Itself* (New York: Viking
Press, Inc., 1941).

Harcourt, Brace & Company—Quotations reprinted
from Gifford Pinchot, *Breaking New Ground* (New York:
Harcourt, Brace & Company, 1947).

Doubleday & Company, Inc.—Quotations reprinted from
Gifford Pinchot, *The Fight for Conservation* (New York:
Doubleday & Company, Inc., 1910).

Charles Scribner's Sons—Quotations reprinted from
Theodore Roosevelt, *Theodore Roosevelt: An Autobiography* (New York: Charles Scribner's Sons, 1920).

Originally published in 1961
by Syracuse University Press, Syracuse, New York

Reprinted with the permission
of Syracuse University Press

First Greenwood Reprinting 1973

Library of Congress Catalogue Card Number 73-7672

ISBN 0-8371-6943-7

Printed in the United States of America

For Daryl

Preface

THIS VOLUME examines the radicalism of the Progressive years
1910–17 through consideration of the political activities and
thought of Gifford Pinchot, a principal leader of the radical
faction of the Progressive Party. Through his work the author
wishes to promote a better understanding of these activities
and this period. The book is based largely on the voluminous
manuscripts in the Gifford Pinchot Papers and the Amos
Pinchot Papers, which the author examined at length in the
Library of Congress. Citations in the text are from the two
Pinchot collections unless otherwise indicated. Bibliographical
Notes in this volume describe the contents of the Pinchot
manuscript boxes which were used as related to specific portions of chapters. Other collections of manuscripts were examined, as were many newspapers and periodicals of the era.
Numerous books and articles in scholarly journals touching
upon the period were also used.

Many persons at the Maxwell Graduate School of Citizenship and Public Affairs, Syracuse University, and at the Library of Congress have helped me in the preparation of the
book and have earned my deep gratitude. I thank particularly
Professor Marguerite J. Fisher of the Maxwell School for her
generous use of effort and time in reading the manuscript and
for her advice; Professor Stuart Gerry Brown, also of the Maxwell School, for reading parts of the manuscript; and the
several people at the Library of Congress who guided me
through the manuscripts of the two Pinchot collections and
whose aid was inestimable.

Further appreciation is expressed to the Research Foundation of the State University of New York for financial assistance; to Mrs. Amos Pinchot for giving me permission to use her husband's manuscripts; to Dr. Gifford B. Pinchot for permission to use his father's papers; to Mr. S. W. Higgenbotham, Director of the Bureau of Research, Publications, and Records at Pennsylvania Historical and Museum Commission, for his many leads to pertinent sources; and to Professor Walter Harding, State University College of Education, Geneseo, New York, and Professor M. Nelson McGeary, Pennsylvania State University, for reading parts of the manuscript.

Thanks are also expressed to my colleague Professor Morton D. Waimon for his encouragement and to Mrs. Maxine Callan for her pleasant co-operation in the typing of the manuscript. Most importantly, to my wife, Daryl, I express fond appreciation for much work in reading the manuscript and for her understanding and patience.

Any errors in the book are my own responsibility.

MARTIN L. FAUSOLD

State University College of Education
Geneseo, New York
Fall, 1961

Contents

GIFFORD PINCHOT

Bull Moose Progressive

Introduction

AT A FEW minutes past noon on a warm spring day in 1938, I watched Gifford Pinchot, who was seventy-three years old at the time, address an assortment of rural and townspeople, mostly Republicans, from the courthouse steps in Indiana, Pennsylvania. He was seeking his third nomination as Republican candidate for the Governorship of the Commonwealth. Twice before he had been nominated and elected. Characteristically, he ran without "regular" Republican backing. The people listened, farmers and businessmen rather attentively, numerous schoolboys, including the author, not so attentively. The speaker faltered; he was not convincing. The majority of the county's Republicans would not support him and would vote the "good" organization slate.

The Republicans of Indiana County, and of the Commonwealth of Pennsylvania, little realized the historic moment which they were witnessing. A son of the state, who typified the twentieth-century man of American government as few had, was making his last large political effort. With defeat he would enter the eve of his life. Although in subsequent years he retained his interest in state and national politics and in the conservation of natural resources, the public memory of him lost focus.

On October 4, 1946 Gifford Pinchot died and was buried in his beloved Milford in eastern Pennsylvania. His death evoked a considerable amount of comment in the nation's press. Note was made that he was considered by some to be the father of forest conservation in America and that he had been twice elected Governor of Pennsylvania. Recognition was given to his recent work with the President of the United States in planning an international conference on the conservation of natural resources. A few members of the press saw passing from the scene only a politico—in a narrow sense. Indeed, at times Pinchot had been narrowly partisan—violently anti-Republican, anti–United States Steel Corporation, anti-Democratic, and antipacifist.

Unfortunately, the press did not give sufficient consideration to what was probably paramount in Pinchot's life and significantly dominant in the life of modern reform—his peculiar role as a prime mover for positive government in national efforts to conserve natural resources, from 1901 to 1910. Many of this century's concepts of enlarged federal responsibility, vigorous presidential stewardship, and scientific planning in government can be traced to their beginnings in Pinchot's fight for conservation. The press also neglected Gifford Pinchot's role as a leading spokesman for Progressive Party radicalism, from 1910 to 1917. Yet these activities influenced the national political structure and ideology far more than his early forestry activity or his subsequent governing of Pennsylvania. The first two decades of the twentieth century fostered this century's early progressive movement; these years saw the growth of a reform movement in the United States that touched the social, economic, and political aspects of American life at the local, state, and national levels. These were years which reflected discontent with industrial giantism abetted in the late nineteenth century by a spirit of laissez faire and social Darwinism.

Perhaps no American represented the total 1901–17 span of the progressive movement as well as did Gifford Pinchot. As Chief Forester of the United States in the Theodore Roosevelt administrations, he implemented scientific and positive government. As an insurgent Republican and then as a Bull Moose Party leader, he continued his fight for progressivism in the now-almost-unnoticed 1910–17 period. During this period—the latter years of that progressive movement—he affected the vital processes of the national life, adding considerably to its liberal tone: to wit, through his roles in a controversy with Secretary of the Interior Richard Ballinger, that some considered to be a *cause célèbre* of the century's first decade; in the authorship of Theodore Roosevelt's declaration, made at Osawatomie, Kansas in 1910, the most radical speech of any former President; in the formation of the National Progressive Republican League in 1911, the focal point of insurgency in the GOP; in the establishment of the Progressive Party in 1912, which set the liberal tone of that election year; in the struggle to maintain the national and state Progressive Party in 1913; in the United States senatorial campaign in Pennsylvania against Boies Penrose, a 1914 continuation of the great political "crusade" of two years before; in the fight for Progressive Party survival and radicalism during 1915–16, in large part forcing President Woodrow Wilson to a final abandonment of the laissez-faire doctrine and to an espousal of the New Nationalism; and in the demise of the Progressive Party, accompanied, however, by a reiteration of its ideology, in the years 1916–17.

The author hopes that a thorough examination of Gifford Pinchot's political activities during the 1910–17 period will provide a new key to understanding and appreciating the significance of the early progressive movement. To the justification for such a study the following seems to attest: First, Gifford Pinchot transferred the struggle for scientific conservation of natural resources from a government bureau to the national political scene as a great plan to ameliorate man's condition. Thus, two of the twentieth century's significant tenets of federal government—conservation of natural resources and scientific government planning—became firmly imbedded in the American political tradition. Scientific government planning, evolving as a form of positive government enounced in the New Nationalism of 1912, portended the nature of future United States government. In the second place, Pinchot's leadership among Republican insurgents in 1912 largely set the measure of the era's progressivism and paved the way for that election year's great debate of liberals—the Progressive Party's New Nationalism versus the Democrats' New Freedom. Thirdly, Pinchot peculiarly epitomized the radical spirit of the Progressive Party, the movement's culmination. Certainly, no man was more consistently committed to the party, from the formation of its precursor, the National Progressive Republican League, in 1911 to its final surrender to the new issue of the period—the First World War. Finally, Gifford Pinchot's enthusiasm for radical progressivism in the 1910–17 years contributed richly to wedding the liberal cause to twentieth-century America. Although latent in subsequent periods, such liberalism sprang forth to meet perennial crises. In the best tradition of the early progressivism came the Muscle Shoals fight and the McNary-Haugen proposals of the 1920's, the New Deal and the Fair Deal of the 1930's and 1940's, and the New Frontier of John F. Kennedy.

*   *   *

Gifford Pinchot was born on August 11, 1865 at Eaglewood, the "great house" of Simsbury, Connecticut. Simsbury dated from the previous century as a vigorous center of manufacturing and farming activity. The "great house" was the home of

Pinchot's maternal grandfather, Amos Eno, noted New York real-estate builder and operator. Its elegance and amplitude marked the life to which Gifford would always be accustomed. The broad, brick, gambrel-roofed house, with side porches and arched dormer windows, exemplified the prosperity of the Civil War era.

Mary Jane Eno had married James Wallace Pinchot on May 25, 1864. After a five-month honeymoon abroad, they returned to Eaglewood, where their son Gifford was born the following year.

James was the son of Cyril Désiré Constantin Pinchot, a former Napoleonic army captain who came to this country as a young man in 1816. Cyril settled in Milford, Pennsylvania, a village on the Delaware River not far from the Poconos. The young Frenchman fared well, coming to own much land, a lumber business, and a general store. James inherited the Milford property, prospered in the dry-goods business, and later established a well-known New York wallpaper firm, Pinchot and Warren. Although he became a part of New York business and social life, he retained his attachment to Milford. There, overlooking the Delaware Valley, he built "Grey Towers," a Norman manor house designed by Richard Morris Hunt.

During Gifford Pinchot's first six years, his family lived at various places of solid social repute in New York City. For one year it was the Fifth Avenue hotel recently built by his Grandfather Eno. A bold real-estate venture because of the building's remote location, the hotel was known as "Eno's Folly." Soon after its construction, however, it played a conspicuous role in the social and political life of New York. To it the Prince of Wales started a "royal procession" in 1860. It was the headquarters of Republican rule of the state and at times of the nation. Particularly famous was its "Amen Corner," where Republican boss "Tom" Platt made his many "deals."

The young Pinchot family spent some winters at 26 East Twenty-third Street and at 233 Fifth Avenue. At the Fifth Avenue residence, which had originally been bought by Grandfather Eno, Gifford's sister Antoinette ("Nettie") was born on December 30, 1868. In these early years the summers were spent most generally at the "great house" in Simsbury or "Grey Towers" in Milford. However, Gifford later noted in his papers that the summer of 1868, which was unusually pleasant, was spent at Bateman's Hotel in Newport, Rhode Island. Newport was just becoming the summer playground for wealthy northern families, and Mrs. August Belmont and Ward McAllister reigned over elaborate dinners, great breakfasts, and aquatic picnics. Young Master Gifford, however, seldom took part in these functions, for he was too young; he was left in the care of his French nurse, Cécile.

As was fitting for families of their social class, the Pinchots and the Enos made frequent European sojourns. At six years of age, Gifford accompanied his parents on an extended trip to France, by way of Leamington and Warwick, England, arriving at the Hotel Bristol in Paris in September. Strangely enough, the Paris Commune uprising, which had just wrecked 31 public offices and 238 buildings in its seventy-three days of rule, did not in the least discourage the tourists. The older inhabitants marveled at the hordes of Yankees who came to "do" the devastated town. "Really, I never knew Paris so full in the summer," exclaimed the average Parisian. Although the blackened and roofless walls of the Tuileries and other ruined buildings remained for years reminders of the mob rule of 1871, the anesthetized city came to life, suddenly and completely. Not long after the Pinchots' departure in 1874, the Parisians put on their great international exhibit.

France was hardly just a tourist stop for the Pinchots, for Gifford's father was only one generation removed from her soil. For three years the family considered Paris their home, occasionally journeying to French resorts and to Italy and Switzerland. The Pinchot household was established at 6, Rue de Presburg, near the Arc de Triomphe. When necessary, James would return alone to his business in New York. Visitors to the Pinchot ménage in Paris were frequent, among them the Enos and General William Tecumseh Sherman, an old friend of the family. The stay in France was blessed by the birth of Gifford's brother Amos Richard Eno on December 9, 1873. During these years Gifford attended the day school at the Institution J. Baudeux, where he learned to speak French fluently.

In the autumn of 1874 the Pinchots returned to 233 Fifth Avenue in New York, when Gifford was nine years old. He would remember clearly the next few years of his youth: happy Christmases; Gibbons and Beach's private school at Forty-fifth Street and Fifth Avenue; summers at the Milford and Simsbury homesteads; insect collecting under the direction of his governess, Fraulein Eugenie Rausen; the three weeks his mother had to do the cooking because the cook fell ill; the fishing for bigmouthed bass at Camden, South Carolina; the John MacMullen School; a scolding by a Nantucket sea captain for getting outside a ship's bulwark; Bridget the cook's expert preparation of partridge, eggplant, cauliflower, and ducks; and family moves to 18 East Twenty-ninth Street and to 212 Madison Avenue.

Special note must be made of two delightful summers he spent at Saybrook, Connecticut, and one in the Adirondacks. Saybrook had only recently been developed as a restricted seaside resort. Sea breezes, blowing from three points of the compass, kept temperatures below 84 degrees. This pleasant climate was quite in contrast to New York City, or even Simsbury and Milford. The Adirondacks, made famous by Currier and Ives prints, first attracted the Pinchots in the summer of 1879. Gifford notes meeting pleasant people that summer, such as President Noah Porter of Yale and Mr. Paul Smith, the famous proprietor of the hotel on St. Regis Lake. More importantly, Gifford's attachment to the forests must have begun during this period. Camping became a delight for Gifford, and his first pin-fire shotgun became a treasure. That summer his father gave him his first rod and taught him to cast.

Gifford attended Phillips Exeter Academy, as was expected of the son of a very well-established New York businessman, philanthropist, and connoisseur. After Exeter, Gifford went off to college at New Haven, Connecticut, where a great-grandfather, numerous uncles, and a cousin had preceded him.

Gifford's father, always close to the wooded estate at Milford, suggested the study of forestry to his son. Gifford gladly followed the suggestion, giving up the idea of medicine or the ministry. There was, however, no forestry school at Yale—or anywhere in the country.

"Whoever turned his mind toward Forestry in those days," wrote Gifford in *Breaking New Ground*, "thought little about the forest itself and more about its influences on rainfall first of all." Pinchot continued:

> So I took a course in meteorology, which has to do with the vegetable kingdom—trees are unquestionably vegetable. And another in geology, for forests grew out of the earth. Also, I took a course in astronomy, for it is the sun which makes trees grow. All of which was as it should be, because science underlies the forester's knowledge of the woods. So far I was headed right.

Pinchot enjoyed life at Yale. Many engagements frequently overshadowed his study of forestry: class deacon, class committees, athletics, contributions to the *Yale Literary Magazine,* the Grand Street Mission, and "a thousand other matters." His laissez-faire economic views were in accord with those of his young blue-blooded peers: "The railroads own the tracks and the cars, don't they? Then why shouldn't they charge what they please?" [1]

During the winter of his senior year Pinchot traveled to Washington to talk to government forest authorities about the prospects for his profession. There, Dr. Bernhard E. Fernow, a trained forester and Chief of the Forestry Division, suggested that Gifford so direct his "studies that they will be useful in other directions also." [2] Others were also discouraging, but Pinchot persevered. He pursued forestry study farther in Europe, mostly at the École nationale forestière at Nancy, France. There, lectures, books, walks, and discussion with foresters were invaluable to his professional education. Of particular influence was Sir Dietrich Brandis, of Bonn, Germany, founder of forestry in British India. Pinchot would never lose touch with Brandis, consulting and visiting with him frequently in later years.

In late 1890 Pinchot returned home, the first native American professional forester. Immediately, he was struck by gigantic waste in American forests. Such waste was magnified by his having known almost nothing about American forest conditions before going to Europe. Whereas Europeans made use of scraps down to pencil size, Americans burned piles of logs to get rid of them. The richest American timberlands could

[1] Quoted in Gifford Pinchot, *Breaking New Ground* (New York: Harcourt, Brace & Company, 1947), p. 4.

[2] Quoted in *ibid.,* p. 5.

be bought for $2.50 an acre. Millions of acres were given as grants to railroads. The Northern Pacific received lands whose area was more than the combined area of Pennsylvania, New Jersey, Rhode Island, and the District of Columbia. Most frequently, when timber was needed it was stolen. Much of the timberland had been ravaged by fires at one time or another.

Pinchot's task as a forester took many directions. Traveling was essential. He readily heeded General Sherman's advice that he see at first hand American forest conditions. An early opportunity came when Dr. Fernow asked Pinchot to accompany him to inspect some hardwood timber in Arkansas. Although grateful to Fernow for the opportunity of seeing the great western forests, an important side development of their trip was the incompatibility of their dispositions—a condition never resolved. It was difficult for Pinchot to erase a prejudice. He felt Fernow preached too much and downgraded too many people.

Much of the forester's time was devoted to writing, speaking, reading papers before professional groups, and, most importantly, putting out a shingle as a practicing and consulting forester. His first professional opportunity came in February of 1892, when George W. Vanderbilt hired him to employ practical forest management on his seven thousand–acre Biltmore estate near Asheville, North Carolina. Pinchot preferred this position to one as Fernow's assistant in the Division of Forestry. Through forest planning, improvement of cutting, controlling of forest fires, and restriction of cattle grazing, Pinchot made practical forestry pay at Biltmore. Frequently, he turned to his European teachers, especially Dr. Brandis, for advice.

In December of 1893 Pinchot, anxious for fresh fields, opened an office in the United Charities Building on Fourth Avenue at Twenty-second Street, New York City. While in the city he became an active member of the University Settlement on Delancey Street. As the settlement demonstrated that human beings, like forests, are sometimes exploited, his original conservative ideas changed greatly. From the New York office his forestry duties continued to be quite varied. He wrote *The White Pine,* practiced forest management on private estates such as the forty thousand–acre Ne-Ha-Sa-Ne Park in the Adirondacks, and served as consulting forester for the state of New Jersey.

By 1895 Pinchot was well established as a forester. The client he sought most, however, was the most evasive—the United States government. As yet there was not a single acre of government timberland under systematic forest management. Furthermore, the prospect of federal legislation supporting such management was meager. The Homestead Act of 1862, the Mineral Land Act of 1866, the Desert Land Act of 1877, and the Timber and Stone Act of 1878 were greatly abused. For example, the Timber and Stone Act made possible the purchase of land by trainloads of vacationing schoolteachers who immediately transferred their titles to lumber companies. This act did not provide for Forest Reserve or forestry practice. An important act passed in 1891 did, however, authorize the creation of Reserves.

In 1896 Pinchot was the only forester on a commission appointed by the National Academy of Sciences, at the request of the Secretary of the Interior, to conceive and report on a plan for a national forest policy. Interestingly, Fernow disapproved the commission's assignment, for his division and the Department of the Interior had been evolving such a plan since 1886. President Grover Cleveland urged that the commission take up the problem of a forest service before recommending the establishment of additional Forest Reserves. To

Pinchot's disgust, the commission ignored the plea, failing to see that use of forests and protection of forests went hand in hand. In 1897, on the commission's recommendation, the President did withdraw 21,279,840 acres of government timberland to be added to the existing 17,564,800 acres of Forest Reserves. By the time William McKinley became President the commission had finally recommended a policy for forest protection. An amendment to the Sundry Civil Act of June 4, 1897 did open the forests to use and administration. The Secretary of the Interior was to "insure the objects of such reservations, namely, to regulate their occupancy and use and to preserve the forests therein from destruction." [3]

On the day after the amendment to the Sundry Civil Act was passed, Secretary of the Interior Cornelius Newton Bliss asked Pinchot to make an examination of and report on the Reserves as a Special Agent of the Land Office. Pinchot has stated in *Breaking New Ground:*

> I was to examine and report upon the suspended Reserves, their condition and needs, their forests, and their relations to lumbering, agriculture, mining, grazing, commerce, and settlement. I was to draw up a set of principles to govern future increase . . . in the Reserves. . . . Finally, I was to report a practicable plan for the establishment of a Forest Service, with specific recommendations for individual Reserves—recommendations which the report of the Commission had not contained.

Pinchot's assignment portended his appointment as chief of the Division of Forestry in the Department of Agriculture. On July 1, 1898 he succeeded Fernow, who "jumped the gun" by joining the faculty of the new forestry school at Cornell. Secre-

[3] Quoted in *ibid.,* p. 117.

tary of Agriculture James Wilson had decided to ask for Fernow's resignation, for the "old" division was not helping practical forestry in the United States. However, Mrs. Fernow, wife of the former Forestry Chief, has insisted that "Forestry stood firmly on its feet and a comfortable position was ready for Mr. Pinchot." [4] The former point is probably the more accurate. Pinchot took over Fernow's position after the Secretary of Agriculture assured him a free hand—an assurance which was fulfilled.

By 1898 Pinchot knew his way around Washington. He had met two Presidents on a working basis, conferred frequently with congressional and administration leaders on land and forestry legislation, and constructed legislation for congressional action. He delighted in his new title, Chief Forester of the United States. It distinguished him from his peers, who were known as division heads.

In rather quick order Pinchot knew his way around his new division. Certainly, he demonstrated rare ability as an administrator; to this most government personnel testified, including Fernow and his biographer, Andrew Denny Rodgers III. The division rigorously studied the silvics of the nation's trees, the relation of forests to stream flow, water supply, evaporation, erosion and irrigation, and forest fires and their history; advanced tree planting; and laid the foundation for regulation of grazing in the Reserves. Much success was attributed to the division's publicity and recruitment programs.

Pinchot was quick to see obstacles and just as quick to try to eliminate them, sometimes rather ruthlessly. One such obstacle was the Interior Department's control of the Forest

[4] Quoted in Andrew Denny Rodgers III, *Bernhard Edward Fernow: A Story of North American Forestry* (Princeton, N.J.: Princeton University Press, 1951), p. 243.

Reserves. He felt that the Interior Department's Public Land Office, which had broad powers over the Forest Reserves, was politics ridden and incompetent and had earned the contempt of the hard-bitten Westerners it generally dealt with. Pinchot launched a campaign to transfer the Forest Reserves to the Department of Agriculture.

Theodore Roosevelt's fortuitous ascending to the Presidency was a happy omen for the Division of Forestry. No mean outdoorsman himself, T.R. was already kindly disposed to vigorous forestry practice. As Governor of New York he called upon Pinchot to help the state put scientific forestry principles into effect. Their relationship was more than professional. Both were in the *noblesse oblige* tradition and loved the vigorous life. When Pinchot was in Albany to consult with Roosevelt, they worked out in the Executive Mansion. They were well matched in both boxing and wrestling.

In his first Presidential message to the Congress, Theodore Roosevelt accepted substantially what Pinchot had written in regard to foresty policy. The message made forestry a great national issue and, almost as important, called for transferring various governmental forestry functions to the Bureau of Forestry [5]—specifically, those which were administered by the General Land Office.

The transfer of the Forest Reserves from the General Land Office was slow in materializing. Even the President found it politic to go along temporarily with the contention that Pinchot could carry out his work concerning the Forest Reserves just as effectively from his bureau in the Agriculture Department. The Chief Forester was somewhat mollified by his additional assignment as Forester of the Interior Department, but the assignment was meaningless. Pinchot became incensed; he knew

[5] The Forestry Division became a bureau on July 1, 1901.

his influence over forestry practice in the Forest Reserves necessitated their transfer to his bureau and worked toward this goal at every chance.

Despite the years it took to effect the transfer and its large attendant responsibility and prestige, Pinchot was a power early in the administration. He was more than the Chief Forester of the United States and a member of the Tennis Cabinet. He became closely identified with the great commissions of the administration. In 1903 he originated, suggested to the President, selected the personnel for, planned the work of, and, as secretary of the commission, organized the investigation conducted by the Commission on the Organization of Government Scientific Work. In the same year he was the guiding force behind the Commission on Public Lands. As he hoped, this commission pointed up the need for the transfer and added pressure for it. Two years later Pinchot played an equally prominent role as a member of the Commission on Department Methods, known as the Keep Commission.

The final impetus which drove the transfer through the Congress was a series of resolutions passed by the American Forest Congress, called into session on January 2–6, 1905 by the American Forestry Association. Most of the actual planning was done by the Bureau of Forestry. Reflecting pressures from the Pennsylvania and Northern Pacific railroads; the National Lumber Manufacturing, Live Stock, and Irrigation Association; the United States Geological Survey; the United States Reclamation Agency; and the General Land Office and a substantial membership of the Senate and the House of Representatives, the resolutions not only called for the transfer but also favored the purchase of Forest Reserves in the east, the repeal of the Timber and Stone Act, and the amendment of the Lieu-Land Law. The Lieu-Land Law had permitted settlers and miners to make lieu selections, releasing to the United States millions of acres of worthless land in exchange for valuable land. In less than one month the United States Congress finally succumbed, transferring the National Forests to the Department of Agriculture, implicitly to the Bureau of Forestry, recreated in the form of the United States Forest Service. Western and States-rights opposition also failed to stop legislation authorizing the Forest Service to make arrests, providing the Forest Service with appropriations by permitting use of its own income, and eliminating the pernicious lieu-land exchange.

Secretary of Agriculture Wilson's instructions to the Forest Service, written by Pinchot himself, established important precedents for governing the eighty-six million acres of public Forest Reserves. The great Reserves were to be unlocked and opened to use. The service was instructed to see that water, wood, and forage were conserved and used wisely by both home builders and industrialists. A portent of the TVA decentralization concept was expressed in the instructions' conclusion: "In the management of each reserve local questions will be decided upon local grounds." [6]

That Pinchot followed the instructions soon became apparent. The preface to the new forestry bible, *The Use of the National Forest Reserves,* announced the new policy: "The timber, water, pasture, mineral, and other resources of the forest reserves are for the use of the people. They may be obtained under reasonable conditions without delay. Legitimate improvements and business enterprises will be encouraged." [7]

The new United States Forest Service, a model of efficiency

[6] Quoted in Pinchot, *Breaking New Ground,* p. 261.
[7] Quoted in *ibid.,* p. 266.

and high morale, was, in general, a catalyst to the federal government. Many factors, some interrelated, tell the Forest Service story: good administration at the top; real authority mandated by law; the delegation of actual responsibility down the line; the availability of large sums of money; a good press; and Presidential backing.

Pinchot was already close to the President, and the success of the service enhanced even more the Chief Forester's administrative and ideological entrenchment in the inner circles of government. Administratively, the President had, by 1909, increased the National Forests to 194 million acres and fought for the necessary personnel and funds to administer them. Ideologically, the President had utilized the Forest Service idea that the Executive is the steward of the public welfare.

The principle of stewardship had significant implications as related to many other aspects of public policy. Theodore Roosevelt illustrated this in his autobiography:

Until the Forest Service changed the plan, waterpowers on the navigable streams, on the public domain, and in the National Forests were given away for nothing, and substantially without question, to whoever asked for them. At last, under the principle that public property should be paid for and should not be permanently granted away when such permanent grant is avoidable, the Forest Service established the policy of regulating the use of power in the National Forests in the public interest and making a charge for value received. This was the beginning of the water policy now substantially accepted by the public. . . .

Pinchot's responsibility in the Forest Service brought him into contact with government agencies dealing with many natural resources. The National Forests were certainly related to stream and inland waterways, to the soil and its condition, to the minerals, and to fish and game; but only in the winter of 1907 did the Chief Forester see the essential unity of the several resources. Pinchot recounts the experience in *Breaking New Ground:*

> To me, it was a good deal like coming out of a dark tunnel. I had been seeing one spot of light ahead. Here, all of a sudden, was a whole landscape. Or it was like lifting a curtain on a great new state.
>
> There was too much of it for me to take in all at once. As always, my mind worked slowly. From the first I thought I had stumbled on something really worthwhile, but that day in Rock Creek Park I was far from grasping the full reach and swing of the new idea.
>
> It took time for me to appreciate that here were the makings of a new policy, not merely nationwide but worldwide in its scope—fundamentally important because it involved not only the welfare but the very existence of men on the earth. I did see, however, that something ought to be done about it.
>
> . . . So far as I knew then or have since been able to find out, it had occurred to nobody, in this country or abroad, that there was one question instead of many, one gigantic single problem that must be solved if the generations, as they came and went, were to live civilized, happy, useful lives in the lands which the Lord their God had given them.

"Conservation" was the word Pinchot applied to his thought— more specifically, "conservation of natural resources." Pinchot took his concept to his faithful assistant, Overton Price; to his father and mother; to Dr. W. J. McGee, the head of the Bureau of American Ethnology; and to Senator Albert J. Beveridge, of Indiana. Then he took it to the President: "And T.R., as I expected, understood, accepted, adopted it without the smallest hesitation. It was directly in line with everything he has been thinking and doing. It became the head of his Administration." [8]

The epitome of Pinchot's responsibilities in the Roosevelt administration was reached in 1908, when he served as chairman of the National Conservation Commission. The commission's task "was to prepare an inventory, the first ever made for any nation, of all the natural resources which underlay its property. The making of this inventory was made possible by an Executive order which placed the resources of the Government Departments at the command of the Commission, and made possible the organization of subsidiary committees by which the actual facts for the inventory were prepared." [9]

On January 22, 1909 Roosevelt transmitted the report of the National Conservation Commission to Congress, describing it as "one of the most fundamentally important documents ever laid before the American people." [10] Two months later, when Roosevelt left his high office, he wrote to Pinchot:

Dear Gifford:

I have written you about others; I have written you about many public matters; now, just a line about yourself. As long as I live I shall feel for you a mixture of respect and admiration and of affectionate regard. I am a better man for having known you. I feel that to have been with you will make my children better men and women in after life; and I cannot think of a man in the country whose loss would be

[8] *Ibid.*, p. 326.
[9] Theodore Roosevelt, *Theodore Roosevelt: An Autobiography* (New York: Charles Scribner's Sons, 1920), p. 409.
[10] Quoted in *ibid.*, p. 410.

more real misfortune to the Nation than yours would be. For seven and a half years we have worked together, and now and then played together—and have been altogether better able to work because we have played; and I owe you a peculiar debt of obligation for a very large part of the achievement of this Administration. With love to your dear mother, I am,

Ever faithfully your friend,
Theodore Roosevelt [11]

Pinchot stayed on as Chief Forester of the United States in the Taft administration. The tenure, however, was abruptly terminated by the Ballinger-Pinchot affair. In more ways than one, Pinchot's leave-taking from federal service marked the commencement of his political career rather than its termination. Roosevelt's Osawatomie address, to follow shortly, demonstrated a vigorous political and ideological activity on Pinchot's part. Indeed, he had come half circle. Raised by governesses and exposed to Darwinism at Exeter and Yale, he had come, after a decade of struggle for positive government, into open battle for political radicalism.

[11] Quoted in Pinchot, *Breaking New Ground*, pp. 380–81.

CHAPTER I

The Stage

THEODORE ROOSEVELT had qualms about a dedicatory speech that he was to deliver at the John Brown State Park, Osawatomie, Kansas on August 31, 1910, during a thirty-one day western swing. Concerning the text of this speech, he wrote to Pinchot: "To go on behalf of the people much further than the people want is considerably worse than useless." Because the former Chief Forester of the United States largely wrote the speech, he had no such qualms. Pinchot replied confidently to the former President: "There is at least equal danger of going ahead slower than public opinion." On the day after the speech, Gifford's brother Amos wrote excitedly to his mother: "T.R. seems to have delivered the Osawatomie speech exactly as Gifford wrote it."

Thus Theodore Roosevelt and Gifford Pinchot embarked upon one of the most inspired political crusades in American history. Two years later it would reach its high-water mark in the fierce three-sided race for the Presidency. Under the banner of the national Progressive Party, Roosevelt would drive his New Nationalism against Woodrow Wilson's New Freedom. Although as a third party the Progressive Party's precedent-shattering second place in the election boded well for its future success, unfortunately, the party's four-year existence

21

was a losing battle for survival. It would not die, however, without leaving an indelible imprint upon America.

The Osawatomie speech,[1] in which Roosevelt defined the New Nationalism, was probably the most radical speech ever made by a former President. It extended the executive steward-ship and government planning concepts of Roosevelt's Presi-dency by demanding more central authority to regulate the so-ciety for the benefit of the people and to protect society from wealthy special interest groups. The influence of Herbert Croly's *The Promise of American Life,* published during the previous year, was apparent. To his Kansas audience Roosevelt advocated the graduated income and inheritance taxes, a re-vision of the tariff, regulation of child and female labor, strengthening of the Bureau of Corporations and the Inter-state Commerce Commission, and, of course, extended con-servation of natural resources.

The interpretations of the purpose of Roosevelt's radicalism expressed at Osawatomie are varied: to unite a disintegrating Republican Party, to appeal to his audience of disgruntled Westerners, to disassociate himself from the apparently con-servative President William Howard Taft, to capture the po-litical limelight, to defer to his immediate coterie of advisers. The latter interpretation is as plausible as any. In this respect Pinchot's radical influence in 1910, as well as in the preceding decade, has not been fully appreciated.

Pinchot had the confidence of the former President. For eight years he had been a very powerful person in the Roosevelt administration; he had been a White House intimate—a mem-ber of the Tennis Cabinet. His policies concerning conservation

---

[1] Quoted in Theodore Roosevelt, *The Works of Theodore Roosevelt* (national ed.; 20 vols.; New York: Charles Scribner's Sons, 1926).

of natural resources had been fundamentally one of the Roosevelt administration's first responsibilities. They had breathed the spirit of executive stewardship and government planning into the Presidency. Professor Henry Steele Commager, in his *The American Mind,* states that the beginning of scientific government planning "may be traced to the various conservation boards and conferences of the Theodore Roosevelt administration."

Although Roosevelt did not reciprocate the almost fetishistic worship Pinchot showered upon him, he admired Pinchot greatly. Had he been elected President in 1912, perhaps he would have considered giving Pinchot the first cabinet position—that of Secretary of State. T.R. had considered Pinchot as the high-ranking official of his own administration. For posterity, he would note in his autobiography:

> Taking into account the varied nature of the work he [Pinchot] did, its vital importance to the nation and the fact that as regards most of it he was practically breaking new ground, and taking into account also his tireless energy and activity, his fearlessness, his complete disinterestedness, his single-minded devotion to the interests of the plain people, and his extraordinary efficiency, I believe it is but just to say that among the many public officials who under my administration rendered literally invaluable service to the people of the United States, he, on the whole, stood first.

*   *   *

As Roosevelt delivered the speech at Osawatomie, William Howard Taft sat in the White House. Two years previously Roosevelt had put him there, steam-rolling him through the Republican Convention of 1908 and recommending him to the electorate. Taft had been a faithful public servant in various capacities during practically all of T.R.'s seven-year reign. He was a progressive, and it was expected that he would carry on in the Roosevelt tradition. Unfortunately, his political ineptitudes overshadowed much in his administration which was progressive. The strengthening of the Interstate Commerce Commission, the vigorous enforcement of the antitrust laws, and the establishment of the Postal Savings Bank were certainly in the progressive tradition. In addition, he asked the Congress for much progressive legislation which was not granted. However, Taft received little credit for such progressivism; his political bungling proved devastating. In the summer of 1910, two instances were fresh in the American mind.

On September 18, 1909 Taft delivered a hastily dictated speech in Winona, Minnesota. Unfortunately, he used the superlative rather than the comparative in describing the recently passed Payne-Aldrich Tariff as the best tariff that the Republican Party had ever enacted. To many Americans his speech was a betrayal. The tariff was the highest in history. The laborers, the white-collar workers, the farmers, and the tenement dwellers, already burdened by a rising cost of living, were incensed. The President had campaigned in 1908 to revise the tariff. He had called a special session of Congress to fulfill that pledge. Taft had managed to convince himself that the downward revisions of the Payne-Aldrich Tariff, while less numerous than the upward, concerned the important items which most affected the cost of living. Also, he was quite partial to the provision in the bill that provided for an impartial commission to establish future rate making on a scientific basis. An insurgent element in the Republican Party, however, read Taft's Winona remarks as anti-Rooseveltian.

As certain party members were furiously contesting the

tariff in the early autumn of 1909, their anti-Roosevelt charge seemed to be confirmed by another political explosion—the Ballinger-Pinchot affair. This incident catapulted a leader into their midst; before the dispute was over, thirty newspaper editors would wish Gifford Pinchot to be elected the next President of the United States.

The Ballinger-Pinchot affair involved a dispute over certain Alaskan coal claims. Implicitly at stake was the principal legacy of the Roosevelt administration—the conservation of natural resources.

Louis Glavis, a youthful Interior Department land inspector in Alaska, suspected Richard Ballinger, Secretary of the Interior, of collusion. Glavis' knowledge of certain of the secretary's actions, before and during his tenure in the President's cabinet, convinced him that Ballinger fraudulently cleared valuable Alaskan coal lands for purchase by thirty-three claimants represented by a Clarence Cunningham and a Morgan-Guggenheim syndicate. Feeling hemmed in by superiors unsympathetic to his cause, Glavis went to the Chief Forester. Impressed by the whole story and suspicious that the Taft administration was less committed to conservation than Roosevelt had been, Pinchot gave the agent a strong letter of introduction to the President. Although the Chief Forester was not the power in the administration that he had been in Roosevelt's day, he was sufficiently well placed socially and politically to assure Glavis an audience with the President. It should also be noted that Pinchot's Forest Service aided Glavis in preparing the charge to be presented to Taft. President Taft received Glavis at his summer home in Beverly, Massachusetts, on August 19, 1909, and shortly thereafter he consulted with Ballinger, Oscar Lawler, the Assistant Attorney General for the Interior Department, and George Wickersham, the Attorney General. After examining their reports, Taft became convinced that Glavis' charges embraced only shreds of evidence. On September 13, as he wound up his vacation, the President unhesitatingly exonerated his Interior Secretary, authorizing him to dismiss Glavis. Ballinger happily responded to the authorization.

Almost immediately, Taft wrote to Pinchot, pleading with him not to make Glavis' cause his own. The President apparently anticipated the sorry consequences which followed: "I am convinced," he wrote his brother Horace, "that Pinchot with his fanaticism and his disappointment at my decision in the Ballinger case plans a coup by which I shall be compelled to dismiss him and he will be able to make out a martyrdom and try to raise opposition to me on Ballinger's account." [2] The President's prophecy was fulfilled. In spite of attempts to appease the Chief Forester, Pinchot did make Glavis' cause his own, and not "under a bushel." In a letter to Senator Jonathan Dolliver of Iowa, which was read on the floor of the Senate, Pinchot admitted that his Forest Service had aided Glavis in taking his case to the President and subsequently to the press. Fearfully, Taft removed Pinchot. In classic understatement, he observed: "I would not have . . . if I could have helped it." [3] The Chief Forester was not distressed by the action.

Pinchot's dismissal and an explosive exposé by Glavis in the muckraking *Collier's Weekly* precipitated a congressional resolution calling for a thorough investigation of the affair by a joint committee. Ever mindful of the power of the press, Pinchot confidently anticipated the public review—if not for

[2] Quoted in Henry F. Pringle, *The Life and Times of William Howard Taft* (New York: Farrar and Rinehart, 1939), p. 492.
[3] Quoted in *ibid.*, p. 509.

himself, for his conservation policies, the threat to which he considered the "most critical and far reaching problem . . . since the Civil War." [4]

As Pinchot anticipated, his prestige and that of his cause rose to a new height with the investigation, even though his performance as a witness was rather ineffective. On the stand he admitted mistakes and frequently lacked evidence to support his adamant assertions. His differences with Ballinger on policy and legality made poor testimony under cross-examination, except, of course, in the eyes of a female contingent in the audience which was headed by his mother. It was Louis Brandeis of Boston, "the peoples' attorney," who brought the "prosecution" through. As Glavis' counsel he completely dominated the scene.

Brandeis' success was not based on the fraudulency of land claims. Indeed, that accusation might well have been dismissed on the basis of differing legal interpretations. Rather, the future Supreme Court Justice exposed the apparently devious behavior of administration officers and their sympathetic majority on the committee. In appealing to the higher court of public opinion, Brandeis' vigorous cross-examination showed them frequently objecting, denying, and evading. On two occasions the public became particularly distressed.

First, Counsel Brandeis was able to prove that the President of the United States had predated an important document submitted to the committee. Early in the investigation Brandeis was struck by the size of the Attorney General's "Summary and Report" which had allegedly premised the President's September 13 exoneration of Ballinger. Contrary to the ad-

[4] Quoted in *ibid.*, p. 507.

ministration's insistence, Brandeis did not believe that the eighty-seven–page report, based on the analysis of voluminous material, could have been constructed in the five-day period between September 6, the date on which Ballinger supposedly turned over to Taft and Wickersham the mountain of data, and September 11, the date of Wickersham's report to the President. After considerable cross-examination of administration witnesses, Brandeis forced the President into admitting that the report was predated. Such a confession at a late stage in the investigation made it appear that the President had misled the public into believing that he had given more consideration to the Ballinger exoneration than really was the case.

Second, Brandeis demonstrated that the letter of exoneration which Taft sent to Ballinger had not been written by the President but by the Assistant Attorney General for the Interior Department, a close Ballinger associate. The authorship of this "Lawler Memorandum" was brought to light when Frederick M. Kerby, a Ballinger stenographer, voluntarily described to the press its secret construction in the Interior Department before it was taken to the President. The fact that the memorandum was withheld from the committee was also damaging to the administration.

The vocal verdict of the public, preceding that of the committee, favored Pinchot and Glavis. The committee, however, sustained Ballinger in a seven-to-five partisan vote. Had the administration been forthright about the predating of the Wickersham report and the ghostwriting of the President's letter, the public might well have turned in its favor. However, the administration leaders and the standpat majority on the committee faltered; they seemed to be hiding something. As stated in a political adage, "The appearance of evil, in public life, is often worse than the evil itself and the explanations are invariably futile." Interestingly, the same committee which exonerated Ballinger accepted most of Pinchot's recommendations for handling the Alaskan lands: that the government not sell the land; that the government lease the land at fair royalties for limited periods; and that the validity of the Cunningham claims be determined by an appropriate court of the United States.

Gifford Pinchot emerged from the great investigation as an undisputed leader of the Roosevelt progressives. To say, however, that such a role was purely manipulated by Pinchot or that it was attributable to Brandeis' cleverness is to miss an important point. Pinchot's role evolved more from his defense of specific conservation policies and the philosophy underlying them. The Roosevelt administration's method of conserving natural resources varied considerably from that of the Taft administration. The actual success of conservation was in direct proportion to the method. Pinchot and Roosevelt fought hard for legislation implementing scientific conservation. On occasion they carried out a stewardship role by withdrawing land from public sale by Executive order. Both actions were marks of a positive state. There is little evidence that the total lands added to the Forest Reserves in the Taft administration were comparable in area to those added during the Roosevelt Presidency. In regard to withdrawal of land from public sale by Executive order, Secretary Ballinger considered such action illegal. Both he and Taft felt that only Congress could enact such withdrawals.

The result of the difference in methods of withdrawal employed by the two administrations was considerably more significant than the change in procedure might indicate. Congress had frequently shown great unwillingness to withdraw land from public sale. Since, in the Taft administration, only the Legislature had power to take such action, withdrawals of additional lands were much less frequent than had been the case in Roosevelt's Presidency. Taft's harsh criticism of Pinchot's and Roosevelt's conservation methods led to suspicions that the end as well as the means was being questioned. "Gifford Pinchot," the President wrote to his brother, "is quite likely to get some transcendentalist who hasn't any knowledge of the law, but who has commended himself in some way, because of some particular view that he has on a matter of sociology or political economy." [5] In more cynical tone he wrote: "Gifford Pinchot is out again defying the lightning and the storm and championing the cause of the oppressed and downtrodden and harassing the wealthy and the greedy and the dishonest." [6] On another occasion he referred to certain of Pinchot's views as being "of lunar character." Taft saw Roosevelt in much the same light: "They both have more of a socialist tendency." [7]

One of the many consequences of the Ballinger-Pinchot affair was the identification of conservation with democracy. Professor Alpheus T. Mason's conclusion in his analysis of the affair, *Bureaucracy Convicts Itself,* is most succinct:

> Democracy becomes reality only as the potential capacities of all men, wherever found and of whatever class, are fully realized and made available, utilized, for the betterment of society as a whole. So regarded, conservation and democracy were, and are, one and inseparable. Just as conservation, in essence, means taking care of things public for public benefit,

[5] Quoted in *ibid.,* p. 479.
[6] Quoted in *ibid.,* p. 506.
[7] Quoted in *ibid.,* p. 492.

preserving them so that the people may have and enjoy them, so also the aim of democracy is that all men, so far as is humanly possible, shall have equality of opportunity, that crippling differences to which men elsewhere have been artificially subjected shall not prevail here.

Against this backdrop Pinchot was ready to move his fight for progressivism from the Forest Service into the national political arena.

CHAPTER II

Enter Politician

THE YEAR 1910 was important for Gifford Pinchot; he accepted the calling of partisan politics. Before the end of the year he was immersed in a great political struggle. For Pinchot, it was a new phase in progressivism—as fervently pursued as that of scientific conservation of natural resources.

About one week prior to his January 7 dismissal, Pinchot defended his position in a letter to Roosevelt, who was currently hunting game in Africa. "In my judgment," Pinchot wrote, "the tendency of the Administration thus far, taken as a whole, has been directly away from the Roosevelt policies." Cautiously, he admitted that the people's interest might yet be recognized by the Taft administration, but he believed that "special interests" were once more in control. The Chief Forester was very careful not to accuse Taft of "deliberate bad faith." Rather, he indicated that conditions were due to "a most surprising weakness and indecision" and to Taft's desire to act as a judge and not as a President.[1] Then, continuing

---

[1] Before assuming appointive office in the Roosevelt administration, Taft held the following judicial offices: Judge, Ohio Superior Court (1887–90); U.S. Solicitor General (1890–92); U.S. Circuit Court Judge (1892–1900).

in his letter, Pinchot seemed to drop the rapier and pick up the sledge hammer. He listed the following evidences of Taft's abandonment of the Roosevelt policies:

1. He permitted himself . . . to be surrounded by a circle of Trust attorneys and other reactionaries. . . .

2. He allowed the attacks upon yourself in Congress. . . .

3. He surrendered to Congress in its attack upon the Executive's power to appoint advisory commissions. . . . Thus he seriously retarded the practical progress of the conservation movement.

4. He surrounded himself . . . by corporation lawyers who were necessarily in opposition to the Roosevelt policies.

5. He affiliated himself in Congress with the leaders of the opposititon to the Roosevelt policies. . . .

6. He established, by his appointments . . . a vicious political atmosphere in his Administration, and revived the spoils system. . . .

7. By the appointment of Secretary Ballinger he brought about the most dangerous attack yet made upon the conservation policies. . . .

8. He failed during the course of the tariff debate to support the Insurgent Republicans. . . .

9. He signed and now defends a tariff bill made by and for the special interests. . . .

10. He indorsed . . . the most conspicuous representative reaction and special interests in the Senate.

11. He indorsed, in his Winona speech, in the person of Mr. Tawney, your bitterest enemy in the House of Representatives. . . .[2]

12. In the same speech at Winona he tried to read out of

[2] James A. Tawney of Minnesota.

the party, Senators Nelson, Beveridge, and Cummins. . . .[3]

13. He had repeatedly set party solidarity above the public welfare, and has yielded to political expediency of the lowest type. . . .

14. He has apparently impaired or abandoned . . . the principles which you established of Federal regulation and control, in the public interest, of water powers on navigable streams.

15. He is placing or has placed himself in a position such that the only alliance open to him is with the special interests.

16. He has allowed the great mass of the people to lose confidence in the President.

The Chief Forester concluded by writing that he had liked Taft, that he had been anxious to help the President, and that he would continue to help as long as Taft was loyal to the American people. Pinchot then questioned whether or not the President was loyal: "The line between the friends of special privilege and the friends of equal chance is daily growing sharper . . . [and] the hold of your policies on the plain people is stronger than ever."

To Pinchot's list of grievances Roosevelt would soon add the removal of the "first public official" of his own administration. Pinchot undoubtedly hoped his dismissal would tip the scales and bring the former President into the growing camp of insurgents. For the moment, however, Roosevelt remained silent.

Most of Pinchot's devotees, however, were not silent. The *Washington Evening Star,* though recognizing the propriety of the President's action, loudly praised the former Chief For-

[3] Knute Nelson of Minnesota, Albert J. Beveridge of Indiana, and Albert B. Cummins of Iowa.

ester in its leading editorial: "He is a high type of citizen, whose devotion to the public welfare is an inspiration. In his own line he is an expert, qualified by a lifelong study, and there is no estimating the worth of his services during the years of his official activity." Pinchot was delighted to see similar sentiments expressed in letters which he received from practically every state and every class of the American public. He indeed had the sympathy of many Americans.

Most gratifying to Pinchot and most significant from the viewpoint of his leadership among the progressives were statements from the leading insurgents. Henry C. Wallace, editor of the renowned *Wallace's Farmer* magazine and father of Henry A. Wallace, hoped that Pinchot would not rest until he probed the whole Alaskan matter to the very bottom. "Conceding the possibilities . . . of over-zeal," he elaborated, "your heart was in the right place and you were making a determined stand for the heritage of future generations." W. R. Stubbs, progressive Governor of Kansas, called the dismissal a tragedy, remarking that when public officials, like Pinchot, "do their duty and protect the people's interest . . . [and] are crushed out of existence by the President . . . the government is in a bad way." Stubbs assured Pinchot that the influences which guided Taft's action "are not in any sense in accord with the progressive spirit of the middle west." Sir Horace Plunkett, the eminent Irish agrarian leader and an enthusiast for American insurgency, pointed to the work that would be undertaken when "the old Chief" came back, advising Pinchot to reflect and plan: "You ought to take time to formulate the campaign which cannot mature until 1912 and probably could be more easily shaped after the election of 1910 than before." Plunkett suggested what was typical of much of the correspondence from well-known insurgents: that Gifford Pinchot had out-

grown the Forest Service, that there was greater work for him
to do, that he had "burned his bridges as the first step towards
the larger contest, and that the American people were with
him in . . . his fight."

In responding to his fellow insurgents, Pinchot indicated
his readiness for political battle by declaring that conservation
meant, above all things, preserving for the people control of
the natural resources. "This," he announced emphatically, "is
the issue which we are to fight . . . now that the lines are being
clearly drawn. . . ." With some degree of false modesty he
concluded, "What has happened to me is of no consequence,
except as it will help us to win."

The contention of some standpat Republicans that Pinchot's
removal would not divorce Roosevelt from the Taft forces was
soon shaken. On March 1, Roosevelt wrote to Pinchot from
Africa:

> The appointment in your place of a man of high character
> in no way . . . lightens the blow; for besides being the Chief
> of the Forest Bureau you were the leader among all the men
> in public office—and the aggressive, hard hitting leader—of
> all the forces which were struggling for conservation, which
> were fighting for the general interest as against special privi-
> lege.

After sorrowfully criticizing Taft for his refusal to battle for
those principles which the former President, Pinchot, and their
associates had stood, Roosevelt inquired about the possibility
of seeing Pinchot in Europe or on his return: "I wish to see
you before I in even the smallest degree commit myself."

Needless to say, zealous Gifford Pinchot, vacationing briefly
in Europe, went off hastily to see Roosevelt, reaching him in
the vicinity of Porto Maurizio on the Italian Riviera on April

11. Pinchot reported in his diary that his talk with Roosevelt was one of the best and most satisfactory they had ever had, "lasting . . . nearly all day until about 10:30 P.M." He reported to Henry Wallace that he brought Roosevelt "up to date," and it is only conjecture that he elaborated on Taft's betrayal of the Roosevelt policies, on the need for more positive government in Washington, and on the grassroots popularity of Roosevelt. The Pinchot-Roosevelt talk on the Italian Riviera was the beginning of T.R.'s ideological journey to the New Nationalism position he would assume at Osawatomie, Kansas, on August 31 of the same year.

Although insurgent leaders appreciated Pinchot's part in making progressive inroads in Republican standpat ranks, they saw Roosevelt as the real key to their campaign. "Our Republican insurgents seem to lack a leader," said Benjamin Lindsey, the famous children's-court judge from Colorado, a state which "was ripe for insurgency." "Everyone is saying that a great deal depends on Roosevelt," and, indeed, Lindsey agreed, feeling that Roosevelt was in a position comparable to that of Abraham Lincoln in his power to aid his country. Yet, "He [Roosevelt] can do nothing," said Lindsey, "unless he makes it clear that he is in full sympathy with the La Follette-Cummins-Beveridge-Pinchot wing of the Republican party." For Lindsey and for most progressives, the state of insurgency would remain unsettled until Roosevelt returned.

Pinchot, anxious to live up to the "greater work" assigned to him by his admirers, proceeded to channel leaderless insurgency into a constructive program. With the zeal reminiscent of his earlier forestry days he strove to translate his fight against privilege into political action. He was cautioned against overzealousness. Medill McCormick, of the *Chicago Tribune,* advised a middle-of-the-road course:

You must do so not only on account of the individuals in
Congress, but in the interest of conversion of voters who
may despise Aldrich and like Burton; . . . who may think
well of Root and admire Dolliver; who may equally dislike
La Follette for a selfish hysteric. An insurgent program can
contain no plan not already well known and even widely
approved. . . .

In regard to the ideas presented by Lindsey and McCormick,
Pinchot had grave reservations. Unlike Lindsey, he refused to
urge insurgents to bide time until Roosevelt made a decision
to throw his weight either to their group or to the standpatters.
Rather, he was determined that Roosevelt would understand
insurgent principles so that he would feel morally compelled
to accept them. And, unlike McCormick, he refused to compromise his radicalism in dealing with the converted insurgents.

By the summer of 1910 Pinchot was optimistic about the insurgent cause. Public sentiment seemed more critical of the
Taft administration than at the time of his January removal.
Such reaction was attributable in part to the outcome of the
Ballinger-Pinchot hearings, particularly in regard to the predating of the Wickersham documents and the authorship of
the letter of exoneration. "Taft seems to have lost even what
shreds of respect for his effectiveness he still retained at the
time of my dismissal," wrote Pinchot to Plunkett. "The Country has made up its mind."

Much of Pinchot's pleasure about the state of the insurgent
cause in 1910 was due to its ideological context. In the summer
of 1910, Doubleday, Page and Company published Gifford
Pinchot's *The Fight for Conservation*. To the author the one
hundred–page book demonstrated the propriety and necessity
of fighting for his conservation principles in the political arena.

Also, it clarified the fundamental issues involved. As a premise of much of Pinchot's and Roosevelt's political behavior in 1910, *The Fight for Conservation* was significant to the progressive cause. It pointed up the many ideas which influenced Roosevelt's 1910 declarations so much.

Pinchot's book was not a systematic treatise or an exhaustive analysis of the problem of conservation. More importantly, it set forth the conservation of natural resources as the issue regarded as most fundamental to all other government questions. Much of the power of its ideas lay in the simplicity of presentation.

The goals sought by conservation of natural resources were few and simple but too often obscured by false issues and unrealistic thinking. Concerning the importance of conservation, Pinchot wrote:

> The planned and orderly development and conservation of our natural resources is the first duty of the United States. It is the only form of insurance that will certainly protect us against the disasters that lack of foresight has in the past repeatedly brought down on nations since passed away.

To justify the stewardship concept of executive action in public problems, Pinchot quoted from Justice Marshall's decision in *McCulloch* v. *Maryland:*

> Let the end be legitimate, let it be within the scope of the Constitution, and all means which are appropriate, which are plainly adapted to that end, which are not prohibited, but consistent with the letter and spirit of the Constitution, are Constitutional.

Concerning the Roosevelt administration and conservation, he wrote:

The greatest work that Theodore Roosevelt did for the United States . . . is the fact that he changed the attitude of the American people toward conserving the natural resources, and toward public questions and public life.

In a Jeffersonian spirit, Pinchot called for a change with the times:

The public welfare cannot be subserved merely by walking blindly in old ruts. Times change, and the public needs change with them. The man who would serve the public to the level of its needs must look ahead, and one of his most difficult problems will be to make old tools answer new uses —uses some of which, at least, were never imagined when the tools were made. That is one reason why constructive foresight is one of the great constant needs of every growing nation.

About the "Old Order," the former Chief Forester observed:

The "Old Order," standing pat in dull failure to sense the great forward sweep of a nation determined on honesty and publicity in public affairs is already wearing thin under the ceaseless hammering of the progressive onset.

And about the "New Order":

The people of the United States demand a new deal and square deal. They have grasped the fact that the special interests are now in control of public affairs. They have decided once more to take control of their own business. . . . They insist that the special interests shall go out of politics or out of business—one or the other, and the choice will lie with the interests themselves. . . .

In conclusion, Pinchot stated:

The conservation issue is a moral issue and the heart of it is this: For whose benefit shall our natural resources be conserved—for the benefit of us all, or for the use and profit of the few? This truth is so obvious and the question itself so simple that the attitude toward conservation of any man in public or private life indicates his stand in the fight for public rights.

Among insurgents, reaction to *The Fight for Conservation* was instant and enthusiastic. Public reviews were generally favorable; they were almost unanimous in appreciating the clarification of conservation and insurgent principles. "Tho there is not a great deal new in the book," stated the *Independent Magazine,* "the clear, fearless treatment of a vital theme, giving in small compass an unequivocal review of the problem reduced to its simplest terms, is a distinct contribution to the literature of the subject." The *Economic Bulletin* understood more correctly the intention of the author: "to line up the public on the question of 'special interests' versus 'equal opportunities.' " Less sympathetically, the *New York Times* felt it was a pity that "Mr. Pinchot does not stick to conservation and leave politics alone." The *Times* apparently did not understand that at the time of the book's publication in the summer of 1910 Pinchot was simultaneously translating his principles into political action through Theodore Roosevelt, the recognized key to insurgent success.

Pinchot's frequent pilgrimages to Oyster Bay, after the former President's return from Europe, were effective. In July he wrote optimistically to a southern insurgent: ". . . [Roosevelt's] position is becoming daily clear as a result of visits of insurgents and progressives to Oyster Bay, and I believe the outcome will be a reconstruction of the Republican party on frankly, genuinely, and completely progressive lines." The culmination of Pinchot's influence on T.R. was the former President's August swing through the West—a swing which was undertaken to gain the focus of public attention, the Roosevelt biographer Henry Pringle writes. Pinchot was delighted about the trip, of course. Not only did he join the former President at important stops in the West, but, more importantly, he impressed his insurgency and radicalism at a propitious time. Because of very recent friction between Roosevelt and Taft over the chairmanship of the forthcoming New York State Republican Convention, the former President was particularly ready for the Pinchot brand of radicalism.

T.R. espoused this radicalism at Osawatomie, Kansas. "I took the Osawatomie speech substantially as you left it," said Roosevelt to Pinchot about the radical speech. "I have never seen a crowd that affected me so much," wrote Pinchot to his mother about the Kansas audience. "They listened to T.R. for nearly an hour in perfect silence—and then they listened to Jim [James R. Garfield, Ballinger's predecessor as Secretary of the Interior] and me with precisely the same attention. . . . [T.R.'s] progressivism has grown steadily stronger."

Mrs. Pinchot, to be sure, was impressed with her son's new role. Gifford's brother Amos was even more excited. Amos had been a close adviser to Gifford throughout the spring hearings and followed closely the western trip of Roosevelt and Gifford. Fired up by western acceptance of the Osawatomie speech, he used it as a basis of recruiting for the insurgent cause, suggesting that conservative eastern minds should absorb a little of the enthusiasm and hopefulness of the West. One such plea, however, falling on the ears of a Wall Street Democrat, was ill received. The recipient noted in reply to Amos that he was interested in factional fights in the Republican Party only as an opportunity to restore Democratic control in the nation. He was even less interested in Roosevelt and felt that the Osawatomie speech was stolen largely from Democratic doctrine. Furthermore, he insisted that the former President was disloyal and hypocritical and lacked character and ability. Perhaps this reaction should have given cause for reflection to both Gifford and Amos.

The Osawatomie speech was not readily forgotten. That people remembered it was made clear when Roosevelt moved to test his political strength in his native New York. Although he successfully defeated the Taft forces in a fight for the temporary chairmanship of the state Republican nominating convention held at Saratoga in late September, the convention adopted a platform quite contrary to the spirit of the Osawatomie speech. The platform not only endorsed the "statesmanlike leadership" of President Taft but also lauded the Payne-Aldrich Act, that record-breaking high tariff which insurgents hated so much. Furthermore, many people, particularly Westerners, could not understand Roosevelt's telling the convention that President Taft should be praised for a "long list of laws . . . [which combined] wisdom with progress." [4]

"The Colonel had unquestionably lost stand in the West on account of the New York affair," said Henry Wallace, adding that he doubted that Roosevelt had accomplished his objective of going into the convention to defeat the "old guard." To Uncle Henry, as Wallace was affectionately called, Pinchot confessed that he too was puzzled over the New York situation and appreciated Wallace's sympathy for Roosevelt's embarrassing position. To a less understanding western communicant Pinchot responded differently: "I personally am afraid that a blunder of very far reaching national consequences was made when the West allowed it[self] to get the impression it did about the Saratoga platform." Pinchot felt that western politi-

[4] Quoted in Ray B. Smith (ed.), *History of the State of New York* (6 vols.; Syracuse, N.Y.: Syracuse Press, Inc., 1922), IV, 184–85.

cians should understand the political facts of life sufficiently well to know that New York Republicans and western Republicans were two different breeds and that T.R. was in the middle. Although T.R. had been the temporary chairman, the spirit of the convention was epitomized by its permanent chairman, Elihu Root, a standpat Republican. Also, Republicans had to reconcile their East-West differences; only then could they capture the Presidency.

Most Westerners, however, did not see the New York situation as Pinchot thought they should. William Kent, progressive California Republican, warned that if T.R. made a few more such breaks he would be down and out. "The Democrats," he said, "are panting with joy and are poking hard questions at us." Amos Pinchot also had strong feelings about the Saratoga affair. "I am frightfully upset," he wrote to James Garfield, "about T.R.'s trying to straddle and I am convinced that he cannot make a go of it. Certainly, it is a terrible disappointment to every one who cares a fig for the Progressive cause." Amos felt Roosevelt compromised on the platform at Saratoga so that he would not be defeated in the fight for the temporary chairmanship.

The unfavorable publicity given to Roosevelt's association with the conservative platform of the New York Republican Convention did not stop Pinchot from predicting publicly great insurgent gains in the November elections. Upon his return from a western trip, Pinchot told the *Denver Express:* "The essential facts in the West are the weakening of party ties, due to a genuine interest in popular government and the spread of progressive ideas." About this development Pinchot reiterated that the people were far more progressive than the leaders. Although the probability of some reverses was recognized, nothing could stop or even delay the movement for any length of time. On the issue of the tariff, for example, Pinchot explained that the people saw it as "unjust, a moral wrong, written by the servants of special privilege for the benefit of their masters, and interested, not to help the small man make a living, but to help the big man make an exorbitant profit." While eastern ties precluded a strong position on the tariff, Pinchot's sympathies seemed to lie with western insurgency: "To say that it is a revenue producer is no defense."

Pinchot feared that the insurgent cause might be threatened by the success it had thus far achieved. To a *Denver Express* reporter he said: "Direct attacks upon progressive policies having failed, enemies will seek to join the movement and try from within to emasculate it, or steer it to disaster." He added:

> Already, conversions without conviction have begun. Political deathbed conversions, performed in public by politicians whose leadership is dwindling may properly be regarded with suspicion. Like certain flowers, these gentlemen turn their faces to the rising sun but their roots hold fast to the same old soil.

Pinchot urged that these newly converted, old-style leaders be kept in the ranks and under observation until they had won their right to progressive leadership.

The 1910 elections brought victory to progressive Republicans in the West but defeat to standpat eastern Republican strongholds. Pinchot immediately attributed eastern defeat to standpat lethargy—or to political unpopularity of the standpat Republican organizations. On the other hand, western insurgent gains confirmed his statement that in the West there was genuine interest in popular government. Specifically, in the New England and in the Atlantic coast states, Republican aspirants for governorships lost to their Democratic rivals in

Connecticut, Maine, Massachusetts, New York, and New Jersey. In the western states, where Republican organizations were more progressive, the Republican losses in elections for the United States House of Representatives amounted to only three, whereas in the four eastern states of New York, New Jersey, Ohio, and Pennsylvania the number totaled twenty-six. The story was repeated in senatorial elections.

Pinchot was optimistic about the election results. "First," he wrote to former Governor George Pardee of California, "I am quite clear that there could be no more vigorous proof that the country as a whole demands progressive policies." As a second good consequence, Pinchot was sure that progressive victories in the West and reactionary defeats in the East, especially in New York, would make more difficult a reconciliation between Roosevelt and Taft. After all, Taft's regular Republican organization had saddled a conservative platform on the New York convention over which Roosevelt presided as temporary chairman—a platform quite in contrast to his Osawatomie speech. Pinchot hoped T.R. had learned a lesson. To former Governor Pardee, he continued:

> The one great difficulty has been that the Colonel was not able to see the situation after his return as we who had been in this country through the year of his absence actually knew it to be. I think he will understand it now as he never has before, and I am sure the result will be very good.

Of course, Pinchot was quite unhappy that Roosevelt's public image was imperiled by the Republican loss in New York State —a campaign with which T.R. had been closely identified. Although Pinchot felt that the reactionary Republicans in New York deserved to lose, he was sorry that T.R. had to be a part of it. He was no sorrier than T.R. himself; because of the stigma of defeat, Roosevelt sensed that he was finished politically.

A conspicuous exception to Republican victory in the West was Indiana. The defeat of Albert Beveridge, who ran for reelection to the United States Senate, struck at potential leadership of the insurgent group. Although the temporary loss of Beveridge's intellect, idealism, and political astuteness dejected Pinchot, he was, ironically, served by the defeat. Beveridge would not be a competitor for insurgent leadership. Attributing his defeat to support of the opposition by influential brewers and other wealthy men and to deep resentment toward the new tariff, Beveridge maintained his composure, telling Pinchot, "While . . . I am surprised, I am not downcast." As defeated candidates frequently do, Beveridge found solace in a moral victory. He felt that the progressive stand which he took in his campaign, even though it was unsuccessful, precluded Indiana's going back to the "old time methods and antiquated ideas."

Although most progressive Republicans shared Pinchot's enthusiasm about the election results, all were impressed by the damage that the Roosevelt and Beveridge defeats had done to their leadership. While the progressive Scripps papers' editorials appreciated this viewpoint, expressing sympathy for Roosevelt and admiration for Beveridge, they realistically looked to Pinchot and Robert M. La Follette, Senator from Wisconsin, as the only progressive Republicans whose stature on the national political scene had remained high despite the recent Republican defeats.

By November 29, Pinchot, though still happy about the Taft-Roosevelt split in New York, was admitting that Roosevelt had been "hit," but he hoped only for the moment. Writing to Governor W. R. Stubbs of Kansas about a recent conference he had had with Roosevelt, Garfield, and Henry Stimson (a

New York attorney), he reported that T.R. was sufficiently depressed so that under no circumstances would he consider himself as the presidential choice of the progressives at the 1912 Republican Convention. Pinchot hastened to add, "I don't feel as strongly about the results of the election in New York, nor do I think that his own prestige has suffered as severe a blow as he believes—I mean taking the country as a whole." William Allen White, owner and editor of the Emporia, Kansas, *Gazette,* agreed with Pinchot that the New York election would not have an ultimate effect "or make him in the least less available as a presidential candidate." White, like Pinchot, did recognize that Roosevelt had been "hit," but he was more critical of Roosevelt himself. "If I had been in the Saratoga Convention," said White, "I should have presented my views . . . as a minority report." However, both Pinchot and White were anxious to get on with the fight for progressive republicanism, and both wanted the former President with them.

CHAPTER III

The National Progressive Republican League

IN THE COURSE of digesting the 1910 election results, most progressives agreed about the need for uncompromising Republican Party reorganization along thoroughly progressive lines. Repeating what he had said so many times about the people being more progressive than the progressive leaders, Pinchot wrote to an insurgent colleague: "Unless the Republican party is able to put itself squarely in line with genuinely advanced political principles, the condition in which it finds itself today is likely to be lasting." Henry Wallace was sure that both major political parties were experiencing a seething movement of unrest. Such were the labor pains of a new political party. Wallace hoped that the evolving party would be called "Progressive Republican." Pinchot was not as extreme as Wallace; he believed reorganization could be accomplished within the Republican Party. First, he felt that a vigorous educational campaign, "carried out through Chautauqua meetings and public addresses of various kinds," would do much to bring backward states into the progressive column.

In addition to advocating such a campaign, Pinchot saw that the initiation by Republican progressives of plans for reorganizing the party was naturally hinged to the forwarding of a progressive as a 1912 presidential candidate. Recognizing that Roosevelt wished not to be considered, Pinchot expressed to William Allen White the opinion that La Follette and Iowa's Senator Albert Baird Cummins seemed to be the most available candidates for the nomination. White responded that Beveridge was as available as Cummins and La Follette, especially in view of the illnesses of the latter two, "but if . . . [La Follette] has recovered, we might well stand for him."

Both party reorganization and the selection of a progressive presidential candidate were, to Pinchot, essential in preparing for the coming battle against Taft. Pinchot was certain that Mr. President was looking forward to renomination and that the recent Republican defeat in his home state of Ohio and the repudiation of the administration throughout much of the country was having less effect than would be supposed. Pinchot advanced his theory of the reason for this minimal effect in a letter to Plunkett: "Chiefly as I believe because of the curious habit our people have formed of charging Taft's mistakes to his advisers, and not to him, apparently on the ground that he is incapable of managing his own affairs and that they are free to like him for his personal qualities wholly without reference to what his incapacities may be." Because of this sentiment among the people, the progressives either had to sit down quietly and let Taft be renominated, "or we have got to fight, and which ever we do we must decide on doing with very little delay."

Forthcoming action was in the form of the National Progressive Republican League. During the last week of 1910, two insurgent senators, La Follette and Jonathan Bourne, Jr., of Oregon, met with Amos Pinchot and a small group of progressives to draw up a declaration of progressive principles. This manifesto was sent, with an invitation to attend a national conference, to progressive leaders in every state. Gifford favored the action. His good friend James Garfield had reservations: "Had . . . [Pinchot] arranged with La Follette to see Roosevelt before taking any further action?" And might Taft become a martyr "if too much time intervened before nominations?" "The longer you wait," added Garfield's wife, "the more opportunity you will have to point out his [Taft's] failure in accomplishing these many things."

In regard to Garfield's first query, Pinchot was satisfied that T.R. was well aware of growing insurgent action. Pinchot was the principal liaison between the former President and the progressive Republicans. As for the prematurity of action, Pinchot could not be dissuaded, giving full aid to the January 21 meeting which gave birth to the National Progressive Republican League. Pinchot was a member of its Nominating Committee and was elected to its Executive Committee. Acting for Garfield in his absence, Pinchot added his name to the list of charter members, reporting to him that there would be no regrets: "The men who have come in are the right kind, and it seems to me the whole business is starting well." In this statement Pinchot was not completely truthful, for he noted in his diary that he did not "trust . . . much" the new president of the league, Senator Bourne.

A Declaration of Principles of the new organization served notice that the league believed that popular government was basic to all public questions. To this end, it advocated: the election of United States Senators by direct vote of the people; direct primaries for the nomination of elective officials; the direct election of delegates to national conventions with opportunity for the voter to express his choice for President and Vice President; amendment to state constitutions providing for the initiative, referendum, and recall; and a thoroughgoing corrupt practices act.

Reaction of the press to the league was varied. Garfield was sufficiently impressed with the *Cleveland Leader*'s statement to send it to Pinchot:

> As a vital force in national politics and as the concrete expression of the purposes and fighting force of the advanced Republicans of the country, the National Progressive League promises to be a powerful aid to development along high ennobling lines. It is a movement which will make many mistakes but it will aim so steadfastly upward that it may well become the dominant element in the Republican party. . . .

Although Pinchot agreed that the league seemed to have made a good impression, he feared organizational weakness, complaining that "it is not being followed up with sufficient vigor, and . . . there is danger of an impression being created in the public mind that it will amount to little." Remarking that he had simply come into the league with the other members, he was now determined to "get after them to help it along." Three weeks later, Pinchot was still discouraged: "So far, its organization is ineffective; it is doing very little, and that very little largely without plan. I am free to say I am greatly disappointed. Perhaps there is a better time coming."

Disappointment in the league was not limited to Pinchot. Progressives such as Henry Stimson, supported by Roosevelt in the 1910 New York gubernatorial race, refused to join the league. The league, said Stimson, was regarded with hesitation and suspicion in New York for two reasons: "First, because it has incorporated in its platform certain measures as the initiative, referendum and recall which public sentiment is not ready for here; second, because there is a lack of disinterestedness of some of its leaders." Stimson pointed out that he was referring to the leadership of Bourne and La Follette and that the feeling he expressed was accentuated by the attitude of some of the league's prominent members toward the planned reciprocal tariff with Canada: "Their opposition toward the Reciprocity Bill is being, as I think, justly criticized as an evidence either of very small mindedness towards a great, progressive problem, or as evidence of the fact that they never were really sincere in their progressivism." Most progressives, including La Follette, believed in the principle of tariff reciprocity. This particular bill, however, was not truly a reciprocal agreement. La Follette was convinced that it would sacrifice United States farmers to Canadian competition while strengthening U.S. trusts, for the bill provided that certain commodities manufactured in the United States would be admitted duty-free to Canada and that certain Canadian farm products would be admitted duty-free to this country.

Pinchot was sorry that Stimson refused league membership and staunchly differed with him on his feeling about La Follette, writing: "I find him one of the best men I have come in contact with for some time." As for Stimson's opinion of Bourne, Pinchot concurred: "I have long felt precisely as I judge you feel. I don't mind telling you confidently that under Bourne's management nothing is being done." In spite of such leadership, Pinchot reiterated that, as a progressive, he felt compelled to come into the league.

On March 3 Pinchot overtly complained to the secretary of the league, Frederic C. Howe:

I feel strongly that the League has got to do something more than it is doing now to maintain even a reasonable prospect of doing the work for which it was organized. There is a very clear-cut feeling among many men, whose opinion is worth while that the League is falling down.

To this criticism Howe replied that the league had been actively at work for less than one month and had concentrated all its efforts on the state legislatures then in session in order to secure the maximum results before they adjourned. He said further:

> We have corresponded with all Governors, familiarized them with the Oregon Laws. . . . In addition to this we have circulatized every member of half a dozen legislatures. . . . Scores of local leagues have been organized and several thousand letters have been sent. . . . The real accomplishment, and it is a most substantial one, has been the crystallization of sentiment about the five articles of our creed. Our actual achievement has been colossal. I cannot claim that this is traceable to the League, but at least it has had the encouragement of concerted nationwide sympathy and has already resulted in more progressive legislation than has been achieved in the preceding twenty years. . . .

*   *   *

From the time of the March 6 Howe report to Pinchot on Progressive League activities, Pinchot took less interest in the league's mechanics and more interest in the underlying reason for its existence: forwarding a progressive presidential candidate. No longer was the league merely "a machine for advocating popular government throughout the country." At a Lincoln banquet in Akron, Ohio, on March 7, Pinchot expressed his major concern: "In 1912, the nominee himself will be more than half the platform. It is obvious, therefore, that the Republican candidate should be . . . [selected] with peculiar care,

and that he must have certain indispensable qualifications."
The following qualifications were spelled out by Pinchot:

First—He must have wisdom, courage and genuine devotion to the welfare of the people.

Second—He must be progressive and stand for popular government.

Third—He must be a leader whom the voters will follow with enthusiasm.

Fourth—He must offer the party he is to lead a fair chance to win.

Pinchot, of course, knew of a candidate who met these qualifications. To his friend George Pardee he repeated what he had said many times since the 1910 elections: that to the vast majority of progressives "La Follette is the only man in sight . . . [and that] nothing will happen unless we go after it, . . . [and] we ought to do that without delay." Pardee agreed with Pinchot's choice of a candidate, but with a reservation expressed by many progressives: that La Follette was the choice "on the supposition that the Colonel will not permit his name to be used."

Pinchot's late February advocacy of La Follette as the progressive choice for the Republican nomination was sincerely motivated. He had, of course, felt differently during much of the previous year. Considering his close affinity to T.R. at that time and his many pilgrimages to Oyster Bay, it is clear that he had nurtured high hopes that Roosevelt would seek the 1912 nomination. Roosevelt's New York defeat changed that. So despondent had T.R. become that even Pinchot looked elsewhere—and found La Follette. Pinchot pushed hard for La Follette's candidacy. On February 24 Pinchot notes in his diary that he asked T.R. if he would support La Follette as a candidate for the nomination and that the former President said he could not do so publicly. From this statement Pinchot deduced that Roosevelt expected to run in 1912 as a compromise candidate. Pinchot told Roosevelt that he "thought he ought not to run" and persuaded T.R. to invite La Follette to New York so that the three of them could talk the situation over. Pinchot delivered the invitation in person, but La Follette would not come.[1]

Robert La Follette and Gifford Pinchot had much in common. Both were fighting progressives and rather doctrinaire in their progressivism. The Wisconsin Idea, as La Follette's state reforms were known, put the Wisconsin progressive in the front ranks of political insurgents. These reforms included the direct primary, corporation taxation, regulation of railroad rates, and regulation of public services. La Follette carried his insurgency into the United States Senate in 1905, earning a particular reputation in his fight for increased federal railroad control, tariff reduction, and conservation of natural resources. Pinchot was particularly appreciative of his work in the latter field.

On April 13, while Pinchot was on a Mediterranean cruise, a conference of progressives was held in Washington, D.C. to unite behind one of the progressive leaders as a candidate. La Follette was urged to become that progressive choice; he demurred; the pressure upon him mounted; hardly a day passed without his being urged to give the final word. Upon Pinchot's return from Europe, he was among those encouraging

[1] Belle C. and Fola La Follette, *Robert M. La Follette* (New York: Macmillan Co., 1953), report that La Follette had a severe sinus complication and thus could not make the conference. M. Nelson McGeary, *Gifford Pinchot: Forester-Politician* (Princeton, N.J.: Princeton University Press, 1960), notes that Pinchot tried on several occasions to bring La Follette and Roosevelt together.

the Wisconsin leader to throw his hat into the ring. Amos gave La Follette ten thousand dollars to use for the campaign if he were to consent. Many of those encouraging La Follette to run assumed that Gifford Pinchot would be the vice-presidential candidate.

A major cause for La Follette's hesitancy was Roosevelt's attitude. After all, T.R. had refused a request by La Follette that Roosevelt give the league movement "the benefit of your great name and influence." [2] La Follette asked Pinchot what he thought of Roosevelt's attitude toward the La Follette candidacy: "Roosevelt will not be a candidate. He has said repeatedly that he could not be a candidate against Taft. And from many talks with him I am certain as I live that he will be found actively and openly supporting your candidacy before the campaign ends." [3] Roosevelt, however, was of little aid to La Follette as the Wisconsin progressive struggled to make a decision about the 1912 race. He was coy. Probably at times he thought that the party was beyond repair, that it must face defeat in 1912 and then re-establish itself under progressive leadership. If he was to give it that guidance in 1912, he did not want to alienate either wing of the party by backing La Follette. At other times T.R. thought he might be the candidate himself in 1912 and, for that reason, he had better not support La Follette.

Regardless of what went through Roosevelt's mind, Pinchot's correspondence of this period attests to his sincere ardor for the La Follette candidacy. "Gilson Gardner," he wrote to his brother Amos on May 17, 1911, "is very hopeful that if

[2] Quoted in George B. Mowry, *Theodore Roosevelt and the Progressive Movement* (Madison, Wis.: University of Wisconsin Press, 1946), p. 174.

[3] Quoted in Robert M. La Follette, *La Follette's Autobiography: A Personal Narrative of Political Experiences* (Madison, Wis.: Robert M. La Follette Company, 1913), p. 524.

La Follette's candidacy can be declared within the next week
or ten days, there will develop a real chance to elect him. I
am not so sure myself but it is obviously the one thing to do."⁴
At this time Pinchot noted in his diary, with much satisfaction,
that T.R. was warming up to La Follette's candidacy. Not only
was T.R. suggesting ways in which La Follette might announce
his candidacy, but he was also becoming decidedly more
progressive.

In late May Pinchot wrote his friend Sir Horace Plunkett,
"The Progressives will undoubtedly make an effort to nominate La Follette, for whom my personal regard grows steadily
greater." To another friend, Pinchot showed impatience: "I
want to see La Follette come out as a candidate for the nomination at once, and generally I should like to have things stirred
up as vigorously and as promptly as possible." To Amos, on the
same day, he expressed anger: "I am going to spend two or
three days more, and make a final attempt to stir up the ani-
mals. If that fails I shall pull out with a clear conscience. At
present writing I am pretty mad and worse disgusted."

Pinchot did not, however, desert his fight for the La Follette
candidacy. Upon reflection he came to a realization that "the
difficulty is very largely with the failure of the Progressives to
keep a united front on the proposed Canadian Reciprocity tariff
bill." Many progressives saw the bill as good, low tariff legislation. Western progressives, like La Follette, felt differently.
With considerable justification they still thought the bill dis-
criminated against agricultural interests in favor of already
overprotected trusts. Pinchot threw his lot with the proponents
of the bill and hoped that La Follette would come to the same
point of view.

Pinchot was particularly disturbed by Taft's call for a special

---

⁴ Gilson Gardner was the Washington correspondent of the Scripps
newspapers.

session of Congress to consider the Canadian reciprocity tariff. He felt that the confusion created by Taft's temporary turn to progressive ideas could only be cleared up by striking action "of some kind on the part of the progressives, and, of course, the least possible thing would be an announcement of a candidate for nomination." Indeed, Pinchot seemed almost obsessed with the need for La Follette's declaration of his candidacy.

Finally, La Follette, feeling that there was sufficient demand for his candidacy, and sure of adequate financial support by the Pinchots and other progressives, publicly announced his candidacy on June 17, 1911.[5] Before taking this step he took the precaution to say to those who became contributors to his campaign, and particularly to Gifford Pinchot, "because of his close friendship for Roosevelt, that it must be understood, if I became a candidate, I should remain a candidate until I was nominated or defeated in the convention." [6] Obviously, La Follette questioned Pinchot's assurances that Roosevelt would ultimately support him in his fight for the nomination. La Follette did so with justification. Only one month later Pinchot was wavering on the La Follette candidacy, telling T.R. that he, the former President, might be nominated by acclamation.

Although ambivalent about Roosevelt's 1912 prospects, Pinchot was happy about the La Follette candidacy. It injected new life into the insurgent drive. The progressive split over the reciprocity tariff, however, still thwarted vigorous progressive action. Critics of Pinchot stressed circumstances in which Republicans supported Taft and the Democratic Congress on liberal issues such as Canadian reciprocity. Indeed, because of ob-

[5] Gifford gave $10,000 shortly afterward and another $5,000 in August.

[6] La Follette, *La Follette's Autobiography: A Personal Narrative of Political Experiences,* p. 526.

structionist tactics of progressive Republicans of the La Follette stamp, some Republicans saw a Democratic victory in 1912. W. H. Blodgett, of the *Indianapolis News,* was one such skeptic. He wrote to Pinchot:

> The people have great confidence in you as King of Insurgents but some of your chamberlains and court attachés have developed into a bunch of chevaliers d'industrie and that has caused the plain ordinary people to think that, after all, insurgency is as barren of good things as an army mule's dream.

That La Follette disappointed Pinchot in his final stand against the reciprocity bill was not denied. Pinchot admitted that he was "keenly sorry that such legislation should pass without the progressive candidate's support." Characteristically, however, Pinchot shrugged off the disappointment: "As a matter of fact," he wrote to his friend Blodgett, in the summer of 1911, "I believe the total effect against La Follette will be comparatively small." The ill effects of La Follette's reciprocity stand seemed to be more than counteracted by the "development of the Controller Bay affair, the Wiley matter, and the passage of La Follette's wool bill." Pinchot concluded:

> All these things will combine before the convention, with other things about which as yet nothing is known to make Mr. Taft's nomination impossible. You can't keep an administration forever on the defensive as to its integrity in regard to the public interest, and not begin to make a dent in the public mind.

It was natural that Pinchot should give prominence to the three current issues he mentioned to Blodgett. Concerning the

Wiley affair, it may be safe to say that Dr. Harvey W. Wiley, Chief Chemist of the United States, was as zealous about pure foods and drugs as Pinchot had been about forestry. To a comparable degree, his crusade was appreciated by the American people. When Taft's Secretary of Agriculture preferred nonsensical charges against Wiley for hiring a distinguished pharmacologist at a per diem of eleven dollars over the congressional limit, the public felt that Wiley was being forced out against the best interest of the nation. "Dr. Wiley," declared an Ohio editorial, "like former Forester Pinchot, enjoys in high degree the confidence and support of the people because he has been fighting the people's battles against special interests. His dismissal from office would be followed by as great a popular protest as was that of Pinchot's." Pinchot was quick to sympathize with the food and drug expert. "Having been more or less in the same place myself," he wrote Wiley, "I know just how you feel. The only difference is that the President fired me and he won't dare fire you."

Pinchot was even more optimistic about La Follette's wool bill. Although, from the standpoint of many progressives, La Follette had taken an unpopular stand on reciprocity, he was soon effecting a Democratic–progressive Republican coalition for the purpose of revising the Payne-Aldrich Tariff, schedule by schedule. Through clever manipulation by La Follette, a woolen schedule act which had passed the House was pushed through the Senate. When Taft vetoed the schedule on the ground that it had not been approved by a scientific tariff board, progressives had good reason to criticize the President for having advocated reciprocity without having first taken similar action. They now generally agreed that Taft opposed reductions that would harm the manufacturers and favored reductions at the expense of the farmer. Pinchot was delighted.

Even before the President's veto he felt that, regardless of the President's action, "the advantage will remain with La Follette and the insurgents." Concluding a letter to his sister, Pinchot "was more satisfied than ever that Taft would not be nominated." Amos Pinchot was also pleased, for he felt that although the people did not understand the insurgent stand on reciprocity they would readily appreciate the fight on the wool schedule.

The Controller Bay issue was not unlike the Ballinger-Pinchot affair, and the prospect of another such exposé delighted Pinchot. The issue came to light when Miss Myrtle Abbott syndicated a rather unsavory story implicating people close to the administration, including the President's brother. It was alleged that Taft secretly signed an order exempting from a government land reserve a large portion of the shores of Controller Bay in Alaska and that the order lacked the usual thirty-day notice made for the benefit of prospective settlers and the publicity which it would have received if it had gone through customary channels. Supposedly, there was also evidence that T. R. Ryan, the accredited representative of the Morgan-Guggenheim syndicate, had full notice of the promulgation. Furthermore, it was conjectured that the records of the Interior Department showed that dummy entrymen, in the service of Ryan, filed, immediately after Ryan's notification, on lands needed for a monopoly of the shores of the bay. Most intriguing was a letter, known as the "Dick to Dick" letter, which Ryan had allegedly written to Richard Ballinger, former Secretary of the Interior:

Dear Dick:

I went to see the President the other day about this Controller Bay affair. The President asked me whom I repre-

sented. I told him, according to our agreement, that I
represented myself. But that didn't seem to satisfy him.
So I sent for Charlie Taft and asked him to tell his brother
who it was I really represented. The President made no
further objection to my claim.

Yours,

Dick [7]

The affair had all the earmarks of another Cunningham
claims case—the case that precipitated the Ballinger-Pinchot
affair. Congress appointed a special committee to examine
the charges. Louis Brandeis, the famous "prosecutor" in the
Ballinger case, was asked to serve as counsel, and with Pinchot's
urging he consented. Senator Miles Poindexter, of the state
of Washington, was sent to Alaska to conduct personally a
thorough investigation on the scene; Gifford Pinchot accompanied him. Amos Pinchot was put to work by Brandeis draft-
ing proposed legislation to eliminate the type of abuses that had
allegedly been committed at Controller Bay. All of this work
was for nought, however, for Poindexter and Pinchot found
no evidence of collusion in Alaska, and Brandeis found no
proof of misconduct in Washington. Although the case eventually fizzled out, Pinchot, in the summer of 1911, was elated
over the prospect of thoroughly discrediting the administration.

W. H. Blodgett, a frequent correspondent and self-styled
critic of Pinchot and the progressives, recognized that Pinchot's
elation about Controller Bay, the Wiley affair, and the passage
of La Follette's wool bill would "cut some figure." "But, after
all," he concluded, "the thing that succeeds in politics, as well
as everything else, is organization. Taft will have the organi-

---

[7] Quoted in Alpheus T. Mason, *Brandeis: A Free Man's Life* (New
York: Viking Press, Inc., 1946), p. 283.

zation. He will have the machine." "You wait," responded
Pinchot, "things look black all through, but, nevertheless, I am
feeling very cheerful and one reason is that I set the principles
I stand for far above party success and it is beginning to look
to me as if they might win brilliantly in the next campaign."

Pinchot was concerned that "the people" should understand
the principles for which the progressives were fighting. In early
June he had written to Gilson Gardner, "It seems to me what
we need now is for somebody to come out and remark in a loud
tone of voice that he is not scared." He finally decided to do this
himself in the form of a published article. Reaction to the decision was varied, from extreme encouragement by his brother
Amos to the warning of Thomas E. Donelly of the Lakeside
Press: "Giff—the public hates a belly acher. . . . It will be the
tactical mistake of your life."

Turning to Louis Brandeis for advice, Pinchot outlined
briefly the points he planned to stress:

> . . . that the next nomination is of enormous importance;
> that the renomination of Taft would probably lead to the
> nomination of a Democratic reactionary, so that whichever
> party won, the people could not win; that Taft proved by
> what he did after his nomination and election that he cannot
> be trusted; that the Republican party is on trial before the
> people with a reputation to retrieve; and that it must stick
> to principle at any cost. You may remember a letter I wrote
> to Khartoon, giving 16 reasons why Taft had abandoned the
> Roosevelt policies. I am proposing to publish that as part of
> the article.

Brandeis liked the proposed outline of the article and agreed
with Pinchot that the latter's insistence upon telling the truth
was sound. Also, he agreed that Pinchot's position of close

co-operation with the Secretary of War and the Secretary of the Interior, Henry Stimson and Irving Fisher, on conservation and other matters would not be hindered by the exposure.

"It's a corker," remarked La Follette about the proposed article. Considering Pinchot magnanimous for his lack of bitterness, he added:

> It is so fair and just, and coming from you just when you had gone through that awful experience [congressional investigation of the Ballinger-Pinchot affair] is a striking portraiture of your bigness. Nothing could be fairer. Indeed, the whole article is ideal in its treatment of Mr. Taft and the progressive cause.

Disregarding the advice that publication would ruin whatever influence he might have with the American people, Pinchot instructed the editor of the *Saturday Evening Post* to place the article in a fall edition of the magazine, "at a time of greater general interest in politics." Upon publication of the article on October 7, 1911, Pinchot felt that he had achieved an insurgent objective of once again placing the issues clearly before the American people.

The *New Orleans Democrat* editorialized that, in launching the open attack, Pinchot spoke as a progressive and as one close to Roosevelt. Pointing out the large number of Pinchot devotees, the editorial recognized the validity of the criticism. It noted that Pinchot felt it his duty as a citizen to help prevent injury to conservation and the public welfare by fighting President Taft's renomination. More specifically, the editorial continued:

> He charges that Mr. Taft began at once to abandon his former friends for the sake of his former foes; that he chose

for his associates and advisers avowed enemies of Mr. Roosevelt and Roosevelt policies he was elected to enforce; that he did not take a hand to assist the latter; and that the developments of his administration made it clear that he had "forsaken both the friends and the principles to which he was pledged." Summing up, and making due allowance for the good things he had done, Mr. Pinchot concludes, "Mr. Taft has himself supplied the proof that he cannot be trusted."

Coming in the midst of Mr. Taft's canvass of the West . . . the ex-Forester's attack is shrewdly calculated to damage the new Taft movement. It is to be followed later . . . by enlistment of Colonel Roosevelt.

Pinchot had far more reason to be happier about the reception of his *Saturday Evening Post* article than about a report he was preparing on the Alaskan Controller Bay investigation. Even while Gifford was still in Alaska, his brother Amos had written, "Go slow on Controller Bay. . . . Brandeis thinks it would be a mistake to bite off too much. The record does not show as much wrong as it promised." From the progressive ranks, Congressman William Kent, of California, had warned Pinchot, "Any exaggerated importance given to this piece of federal property will hurt our cause." Although just prior to his return from Alaska Pinchot had written to Roosevelt that he was still convinced that "it was a serious mistake to exclude from the National Forest the shores of Controller Bay," his public statements about the investigation consisted of vague generalities. Brandeis put the lid on the Controller Bay charge in his November 8 report to Congressman James M. Graham, chairman of the House Investigating Committee:

Although the actions of the Administration lack frankness, and seem hostile to sound policy and real conservation, nevertheless evidence is lacking on which to convict the Administration of illegal conduct. It is evident, however, that the opening to private acquisition of harbor and terminal sites in Alaska at this time is contrary to public policy, and hazardous to industrial development in the interests of the people of the territory.

Even more pronounced than his optimism over his *Post* article was Pinchot's feeling about recent progressive action. "It was the best kind of good news that the recent meeting of progressives at Chicago had put Senator La Follette forward as a candidate for nomination for President." On October 16, at a conference of leading progressives, representing thirty states, the following resolution had been adopted:

> The record of Senator La Follette in state and nation makes him the logical candidate for President of the United States. His experience, his character, his courage, his record in constructive legislation and administrative ability meet the requirements for leadership such as present conditions demand. This conference endorses him as candidate for the Republican nomination for President and urges that in all states organizations be formed to promote his nomination.[8]

La Follette was also happy about the action at Chicago, except for a discordant note sounded by James R. Garfield, a close friend of both Pinchot and Roosevelt. "He came to the meeting," recorded La Follette in his autobiography, "direct from New York, where he had been closeted with Roosevelt. He was careful to say that he spoke only for himself, but he was singularly persistent in opposing any endorsement of my

[8] Quoted in La Follette, *La Follette's Autobiography: A Personal Narrative of Political Experiences,* p. 532.

candidacy." When the *Outlook,* under Roosevelt's editorship, published a statement on October 28, referring to the Chicago endorsement as a recommendation rather than a committal of the movement to any one man, La Follette's distrust of Roosevelt and his disciples, Garfield and Pinchot, was revived.

In connection with Garfield's action and the statement of the *Outlook,* it is interesting to note that, subsequently, Pinchot also began to equivocate on the La Follette nomination. On November 10, Pinchot noted in his diary that he had a "long talk with Gilson [Gardner], who is delighted with Bob's progress but thought T.R. may not want him nominated." On the following night Pinchot recorded that former Senator Beveridge "thinks Taft can't be nominated, nor La Follette either." The influence of these men was immediately reflected in Pinchot's own correspondence. Without endorsing La Follette, he now emphasized Taft's inability to achieve the renomination and the necessity for the Republicans to nominate a candidate who would be satisfactory to the progressives. Pinchot continued to manifest the same attitude; speaking highly of La Follette, he also mentioned Roosevelt as a potential candidate. In a rather confused state, Pinchot wrote to Sir Horace Plunkett that change in the political situation was marked by "a decided increase in the strength of Roosevelt's position, the decided slump in Taft's, and the remarkable progress made by La Follette."

Perhaps most influential upon Pinchot was James Garfield. The tone of his letters to Pinchot and their correlation with Pinchot's correspondence and activity are significant. From the time of the progressive Republican conference at Chicago on October 16, Garfield spoke disparagingly of La Follette's campaign. On October 28 he wrote critically to Pinchot of La Follette's failure to carry his campaign to the East, where he could have presented "a constructive business program . . . [at] a critical moment when Taft has alienated the entire business world." A week later Garfield told Pinchot that "unless there should be a very marked change in the sentiment toward La Follette, he could not win in Ohio."

On November 23, Garfield reported to Pinchot on an Ohio progressive Republican meeting: "It clearly showed that while there was almost unanimous opposition to Taft, La Follette was not acceptable. The response to Theodore's name was instantaneous and unanimous. I am really astonished to see how the feeling for him is spreading." Garfield concluded further that there would be a fight in Ohio for the election of progressive delegates not pledged to any specific candidate. This action would, of course, enable progressive Republican delegates to support Roosevelt. Coinciding with Garfield's statement on unpledged delegates, Roosevelt forces urged the Ohio progressive leaders to withhold a call for a resolution endorsing La Follette until the regular state conference, to be held on January 1, 1912.

That Pinchot respected Garfield's maneuvering for Roosevelt in Ohio is revealed by a communication of November 30. "Fackler [La Follette's Ohio manager] wants me to make a talk for La Follette in Ohio soon," Pinchot wrote to Garfield, "and I have agreed to do so. If I come to Cleveland, it might embarrass you, so I have arranged to stop off for a few hours at Cincinnati on December 5, and make a short talk." Garfield replied immediately to Pinchot, stating that he did not mind Pinchot's speaking out in Ohio. "The only thing," he wrote, "is to make clear that the progressive fight is not simply a La Follette fight."

While Pinchot and those close to him saw La Follette's campaign faltering, such was not the case in the La Follette headquarters. "I am convinced," wrote La Follette's manager to Amos Pinchot, ". . . that we can win this fight. I am sure this is not optimism, but is the result of development and information that seems entirely trustworthy and dependable."

It is difficult to interpret motives in politics, but the sudden shift of support by Roosevelt and Pinchot incites curiosity and an attempt at interpretation. Before December of 1911 Roosevelt was not openly interested in the nomination, and Pinchot was urging the candidacy of La Follette. By December 1, Roosevelt seemed anxious to run if it could be shown that he had support, and many conferences ensued in the attempt to ascertain the extent of the aid needed and available. As a principal participant in the conferences, Pinchot gave every indication of shifting his support from La Follette to Roosevelt. The reason for Roosevelt's seeking the nomination, after having expressed the opinion that the Republicans would be defeated in 1912, is partially explained by Professor George E. Mowry, in his book *Theodore Roosevelt and the Progressive Movement*. Mowry feels that Roosevelt's irritation with Taft had broken all bounds with the institution of the steel suit by the Taft administration. As President, Roosevelt tacitly sanctioned the purchase of the Tennessee Iron and Coal Company by the United States Steel Corporation; certainly, he did not think that the U.S. Steel Corporation was a monopoly. The former President defended this position in his magazine, the *Outlook*. Upon finding his article well received, Roosevelt regained much of the confidence that he had lost in the November election of 1910. He was now anxious to go after Taft. Added to Professor Mowry's interpretation might have been T.R.'s realization that the country was in a progressive mood, as evidenced by its acceptance of the Progressive League and by considerable approval of the La Follette candidacy.

The key to understanding Pinchot's shift of support from La Follette to Roosevelt lies with the latter. Indeed, we might say further that until this point in time Roosevelt was the key to Pinchot's prominent professional and political life. As President, Roosevelt had been clearly responsible for placing Pinchot and his conservation principles before the public, and as former President he inspired Pinchot to an almost fanatical zeal for maintaining Roosevelt's principles within the Taft administration. When working with the Taft administration had failed, Pinchot turned to politics, hoping, in that capacity, to be in a position to better fight for Roosevelt's interests and principles. In the summer of 1910 Pinchot saw hope in a combination of insurgent radicalism and Rooosevelt's political appeal—a combination designed to stop Taft in 1912. It appeared that, through Roosevelt's 1910 western swing, which included the Osawatomie speech, Pinchot was having his way. Then came, in succession, the Roosevelt-chaired Saratoga Convention which underwrote the Taft administration's program and the defeat of Roosevelt's gubernatorial candiate in New York. Reluctantly agreeing with Roosevelt that the former President should remain quiet politically—that he could not be a candidate in 1912—Pinchot looked elsewhere for a progressive leader. From the vantage point of the 1960's, Pinchot's shift to La Follette—a courageous insurgent leader in the Senate— seems logical. Pinchot worked hard for La Follette and the progressive cause, but at this time he remained close to Roosevelt—frequently a guest at Oyster Bay or a caller at Roosevelt's *Outlook* office. When Roosevelt finally decided to enter the race, it is not difficult to understand that Pinchot would be in his corner. Furthermore, from a practical political viewpoint, Pinchot had boundless faith in Roosevelt's appeal to the country.

Publicly, Pinchot continued to praise La Follette, but on December 8, in a speech endorsing the Wisconsin progressive before the Chicago Press Club, he showed public signs of wavering. Although he aptly described La Follette as a Senate leader of insurgency, his description of the origin of La Follette's candidacy was ambiguous: "At that time we all believed, La Follette with the rest, that the man . . . could not win the nomination for himself. . . . Now we know that the man, who for the sake of principle was willing to volunteer in a forlorn hope, has a good chance to capture the fortress." As previously, Pinchot continued to imply that Roosevelt would not be a candidate. "I do not assert," Pinchot concluded, "that La Follette is yet sure of the nomination, but now that circumstances have made Mr. Taft's renomination either impossible or extremely improbable, the attention of the country is turning swiftly and eagerly to Bob La Follette of Wisconsin."

On January 1, 1912, at an Ohio state conference of progressives, the Roosevelt and La Follette contest was brought into the open. A few days before, La Follette had entered the state on a speaking tour. His lieutenants, having previously postponed his progressive endorsement at the request of the Roosevelt forces, now planned to end La Follette's electioneering effort with unanimous vote for or endorsement of him by the conference. Obviously, the Roosevelt men would have to declare themselves for Roosevelt or be committed to the Senator's candidacy. Pinchot, publicly committed to La Follette yet so anxious to please Roosevelt and Garfield, was forced to a decision—that decision being to fight the resolution endorsing La Follette. Leading the fight, with Garfield's aid, Pinchot succeeded in substituting a resolution declaring the conference's intention of nominating "a progressive Republican for President, recognizing as fellow progressives all who hold the principles for which we stand whether they be for the Presidential nomination of Robert M. La Follette or Theodore Roosevelt, or any other Progressive Republican."

Publicly, Pinchot appeared to be still in La Follette's camp on the following day, declaring that "the Ohio action was a means of uniting Ohio progressives against Taft and that La Follette would be nominated by the Republican convention." Experienced politicians everywhere, however, interpreted the action as a declaration by T.R. that he would run if enough support was forthcoming.

Having left the Ohio conference for a rest in Michigan, Pinchot was pursued by newspaper reporters who related further equivocations on Pinchot's part:

> Gifford Pinchot . . . denied that he had made any statements in speeches or interviews, that Theodore Roosevelt had told him that he would not accept the presidential nomination if it were tendered. "I know nothing of Mr. Roosevelt's affairs, either as to whether he could accept the nomination, or whether he believes he could be elected." [9]

Pinchot's close friends sought clarification of his position as related to the candidacy of Roosevelt and La Follette. Explaining to George Pardee that Roosevelt was not openly a candidate, Pinchot was obviously pleased with his own action at Ohio:

> My idea of the perfect situation is what I have been trying to bring about in Ohio, viz.: . . . A community of interests between the Roosevelt and La Follette forces, with distinct intention that when it becomes necessary later on to make a final choice between the two, that choice shall have been

[9] Quoted in *ibid.*, p. 577.

determined by the two principals themselves. When that is done, we can all follow it, and a course possibly dangerous to progressive success—a split between the La Follette and Roosevelt forces—will thus be taken out of the field of possibility.

Pinchot hoped that the community-of-interests plan would be followed throughout the country.

"Unless I am mistaken," said Pinchot, "we are ready to get . . . [the progressive vote] now which ever way they jump." Although maintaining a public appearance of supporting La Follette, Pinchot was sure that the progressives would jump to Roosevelt. "The demand for Theodore has been increasing by leap and bounds," he wrote to his sister, "and it is altogether within the range of possibility that the convention will stampede for him at Chicago." In fact, this letter coincided with a declaration of support for Roosevelt made by Governor Stubbs of Kansas, "among the most progressive of prairie states."

La Follette recorded in his autobiography his state of confusion during this period:

> One day it would seem certain that my candidacy had already been betrayed by the friends of Roosevelt who were in my organization; the next day I would be assured that he would announce his refusal to be a candidate; that there would be no division within the Progressive ranks and that his supporters would be my supporters.

On January 14, La Follette reported in this book, Fackler, his Ohio manager, brought to him a proposition from Walter Brown and Dan Hanna, both Roosevelt men, for a working combination of La Follette and Roosevelt forces. La Follette wrote:

They proposed that the campaign be carried on in Ohio with La Follette as the candidate, but that in each congressional district one Roosevelt delegate should be placed upon the ballot with one La Follette delegate. Roosevelt was not to be known as an open and avowed candidate.

La Follette related that the inducement held out was that they would furnish all the money for the campaign, with the stipulation that La Follette progressive literature be destroyed. That Pinchot was aware and in favor of the scheme is indicated by a letter he dictated shortly after: "The idea is to elect La Follette delegates in districts where the La Follette forces dominate and Roosevelt delegates in the districts where the Roosevelt sentiment dominates." La Follette reported that shortly after the Brown-Hanna proposition Pinchot insisted upon his acquiescence. La Follette answered:

> . . . that my candidacy should not be made a shield and cover for Roosevelt; that if he [Roosevelt] was to be made a candidate, he should come out in the open; that I would never consent to be a stalking horse for Roosevelt or any other man; that for many years I had fought a clean, straight fight for definite Progressive principles; that I had been urged by Progressives to stand as the presidential candidate for that reason; that I would not compromise these principles or permit my name to be used in any way to secure delegates for any other candidate; that he [Pinchot] understood all this before he contributed in support of my campaign; and that, as I repeatedly asserted, this would be my position to the end.[10]

On January 18 Pinchot called a conference of contributors to La Follette's campaign, insisting that the Brown-Hanna

[10] *Ibid.*, pp. 586–87.

scheme be carried out. Although he still assured the group that Roosevelt was not a candidate, Pinchot was voted down. Amos Pinchot was with La Follette, saying to him:

> I agree with you perfectly that there should be no combination with Roosevelt. I have no doubt whatever about his having been an active candidate all along, but I am sure Gifford is honest in the position he is taking. Roosevelt has always been able to pull the wool over his eyes.[11]

On January 22, at Carnegie Hall, Pinchot introduced La Follette as the candidate he supported for the Republican nomination. But, as in his December 8 introduction of La Follette before the Chicago Press Club, Pinchot went out of his way to stress the fact that his candidate had been selected as a device for holding progressives together after the 1910 Republican defeats. "That was the condition of affairs some months ago. Now we know that the man . . . has a good chance to capture the fortress." Significantly different from his December 8 speech, Pinchot's remarks contained no reference to his belief that Roosevelt would not be a candidate. That night Pinchot noted in his diary that a "way must be found to let Bob down easy."

By January 27 Pinchot was saying privately that Roosevelt could not avoid the nomination. Although Roosevelt would not openly declare his willingness to run, Pinchot felt that the one hope of a progressive nomination lay with him. "Of course," he said in a note to Plunkett, "I am committed to the La Follette candidacy, and shall remain so. Without it, I doubt if this whole Roosevelt Movement would have come up."

By late January even Amos was agreeing that La Follette's campaign was failing and that "Fighting Bob" was staying "to

[11] Quoted in *ibid.*, p. 593.

make people think, and break down the harmful and popular idea . . . that old injustices of the world are irremediable." La Follette appreciated Amos Pinchot's sympathetic understanding: "Whatever comes out of this game that is now being played in violating every rule of honesty and decency nothing can shake my confidence in either your loyalty or your insight."

Gifford Pinchot took his first overt action against La Follette at another conference of La Follette campaign contributors, which he called to meet on January 29. At this time Pinchot presented La Follette with the alternatives of withdrawing in favor of Roosevelt or of withdrawing and leaving the individuals in the group to take what course they chose. When La Follette refused to submit, Pinchot withdrew his support. He told the group that he would not come out for any other candidate unless they decided to switch support. He warned La Follette, however, not to fight T.R. Amos joined his brother, as did Gilson Gardner and Medill McCormick. Others at the meeting assured La Follette that they would continue to support him to the end. Three days later Amos wrote to La Follette, sadly accounting for his vote:

> I regret as much as you do Colonel Roosevelt's attitude toward the nomination. But more than I can tell you, I fear that the course which you decided at our conference . . . will help the nomination of a reactionary at Chicago, and in the meantime split up the Progressives throughout the country.

An opportunity for Pinchot and other Roosevelt followers to abandon subtly the La Follette campaign was presented on February 2, when La Follette spoke at a banquet given by the Publishers Association in Philadelphia. Fatigued by his strenuous campaign and concerned about an operation his daughter was to undergo on the following morning, La Follette could not stand up to the speaking assignment. He lost himself in a two-hour harangue against the large newspapers represented by his audience and, after many persons in the audience walked out on him, finally brought his fumbling speech to an end. He then fell into his seat, a sick man.

A few days after the La Follette speech, Pinchot wired the Minnesota Republican League: "In my judgment, La Follette's condition makes further serious candidacy impossible." Seeing no way out except by bolting the La Follette campaign, Amos also made the final break, theorizing that "he [La Follette] has no right to ask his friends to take a course which they conscientiously believe will destroy the Progressive movement for the time being." Both Pinchots were encouraged to make the break by a "release" which La Follette was thought to have issued to his supporters through Walter Houser, his manager —a release which La Follette subsequently denied having issued.

In a letter to La Follette, Pinchot reviewed the whole case in detail. La Follette's candidacy, he said, was advocated for two clear reasons: first, to hold the progressives together as an effective fighting force; and second, to prevent the renomination of a reactionary Republican as a candidate for the Presidency. These ideas, said Pinchot, were incorporated in the Chicago Press Club speech of December 8 and in the Carnegie Hall speech of January 22, with the approval of Houser for the first message and the approval of both Houser and La Follette for the second. Houser also approved the Ohio resolution of January 1, which recognized the probable candidacy of either La Follette or Roosevelt for President. Pinchot stated further that La Follette then reversed his stand and decided to co-operate in no way with progressives favoring the Roosevelt candidacy. Inasmuch as this reversal of policy was detrimental to the progressive cause and La Follette's only stated objection to Roosevelt was that he did not consider him a progressive, Pinchot felt obliged to withdraw his support from the Wisconsin Senator. Reference was made to La Follette's health, but the issue was not stressed by Pinchot as a major consideration for his action.

On the following day La Follette's Massachusetts manager, Mrs. E. C. Evans, pleaded with Pinchot to write a more magnanimous letter, one in which he would credit his change of support to political developments—not to the condemnation of La Follette. Somewhat hysterically, Mrs. Evans wrote of La Follette's being "stabbed" and having the knife turned "in order to demonstrate . . . [Pinchot's] own impeccability." Immediately, Pinchot wired that he could make certain changes, and two days later he requested that the original letter be returned. Interestingly, Mrs. Evans replied that Pinchot might send an amendment or a retraction which could either be filed with the earlier letter or, with La Follette's consent, be substituted for the original letter.

Obviously, since the letter had already reached La Follette, it was too late for a change. "There is nothing I can do about it," Pinchot wrote to Mrs. Evans. "I am sorry." He hastened to make it clear, however, that he had made no mistake; he had said nothing untrue in the letter: "On the contrary, it expressed my clear cut and definite conviction." Unequivocally, Pinchot had at last thrown his complete support to the Roosevelt candidacy for the Republican nomination. To that end he was happily committed.

CHAPTER IV

"... Like a Bull Moose"

"PINCHOT IN OPEN FOR ROOSEVELT," declared the *Washington Post* of February 19, 1912, adding that such a declaration could well mean the former President's election. The *Post* continued:

> In view of the close personal relations of the former President and Mr. Pinchot, there are many public men who last night accepted this statement as evidence sufficient to them that Colonel Roosevelt intended to be a candidate before the Chicago convention.
>
> .   .   .   .   .   .
>
> That Mr. Pinchot would take any position that might embarrass Colonel Roosevelt, or that he would issue such a statement as that given by him last night without first having consulted with Colonel Roosevelt, scarcely can be assumed.

Press accounts reported further that Pinchot's new stand was based on an assumption that the original purpose of La Follette's candidacy, to hold the progressives together and to prevent the nomination of a reactionary, could no longer be accomplished and that "the imperative need for another leader has been made plain."

Because of Pinchot's position, the *Washington Post* indicated that "the speech to be delivered by Roosevelt at Columbus, Ohio [before the Ohio Constitutional Convention on February 21] will be awaited with more than the usual interest that attaches to what Colonel Roosevelt has to say." What Roosevelt would say at Columbus had been given additional weight by the February 10 publication of a declaration of seven progressive governors asking the former President to enter the race. Indeed, Pinchot was very much interested in the forthcoming address. He hoped, of course, that it would be based largely on a platform which T.R. asked him to write. Upon discovery that Roosevelt had prepared his own draft of the Columbus speech, Pinchot expressed disappointment. He noted that this draft contained little material which was positive "and gets nowhere as a progressive document." Between February 10 and 14, Pinchot, with much aid from Amos, made some progress in changing the speech. Amos wanted T.R. to take more specific positions, to defend "the people" more vigorously, to hit the great and vital issues, and to speak more plainly. On February 15, T.R. wrote to Amos that he accepted about two thirds of his and Gifford's suggestions. Roosevelt, of course, consulted also with other elements of the Republican Party about the Ohio speech. Gifford and Amos feared, with good cause, that such consultation would result in T.R.'s assuming too much of a middle-of-the-road position. Although Roosevelt adhered to all of the liberal doctrines that were expressed at Osawatomie, he qualified his assertions with assurances of fair treatment to the business world, hoping to win over a great portion of the conservative Republicans.

Roosevelt might well have succeeded in appealing to the

divergent elements of his party if he had not also included in
his address a plan for the democratization of the judiciary. The
former President advocated that court decisions should be submitted to the vote of the people, and, if ratified, they should
stand; but, if not supported by popular vote, they should not
become effective. This scheme to permit "the recall of judicial
decisions" alienated most of the conservative element. They
declared that this was nothing more or less than appeal to mob
rule. The opponents also argued that it was impossible to maintain enduring institutions in the United States under such a
system. With little restraint Roosevelt talked of his scheme at
Columbus: "The judges have decided every which way, and
it is foolish to talk of the sanctity of judge-made law which
half of the judges strongly denounce." With equal lack of restraint, stalwart Republicans who had promised their aid to
Roosevelt requested to be released. Within Roosevelt's own
camp, it appeared that only radicals of the Pinchot stamp were
delighted. Having approved this portion of the draft, Pinchot
firmly defended his approval:

> What it amounts to is nothing more than this: that when
> one body of public servants, the legislature, declare that a
> certain law is in the interest of the public welfare and con-
> stitutional, and another body of public servants, the judges,
> declare that it is not constitutional, then the question of
> which is right shall be determined by the people who make
> the constitution.

Undisturbed by rejection of his address in conservative circles,
Roosevelt, three days after the Columbus meeting, announced
his intention to do battle for the Republican nomination.

Though glad about Roosevelt's stand and anxious to get
into the fight, Pinchot was, nevertheless, worried about the
prospects. He reflected this in a letter to a friend in Seattle:

I am confident that unless Colonel Roosevelt's friends do make an effort to secure delegates for him, the difficulty of securing his nomination will be greatly increased. The power of the administration through patronage is very great. . . . The thing to do is for the men who want Roosevelt to be nominated to begin at once the work of securing delegates for that purpose.

Pinchot's concern was not limited to the delegates. Writing to his brother Amos, he declared that "Senator Dixon was justified in asking for a $100,000 fund before taking charge of the Roosevelt campaign," and "Roosevelt's supporters must immediately contribute."[1]

Pinchot made every effort to present Roosevelt's case to the people in a search for Roosevelt delegates to the National Republican Convention. During the ensuing months his campaign took him across the country. The prenomination campaign was made unusually vigorous by the fact that for the first time in the history of presidential elections the voters of thirteen states were privileged not only to select the delegates to the convention by direct primary vote but also to instruct them in the same way as to the candidate for whom they should cast their ballots. There were almost four hundred popularly instructed delegates from California, Georgia, Illinois, Maryland, Massachusetts, Nebraska, New Jersey, Ohio, Oregon, Pennsylvania, South Dakota, and Wisconsin. Feeling that Roosevelt was the popular choice, Pinchot and other Roosevelt campaigners naturally concentrated their efforts in these states.

In early March, Pinchot was confident upon his return from a swing into the northwest. He did, however, see cause for some concern in two instances. For one thing, the La Follette

[1] Senator Joseph M. Dixon was Roosevelt's campaign manager.

campaign manager was making a nuisance of himself by insisting that Roosevelt was not giving La Follette a square deal. Pinchot wrote to Amos about the second problem:

> Many of the Progressives are sore because a lot of the old line men are out for Roosevelt, and there is no doubt that the fight for the control of the states is the most important factor in the situation.

Concluding that he was sure of Roosevelt victories in Minnesota and Illinois, Pinchot pointed his campaigning to New Hampshire and Pennsylvania.

Pinchot's concern about La Follette's betrayal charge was justified, for, in spite of Roosevelt's strenuous efforts to counteract La Follette's strength, the former President lost the Wisconsin primary by a margin of almost two to one. Add to this defeat Taft's convention victories in the solid South and in the important states of Indiana, Kentucky, Michigan, and New York, and it is evident that Roosevelt followers had considerable reason for concern.

To Pinchot, bearing the brunt of the La Follette charge, there seemed to be no letup. "You who know about the La Follette business," wrote his good friend George Pardee, former Governor of California, "ought to give the true inwardness of his [La Follette's] withdrawal to the public. . . . Out here the Taft papers are making a great deal of capital out of the 'betrayal of the Senator.'" Apparently, California—where La Follette was most active—became a personal concern of Roosevelt. "The Colonel suggested this morning," said Pinchot to Roosevelt's campaign manager, "that I ought to go to California . . . on the ground that I can testify personally concerning the La Follette mix-up, and perhaps help to counteract what La Follette is doing in checking Roosevelt sentiment."

The La Follette candidacy, of course, was not to be readily dismissed. La Follette was determined to keep faith with his followers and stay in the race for delegates. Also, he knew he could keep many delegates from Roosevelt. The considerable Republican support he had attracted as recently as January was not easily dissipated, in spite of T.R.'s grassroots appeal; many were tenaciously loyal to La Follette. E. W. Scripps, of the Scripps newspapers, reflected such loyalty in his correspondence with Amos. "Personally," he wrote, "I have sometimes regarded Mr. Roosevelt as being 'half a loaf,' and as such he is better than no bread at all. . . . It is because La Follette, not only by his word, but by his life activities, has demonstrated that he has views somewhat similar to my own that I am supporting him." Governor Hiram Johnson, of California, reacted quite differently. He wrote:

> [La Follette] . . . intends to remain in this state for nearly four weeks until date of the Primary, indulging in charges and counter charges. . . . He is using every crooked paper in this state. . . . All of them, of course, are for Taft, but that does not prevent the impeccable Senator from acting with them.

The general pessimism that pervaded the progressive ranks did not discourage Pinchot. When the clouds were darkest and it looked as though President Taft would win with only negligible opposition, Pinchot wrote bravely that he liked the looks of the political situation:

> All the information I can get is favorable. In the South, we are getting more than I supposed would be possible. In the East, I believe Roosevelt will get Maine, New Hampshire, part of Vermont, and a part of Massachusetts. In Pennsylvania we ought to divide the delegation if we don't do

better. In New York, I hear [much about] . . . Roosevelt, although the Taft people are counting all but two. In other words, so far as I can see, the facts are with us while the newspapers are almost universally against us.

Apparently, there had been some justification for Pinchot's optimism. A few days after the above statement was made, the Pennsylvania Flinn machine utterly routed out the regular Penrose organization, winning most of the nominations for state officers and contributing sixty-five pledged delegates to the Roosevelt cause. "I am feeling so cheerful," said Pinchot to Roosevelt at this point, "over Pennsylvania and the general outlook that it is hard to get down to business." In mid-April, certainly before a trend could be perceived, Pinchot was extremely optimistic in writing to his sister: "The fight is about over. . . . I think we may all be very easy now that T.R. will be nominated and, if nominated, elected with a whoop."

Indeed, Pinchot was almost prophetic in his feeling. From the date of his latter statement until the middle of May, almost every week witnessed a Roosevelt victory. In short order, California, Minnesota, Nebraska, Maryland, and South Dakota followed one another into the Roosevelt camp. The total number of delegates opposed to Taft's nomination mounted until, by the middle of May, Roosevelt's chances of obtaining the nomination looked very good. As for Pinchot's contributions to Roosevelt's preconvention campaign, Senator Francis J. Heney, of California, testified: "We had a glorious victory here and everybody agrees that you contributed very largely to it by the speeches you made."

When, on the eve of the convention, Roosevelt won in Taft's home state of Ohio, Pinchot not only saw Roosevelt being nominated and elected but also saw himself "getting more for conservation during the coming four years than seemed in any way possible three months ago." Continuing this line of thought in a letter to his sister, Pinchot added, "Roosevelt ought to have an almost stupendous prestige when he comes in this time, and I shall expect to see him more completely dominating Congress than anyone has yet in your memory or mine."

Not all progressives shared Pinchot's optimism. More realistic observers estimated that one third of the delegates were uncommitted and felt that with Taft controlling the convention machinery, they would probably support the President. There was little doubt, however, that Roosevelt was the popular choice of the Republicans for the nomination. In those states in which Republicans had voted in primaries, Roosevelt received 278 of 362 votes.

The week following the writing of Pinchot's most recent enthusiastic letter to his sister must have been a week of reflection for him. Apparently, Pinchot came to the same conclusion as that reached by many progressive Republican politicians: that defeat was possible and that progressives might be forced to leave the convention. He wrote to Roosevelt on June 8 about the platform: "So far as I can gather things seem to be going well, but if we should have to bolt [the convention] then I take it Amos is exactly right when he says that a still more progressive platform will be necessary. I feel good and ready either way."

More practical politicians, however, were not willing to accept the alternative of a bolt. Indeed, before accepting such a bold plan, they were not adverse to making ideological concessions. Critical of Pinchot, many politicos loathed him for the political inexpediency of his views, particularly because of his influence on Roosevelt. His advocacy of proposals such as the recall of judicial decisions was repugnant to progressives of the "Boss" Flinn school in Pennsylvania. When one of the practical politicians expressed a double desire "to kill Lincoln Steffens" and "bottle up Pinchot," [2] even Roosevelt was agreeable to at least the first part of the suggestion. In spite of obvious ideological differences, a surface harmony prevailed within progressive Republican ranks, although at times it was exposed to considerable strain.

When the Republican Convention finally met in Chicago, progressives had more immediate problems than platform differences. Of the delegates elected to the 1,078 seats in the convention, Taft had committed to himself the vast majority of the delegates from the "rotten boroughs"—the southern states which had never cast an electoral vote for a Republican candidate for President. Roosevelt, on the other hand, had the support of the great majority of delegates from the states which are normally Republican and which must be relied upon at election time if a Republican President is to be chosen. Of the 1,078 seats, however, 238 were contested. In preconvention days neither candidate held a majority of the delegates. The progressives' problem of securing a majority for their candidate was particularly significant because of one insuperable advantage held by the Taft forces: The National Committee, which selects the temporary roll of the convention, had been appointed at the close of the last Republican Convention. The last convention, having nominated Taft, obviously appointed a National Committee sympathetic to him. Thus the temporary roll of the 1912 convention showed a distinct majority for Taft.

On the eve of the convention, Roosevelt arrived on the

[2] Quoted in Mowry, *Theodore Roosevelt and the Progressive Movement,* p. 225.

scene to lead the battle: "It is a fight against theft and the thieves will not win." Asked how he felt, he replied dramatically, "I'm feeling . . . like a Bull Moose." [3] The term would not be forgotten; the Bull Moose would become the emblem of the third party which rose from the Republican ruin being precipitated at Chicago.

From the opening of the convention, the Roosevelt forces fought desperately for what they described as "the purging of the roll" of Taft delegates whose names had been placed upon it by fraud. At every turn, however, the Roosevelt people were outnumbered; Taft's control of the convention remained intact.

The preliminary engagements, concerned with determination of the permanent membership of the convention, occupied the first days. Meanwhile, the temper of the Roosevelt delegates "burned hotter and hotter." Roosevelt, from his headquarters at the Congress Hotel, could not stem the tide. Ultimately recognizing the futility of seeking the nomination under existing convention machinery, Roosevelt commissioned Pinchot to circulate the following statement among leading delegates:

We are endeavoring to preserve the Republican party and to prevent the representatives of Taft from committing its assassination. . . . We have, therefore, submitted to the temporary organization while protesting against its legality and its foundation upon fraud and political theft. We will continue in the hope that the great body of the Convention will

[3] Quoted in Pringle, *The Life and Times of William Howard Taft*, p. 801.

not be parties to the final consummation of the fraud. We shall therefore proceed in the usual manner, appear before the credentials committee, put the committee in possession of all the facts so that its members shall have full opportunity to render a just decision when the report of that committee is presented to the Convention. If the delegates who have been fraudulently seated in this convention are allowed to sit as judges in their own cases and to vote upon the report of the committee on credentials, whether seating themselves, in whole or in part; then we will refuse longer to submit . . . in the contingency contemplated, we, the real and lawful majority of the convention, will organize as such and will nominate Theodore Roosevelt.

Certainly, there were progressive elements urging moderation and compromise, but Roosevelt, urged by Pinchot and other radicals, stood firm on the ground that the "roll must be purged." Organization leaders knew, of course, that yielding to his demand would result in a Roosevelt nomination. The Roosevelt struggle with the Committee on Credentials was in vain. At least, he demanded, the committee should seat seventy-two of the Roosevelt delegates, who had been so unjustly rejected by the National Committee.

Amos, in an account of the Chicago convention, noted that even though the standpatters appeared to completely dominate the convention, Senator Dixon, Roosevelt's campaign manager, was confident to the end. Apparently, Dixon and George W. Perkins, a close Roosevelt associate, were relying on a sufficient number of votes bought from southern Negro delegates to put Roosevelt over. The scheme folded when the Taftites bid higher. Amos stated in his *History of the Progressive Party,*

1912–1916 that he "never told Roosevelt about the strange little backwater in the river of righteousness on which the progressive craft was sailing so gallantly."

When it became unmistakably clear that the Taft forces would retain their control of the convention, the progressive delegates united in dramatic action. Speaking with "feeling," Henry J. Allen, of Kansas, announced the intention of the progressives to engage no longer in the actions of a convention existing in fraud. The progressive delegates would remain in their seats, but they would neither vote nor take any part in the proceedings. In ominous quiet Taft was nominated.

The closing minutes of the Republican Convention were not marked by the noisy jubilance of a united and confident party. The delegates well understood that without the support of Roosevelt and the insurgents the Taft candidacy was hopeless. At that very moment, the progressives were organizing the coup de grâce for the Republican Party.

On Saturday following the convention it was announced from Roosevelt headquarters that a new party would be formed that night at Orchestra Hall. The meeting was opened by Governor Hiram Johnson, of California, with a fighting speech to an already half-hysterical throng. Equally passionate anti-Republican tirades followed. Roosevelt himself was finally escorted onto the stage. In colorful prose he warmed to his adulating audience, renouncing his Republicanism and declaring his willingness to be the standard-bearer of a new Progressive Party—the Bull Moose Party. The crowd roared apaproval; the crusade had begun; a Progressive Convention would be held later to draw up formally a slate and a platform.

Although Pinchot, like most Progressives, at first had grave doubts about a Roosevelt victory, he was convinced that Roosevelt had started a movement which would mean the cleaning up of political life for decades to come. "Win or lose," he wrote to Henry Wallace, "I am with him to the end."

At this point, winning or losing depended, more than anything else, on action by the Democrats at their convention in Baltimore. Most Progressives agreed with Pinchot that "if the progressives win there, we shall have a hard time." When, after a long struggle, the Democrats nominated Woodrow Wilson, a true progressive, any chance for a Roosevelt victory diminished perceptibly. In view of almost certain defeat for his candidate, Pinchot established for himself a point of reference. Again, he wrote to Henry Wallace:

> We need, and have long needed, one party as to whose independence of the interests there can be no question. As things stand now, neither the Republicans nor the Democrats are able to fill that need. Wilson is an admirable man . . . but I do not believe his surroundings are satisfactory. . . . I am certain that the wise way out is the way Colonel Roosevelt is following—the creating of a clean new party as to whose affiliations there can be no doubt. . . . I don't believe that victory this fall is an essential condition of the success of the movement by any means. What is wanted mainly is a clear-cut fight for progressive principles, and whether we win or lose, I think there is no doubt that the average man will be better off. So I am going ahead with . . . vigor and enthusiasm.

Shortly after writing the above letter, Pinchot was expressing a new confidence. To his sister Lady Johnstone he wrote, "A week ago I thought he had not a chance to win. Now I am well satisfied that he has an excellent chance, and I am much pleased with the outlook."

Unfortunately for Roosevelt, few Progressives were as loyal to him as was Pinchot. To many progressive Republicans, apparently a family quarrel was one thing, a separation something else. Of the progressive Republican Senators, La Follette, of Wisconsin, Works, of California, Crane, of North Dakota, Brown, of Nebraska, and Nelson, of Minnesota, declared themselves against Roosevelt; and Borah, of Idaho, Bourne, of Oregon, Crawford, of South Dakota, and Cummins and Kenyon, of Iowa, announced that, although they were for Roosevelt as against Taft, they were not for a third party. Professor George E. Mowry suggests that by the first week in July even Roosevelt regretted his June bolt from the Republican Party but, having committed himself, had to go through with the campaign.

A committee was set up to initiate the new party. A few weeks later Senator Dixon issued a call to Progressives to meet in convention at Chicago on August 5 to organize the new party. In the period between the call and the convening of the convention, several rather complex problems had to be resolved. In certain states where presidential electors had been selected prior to the Republican Convention, Roosevelt men had been selected. Although selected as Republican electors, many of them were determined to stick with Roosevelt even though he would not be the Republican nominee. At first, Roosevelt encouraged them, urging them to resist resignation; he soon changed his mind, however. Administratively, it would have been difficult and of dubious constitutionality to have Roosevelt Progressives serve as Republican electors. Then, too, any process of using Republican electors would have tended to identify him with that party, inevitably losing for him some Democratic support.

There was also the serious question of whether or not

Progressive tickets should be established at state and local levels. Many Progressives felt that the new national party would be only as strong as its grassroots organization. Less ardent Progressives were not too concerned; they advocated continued participation by Progressives in local Republican organizations, with support for Roosevelt in a national Progressive Party. The radical wing of the party naturally opposed fusion; these men felt that this type of arrangement would, for example, portray insurgents in Pinchot's home state of Pennsylvania doing business with Senator Boies Penrose, the very epitome of standpat Republicanism. Roosevelt sided with the radicals, calling for Progressive slates in all states except those in which Republican organizations were unequivocally supporting his candidacy. Another reason for establishing separate organizations was the recruitment of Democrats; to make the Progressive Party universal and not just another Republican organization, it was determined to have some Democrats nominated on Progressive slates for state offices. Most states prepared to run a full national Progressive ticket. Twenty-two would run Progressive gubernatorial candidates. Less would run candidates for minor state and local offices.

During the period between the call and the convention, Pinchot and other Progressives met in New York to organize the Progressive Party. Pinchot, Perkins, Munsey, Senator Dixon, Medill McCormick, *Chicago Tribune* publisher, James Garfield, and Edwin A. Van Valkenberg, editor of the *Philadelphia North American,* were among the leaders. Pinchot busied himself particularly with the development of a radical platform to be adopted by the convention. With the assistance of Dean William Draper Lewis, of the Law School of the University of Pennsylvania, he drew up a draft of a platform, which he submitted on June 25 to Roosevelt and other

Progressives, suggesting that revisions be sent to him. Concerning the tone of his platform proposals, Pinchot was happy with Roosevelt's concurrence with their radical nature. Writing to Lewis about the need for a radical stand, Pinchot had warned:

> He [Roosevelt] is taking a very advanced position, and I am more and more persuaded that our platform must do the same. As a matter of fact, unless it does do, we shall be left without any satisfactory issue but the Colonel himself, while if we do take thoroughly advanced ground, we shall have a means of appeal to the average man which cannot fail to be powerful.

Roosevelt was not receptive to all of Pinchot's platform ideas. He did accept Pinchot's demands for minimum wage legislation, the short ballot, woman suffrage, and even preferential presidential primaries; but more radical measures were not appreciated. Completely unacceptable was a suggestion by Pinchot that Roosevelt's new administration should substitute the export of natural resources in manufactured form for their export as raw material. "Thus," said Pinchot, urging Roosevelt to accept the suggestion, "our exports would consist principally of labor, which is always replaceable, and, not as now, of natural resources, many of which cannot be replaced." Roosevelt did not consent to Pinchot's proposals for an immediate national workingmen's compensation act and the creation of a department of social welfare. The Pinchot Papers also give evidence that Pinchot unsuccessfully approached Roosevelt with the radical political innovation of the presidential recall.

It must be pointed out that Pinchot was not alone in his fight for liberalism. On the important issue of the Sherman Antitrust Act, which best manifested the positions of two factions evolving in the new Progressive Party, such sound liberals as Judge Learned Hand and Herbert Croly agreed with Pinchot, insisting that the platform call for a strengthening of the act.

The struggle to include a strong antitrust plank in the platform illustrates well the struggle for party control between two groups with conflicting ideologies. At the opposite end of the pole from Pinchot stood the party's financial godfather, George W. Perkins, who believed ardently that a restoration of competition through government regulation, as opposed to trust dissolution, was possible and desirable. Pinchot doubted the workability and sincerity of Perkins' regulation concept, fearing that it was a scheme of financial titans to get a strong hold on government.

Amos Pinchot had particularly serious reservations about Perkins' entire relationship to the Progressive Party. In *The History of the Progressive Party, 1912–1916,* Amos saw Perkins' financial background as a significant factor in the new party's leadership. As the chairman of the United States Steel Corporation's Finance Committee and as organizer of the International Harvester Corporation, Perkins, in his role in the Progressive Party, seemed to represent the stake of Morgan interests in a new Roosevelt administration. The House of Morgan would expect to enjoy again the harmonious relationship with the administration which had existed during the Roosevelt Presidency. Amos felt that, as President, Roosevelt had relied on heavy financial contributions from the steel industry in the 1904 campaign; that he had permitted the United States Steel Corporation to purchase the Tennessee Coal and Iron Company, thus freeing the Steel Trust from the last vestiges of competition; that he had used many Morgan men in his cabinet; and that his first choices of a successor to his high office were Morgan lawyers Elihu Root and Philander Knox. Amos believed that in a new Roosevelt administration the Morgan interests wanted nothing less than the perpetuation of their monopolization of steel. To Morgan men, Taft had been dangerous, "having in his four years wrought . . . havoc with the Steel Corporation."[4] They believed Taft to be committed to a militant prosecution of the Steel Trust. The spectacle of Morgan men manipulating the new "Party of Righteousness" was repugnant to Amos and Gifford. Throughout the party's existence they were to fight Morgan influence, commencing the struggle at the Chicago Progressive Convention on August 5.[5]

For the moment, however, the Bull Moose Progressive Convention opened in an aura of harmony and enthusiasm. Dedicated, conscientious, and respectable citizens proclaimed their new cause. They were in Chicago to amend the Republic's loss suffered in the Republican Convention. They were not conscious of the incongruous appearance of financial titans and political bosses, such as Perkins and William Flinn, and the more disinterested Progressives, like Pinchot. They were only conscious of a cause and a leader that, to them, were inseparable, as manifested by Roosevelt's "Confession of Faith."

Realizing now that only reformers would back him, Roose-

[4] Amos Pinchot, *The History of the Progressive Party, 1912–1916,* ed. Helene M. Hooker (New York: New York University Press, 1958), p. 175.

[5] John A. Garraty, in *Right-Hand Man: The Life of George W. Perkins* (New York: Harper & Brothers, 1960), gives as the principal reason for Perkins' association with the T.R. 1912 campaign Roosevelt's drive for regulation of trust rather than Sherman Act dissolution. Garraty notes also that T.R. was distressed by the Taft administration's implication that in 1907 he had been manipulated by Morgan into permitting the U.S. Steel Corporation purchase of the Tennessee Coal and Iron Company.

velt's appeal was without restraint. Taking on Democrats, Republicans, the courts, and the titans of industry, his "Confession of Faith" was directed to and for the people: They must govern; they must have the direct election of United States Senators, direct primaries, corrupt practices legislation, the short ballot, the referendum, the initiative, the recall, publicity of election expenditures, woman suffrage, a national industry commission to regulate interstate industry, a federal securities commission to supervise the issuance of stock, a permanent tariff commission, government ownership of Alaskan railroads, minimum wages and maximum hours, unemployment insurance, and old-age pensions. It was a crusade almost without precedent in United States political history. Seldom had a responsible political leader asked for so much reform. Understandably, his followers vented their emotions by alternately cheering and singing "Onward Christian Soldiers." They were in ecstasy, readying themselves to carry the Progressive message across the nation.

The crusade at Chicago was soon marred—only slightly, but indubitably—by the question of the antitrust plank. In an unpublished manuscript, found among the Amos Pinchot Papers, Amos talks about it:

All night long, the Resolutions Committee labored with the new platform. Whenever they had completed a plank, they would send it up to the Colonel's suite, where he, Munsey [the millionaire newspaper owner], and Perkins, armed with blue pencils, revised the planks and shot them back to the Committee, which in most cases obediently carried out the will of their leaders, and adopted the planks in their new and expurgated form. When, however, early toward morning, the Sherman law came up for discussion,

it was apparent that the Committee proposed to kick over
the traces and take the bit in its teeth. Professor Charles
McCarthy of Wisconsin and various radical minded Committeemen believed that the Sherman law would be read
out of the new party, unless it were endorsed by name in
the platform. During the preceding year a series of meetings
had taken place in Washington at which Brandeis, La Follette, Gifford Pinchot, Senator Bristow, Gilson Gardner,
Senator Cummins, myself, and others, discussed the Sherman
law in all its implications; and, as a result, when the Resolutions Committee of the Progressive Party met, in 1912, there
was presented to it, and finally passed, the following formula
for strengthening the Sherman Act, which was important,
not only because it added some force to the Sherman law, but
also, because it amounted to recognition and approval of this
pivotal statute:

> "We favor strengthening the Sherman Law by prohibit-
> ing agreements to divide territory or limit output; refusing
> to sell to customers who buy from business rivals; to sell
> below cost in certain areas while maintaining higher prices
> in other places; using the power of transportation to aid
> or injure special business concerns; and other unfair prac-
> tices."

Amos relates further that when this "Regulation of Interstate
Corporations" plank was presented to Roosevelt, Perkins,
Munsey, and Beveridge, it was returned to the Resolutions
Committee without the antitrust provision. He further notes:

> But the Committee, by this time fatigued by its hectic la-
> bors and piqued by the repeated over-rulings of its decisions
> by men who took upon themselves the role of proprietors of

the party, disregarded the rule of the blue pencil, and reinstated the deleted paragraph which, with the rest of the platform, was at once taken to the Convention.[6]

William Draper Lewis, who had worked closely with Gifford Pinchot on the preconvention platform, presented to the convention the Resolution Committee's platform—including the endorsement of the Sherman Law and the prohibition of specific insurance practices. George W. Perkins then hurriedly conferred with Roosevelt, who instructed O. K. Davis, secretary of the party, to delete the paragraph dealing with the Sherman Law. Accordingly, the platform was printed by the newspapers and later for campaign distribution without mentioning the Sherman Antitrust Law. The omission of the Sherman plank confirmed immediately the suspicions of many delegates that Perkins was a "bought man."

Because of the omission of any reference to the Sherman Act, the platform was interpreted by many reporters as opposed to the classification of trusts and combinations. With Perkins' approval, the document did condemn the evils of inflated capitalization and unfair competition; and it proposed, in order to eliminate those evils while preserving the unquestioned advantages that come from combination, the establishment of a federal commission to supervise corporations engaged in interstate commerce.

Other sections of the platform included the direct popular election of United States Senators, the short ballot, initiative, referendum and recall, direct primaries, nation-wide preferential primaries for the selection of candidates for the Presi-

[6] Garraty, in *Right-Hand Man: The Life of George W. Perkins,* notes that the Resolutions Committee approved the Roosevelt revision of the plank. Garraty adds, however, that there were various interpretations of the affair by contemporaries who were there.

dency, an easier method of amending the Federal Constitution, woman suffrage, and—perhaps the most radical innovation—the recall of judicial decisions "in the form of a popular review of any decision annulling a law passed under the police power of the state." [7] In the field of social justice, the platform pledged the party to the abolition of child labor; publicity in regard to working conditions; minimum wage laws; the eight-hour day; compensation for industrial accidents; continuation of schools for industrial education; and legislation providing for working conditions which would prevent industrial accidents, occupational diseases, overwork, involuntary unemployment, and other injurious effects incident to modern industry. With few exceptions, the platform followed closely the liberal doctrines of the Pinchot element of the Progressive Party. Altogether, it was the most radical platform that any major United States political party had yet presented to the electorate.

By late afternoon of August 7 the Bull Moose Party had accomplished its purpose: it had its platform and slate. Understandably, the convention turned to Governor Johnson, of California, as the vice-presidential nominee. Western support for Johnson would balance Roosevelt's appeal to the East. Johnson had also attained wide popularity for his prosecution of political grafters and bosses in San Francisco. His recent election to the Governship in his state was fresh in the minds of the Progressives. Most importantly, he was available; not many governors were. As early as May, Pinchot had sounded out Johnson and, finding him willing to run, prepared to nominate him if the opportunity arose. Consequently, Pinchot gave one of the nominating addresses.

At 7:00 P.M. the convention chairman, Albert Beveridge,

[7] Harold J. Howland, *Theodore Roosevelt and His Times* (New Haven, Conn.: Yale University Press, 1921), p. 225.

announced the slate and introduced the candidates. The convention accorded them one of the most enthusiastic ovations in presidential convention history. Immediately upon his stepping forward, Roosevelt's adulators broke out with "The Battle Hymn of the Republic." For once, their candidate was at a loss for words, so overwhelmed that he could only thank his followers and quietly accept "the great honor" conferred upon him. In an aura of high excitement, the convention adjourned, sending forth crusaders to battle for the Lord in the coming campaign.

On the following day, August 8, the National Committee met to select a nine-man Executive Committee. To the distress of Gifford and Amos, George W. Perkins was named chairman. The Pinchots, along with William Allen White and Meyer Lissner, had fought his election, but Roosevelt's support of Perkins for the job was too great an obstacle to overcome. Although Perkins' recognized organizing ability and his desire to finance the party made him a good choice, his association with the House of Morgan made him suspect.

*   *   *

Long before the Bull Moose campaign began, Pinchot had been aware of the major problems. "We all realize," he wrote to his cousin W. D. Eno, "that Wilson's nomination has somewhat complicated the third party movement." Still, Pinchot had seen the battle as being worthwhile:

> I believe the one right thing to do is go ahead vigorously. Wilson is an admirable man, but his party is still tied up with the same old influences. Tammany is vigorously behind him. So are the old leaders, who stand for the same things in the Democratic party that Crane and Penrose do in the Republican party.

To his good friend Louis Brandeis, who was supporting Wilson, Pinchot presented another interpretation of the Progressive cause:

> Republican and Democratic platforms, being old-line statements of old-line points of view, we shall find in the new platform a more advanced position toward genuine industrial righteousness than anything that has ever appeared on this side of the ocean.

To leaders within the Progressive ranks, Pinchot expressed himself still differently: "Whether we win or not," he said to Gilson Gardner, ". . . is not a question, although I personally feel that we might have at least a good fighting chance. It might be better in some respects if we did not." Here, Pinchot implied agreement with Gardner's emphasis that the Progressives might make more of a contribution as the new opposition rather than the majority party. By late August, however, Pinchot was again warming up to the possibility of a Roosevelt victory. Having attended a Progressive meeting in the District of Columbia, he reported success to Roosevelt: The meeting "was ten times as enthusiastic as I supposed would be possible. I don't want to be over-enthusiastic, but certainly things look well."

Pinchot's efforts in the campaign fell within three general areas: writing for publications and campaign pamphlets; advising the Progressive candidate and his staff; and, lastly, campaigning actively. All three areas called for particular political acumen. As a leader of the party's radical element, it was not easy for Pinchot to gear his campaigning to the conservative Perkins leadership.

Pinchot had particular difficulty in answering the Democratic charge that Roosevelt's election would mean rule by the United

States Steel Corporation, an organaization with which Perkins had been closely allied. The Wilson forces also charged that the Roosevelt concept of regulation of trusts, rather than their dissolution, was a master state scheme of control which was almost without limit in its power to direct the economic life of the nation. They held that freedom of industrial activity was necessary for a healthy economic life. With considerable skill Democrats argued that Roosevelt's approach to regulation of great industrial concerns would lead to more, not less, monopolization. They believed that only dissolution of trusts under the Sherman Law would restore true cempetition. Almost hypocritically, Pinchot attempted to refute their arguments by going down the Roosevelt-Perkins road on trust legislation. "We want," campaigned Pinchot, "the trusts regulated and the big special interests driven out of the control of our government."

Amos was more vocal in his disapproval of the United States Steel philosophy of government regulation. He felt that its presence in the guise of Perkins made the new party dangerously vulnerable. He begged Roosevelt to consider "the almost certain consequence of Perkins' activities" in the party. Besides, argued Amos, if Roosevelt's retention of Perkins in influential party circles was an attempt to appeal to the business interests, T.R. erred tactically, for his own radical stands on many issues had already alienated this faction. Also, Amos felt that Roosevelt's support of Perkins was a "cruel injustice" to the intelligent, decent people who were giving so much to the party. Roosevelt would not listen to Amos, however. Some twenty years later Amos concluded, in his account of the party, that Roosevelt was no statesman; the former President was too politically oriented to take a firm position on trust dissolution.

As the situation is viewed from the 1960's, both the Pinchot

Progressives and the Democrats lacked justification for their early chastisement of Roosevelt's regulation of business policy. Much of the New Nationalism was a recognition that twentieth-century "bigness" in industry precluded dissolution of trusts. Dissolution was a Jeffersonian concept applicable only to the nineteenth century. The complexity of the twentieth century called more for the Hamiltonian concept of centralization and regulation.

Also troublesome to Gifford Pinchot was the Democratic prediction that the election of a Progressive President would cause legislative chaos, since the Congress would be Democratic or Republican. In addition, the Democrats scored heavily when they attacked Roosevelt's faith in high tariff protection. As a campaigner, Pinchot attempted to divert attention from the telling arguments of the opposition by having himself presented as the man who "awakened the nation against the unscrupulous, wholesale grabbers of natural resources." With such an introduction, Pinchot would proceed to point out that Taft's reactionary actions on conservation of natural resources—in the famous Ballinger-Pinchot affair, for example —were representative of his conservative administrative policy and that in a campaign imbued with reform the President could be considered eliminated. As for the Democratic candidate, Pinchot publicly had grave doubts about the Wilsonian experiment. Granting that Wilson might be a "good hired hand," Pinchot questioned his ability to lead the fight to save natural resources, the source of all monopoly. As proof that Wilson could not lead the fight, Pinchot pointed frequently to recent Democratic action in the Senate:

Last winter in the Senate the Democrats and reactionary Republicans got together in an effort to break down the system of national forests. They did it in the form of an amendment to the agricultural bill, which was innocent enough on its face, but it is enough to say that the effect of their proposition would have been to turn over to the water power grabbers and the timberland thieves forests worth about $1,000,000 and water power about $600,000.

In addition, Pinchot also blamed the Democrats and reactionary Republicans for cutting appropriations for the Forest Service. Even Wilson, Pinchot would then conclude, admitted that the Progressive Party was a sign of general discontent with such regular-party action.

Pinchot's untold expenditure of campaign effort in 1912 was largely attributable to his twofold commitment to the Roosevelt candidacy and to Progressive principles. Of the two, an incident on October 14 demonstrated that particular emphasis was placed on the former. On that day, as Roosevelt was about to deliver a speech in Milwaukee, Wisconsin, the former President was wounded by a would-be assassin, John Chrank. Without knowing the seriousness of the wound, Roosevelt announced dramatically his intent to deliver his speech, "or die." Upon hearing of such bravery, Pinchot wrote sentimentally to T.R., "It may seem like a queer thing to say, but your being shot has been one of the finest things that has ever come into my life on account of the way you have handled the whole situation." [8]

One week before the election, Pinchot expressed publicly his confidence in Progressive victory—a victory to be based on the votes of the "vast majority of the men and women who work with their hands." Reaching the climax of his cross-country campaign in Pennsylvania, Pinchot chided the stand-

[8] Quoted in McGeary, *Gifford Pinchot: Forester-Politician*, p. 231.

pat Penrose machine for unscrupulous tactis. He told Pennsylvanians:

> Wherever I have been in Pennsylvania the enthusiasm for Roosevelt and the Washington Party [the Progressive Party in that state] had far exceeded my highest hopes. Indeed, wherever I have been throughout the nation the power of this movement for decency and a Square Deal is amazing. The spirit of the workers is beyond all praise.

In actuality, a Roosevelt victory was almost impossible. Since Wilson's nomination precluded any great exodus of progressives from the Democratic Party, Roosevelt had to depend upon the support of Republican progressives; they were too few. Many progressive Republicans in the West either were opposed to Roosevelt or gave him little support. His paternalistic New Nationalism, an urban rather than a rural philosophy, was antithetical to the low-tariff, trust-busting doctrines of the farming West. Then, too, many city dwellers throughout the country believed sufficiently in competition to be suspicious about the missing antitrust plank. Also, organizational weakness inevitably hampered the new party in its first national campaign.

When the votes were finally counted, Taft carried two states —Utah and Vermont—with 8 electoral votes; Woodrow Wilson carried forty states, with 435 electoral votes; and Roosevelt carried five states—Michigan, Minnesota, Pennsylvania, South Dakota, and Washington—and 11 of California's 13 votes, giving him 88 electoral votes. Taft's popular vote was 3,484,956; Wilson's was 6,293,019; while Roosevelt's was 4,119,507. The results were not in the least depressing to Gifford Pinchot. On the contrary, he was basking in victory over the Republican Party:

The Progressive party has established its position. In a campaign of three months it has won its place in the front rank. Nothing like it has ever been done before. This is the first victory. We are going ahead to the next without breaking our stride. We cannot be checked for long, and we cannot be stopped at all, for we are fighting for the one thing that always wins in the end, the progress of mankind.

Two days after the election, Pinchot suggested to Senator Dixon, chairman of the Progressive Party, that the following statement be issued about the party's future:

The Progressive party is not relieved from responsibility by the result of the election. As the second of the great national parties, our obligation . . . is as clear as if we had won this first battle. Accordingly, we propose to formulate and present to Congress and state legislatures bills to carry the planks . . . into practical application.

In a three-month campaign we have advanced our legal standing to that of the second or minority party in the United States. . . . If the majority party in Congress or state legislatures proposed to take action hostile to the public welfare, we of the Progressive party, through our Senators and representatives, through our committees on legislation, and in other ways, should oppose it to the limit of our power; but any legislation genuinely in the public interest, originating from any party or from any source, we will support and defend. . . .

Personally, Pinchot felt that the election had proved three things: "Bill" Taft had been defeated; the Bull Moose Party was in second place; and the new party's strength made it certain that "the Progressive policies are the controlling policies in this nation from now on, and any party that neglects them does so at its peril, and perhaps that is the biggest achievement of all." The second point of interpretation, of course, warrants some brief analysis. That the party had achieved second place was questionable. Progressives running for state and local offices did not match the Roosevelt percentage of votes. Only one governor, approximately 12 congressmen, and about 250 local officers achieved Progressive success. Considering the necessity for vigorous grassroots organization in a national party, the Progressive Party was not actually the second party. Pinchot's last point of interpretation was far more sound. The Progressive radical campaign contributed much to the radical tenor of the whole campaign and, consequently, of the Wilson administration.

Pinchot did not linger too long on past failure. His interests were rapidly focused upon the party's future. He tendered extensive suggestions to Roosevelt:

> First, that the headquarters of the Progressive party should be moved to Washington; because . . . our . . . tasks—relating to legislation—can be carried on better here . . . and because . . . organization—can be handled as well from here; and because the third task, publicity, can be carried on far better from Washington. . . .
>
> Second, Dixon ought in my judgment to be put in charge . . . with the principal task of keeping the Progressives . . . interested and eager until the next Congressional and Presidential elections.
>
> Third, Perkins should be kept in the background from now on. . . . I am not disposed to minimize the hard work he had done, or the value of his contributions in money, or his great service in holding Munsey in line. On the other

hand, I believe that the heaviest single load the Progressive cause has had to carry in this campaign has been Perkins, and in saying so I am expressing the opinion of very many men beside myself.

Flinn [the Pittsburgh political boss and the Pennsylvania Progressive leader], who at one time seemed to occupy a similar position, appears to have justified his connection with the Progressive party most everywhere, at least so far as my experience goes. . . . What Flinn has just accomplished, Perkins has not been able to do.

Fourth, there should be attached to headquarters wherever located, one man who is a trained executive of high grade.

Thus it became evident that Pinchot was determined to lead the liberal element in purging the organization of conservative leadership. Just as evident was the fact that Roosevelt did not intend to have his financial benefactor, George W. Perkins, pushed aside. He so wrote to Pinchot:

O Mr. Secretary of State that was to have been. Substantially, I agree with your letter. My reservation is about Perkins. Like Flinn and myself he has been partly a burden and partly an asset. But frankly I don't think we could have carried on the fight at all without him any more than we could have done anything in Pennsylvania without Flinn. I thoroughly believe in both.

Two days later Roosevelt qualified his letter to Pinchot, stating that he had been attacked because of many Progressive leaders, such as Flinn, McCormick, and Dan Hanna, son of late Ohio boss, Mark Hanna. It is interesting to note that Flinn, in this letter and in subsequent letters from Roosevelt to Pinchot, was placed first among the Progressive bosses whom

Roosevelt thought caused the most criticism. In this manner, Roosevelt always implied that Flinn, supported by Pinchot, was as great a burden to the party as was Perkins. Roosevelt continued to Pinchot:

> After any defeat, there is always a tendency among leaders to quarrel, and each one to try to put the blame upon someone else; this at the very time when it is most essential that there should be a united front to the enemy. There are only a few men, like Ben Lindsey and like Perkins himself, who are wholly free from this tendency.

Pinchot was surely caused a great deal of anguish by Roosevelt's having placed Perkins in the same category with the venerable Judge Lindsey. Roosevelt continued his defense of Perkins:

> . . . If Perkins had been excluded from all share in the management, if we had lost his very great organizing ability, his devoted zeal, and the money which he so generously gave, and the money which men like Munsey gave because of their associations with Perkins . . . why I think our whole campaign would have gone to pieces.

Roosevelt explained in his letter to Pinchot that he felt the Progressives were facing an incredibly difficult situation. To continue to fight the old political parties would be difficult because they had stolen the issues and because they were well organized. "We have not," he wrote, "the clear cut issues as to which we take one side and our opponents the other side." Also, he continued, "The strength of the old Republican party is shown by the fact that, although we carried the primaries two to one against Taft at the polls, about as many Republicans voted for him as for me. We only got about ten per cent or in that neighborhood of the Democrats." In view of the lack of clear-cut issues and the need for organization, Roosevelt concluded his voluminous defense:

> I will not throw to the wolves one of the staunchest allies and supporters we have had, the man who has worked for us with the utmost disinterestedness and effectiveness, and sacrificed himself, the man who has not taken a holiday for nine months and who had devoted himself at great personal loss to his cause, with a whole-heartedness and unremitting labor such as he never showed when he was in business and when his own personal profit was concerned.
>
> I trust there will be no fight. Not a voice should be raised against Perkins continuing as Chairman of the Executive Committee. If there is, I trust it will be behind closed doors and that no leader of the Progressive party will furnish aid and comfort to the enemy and excite the jeers of the reactionaries by speaking, except among themselves, of these differences of opinion.

Thus the essence of Pinchot's letter concerning the Progressive Party, the reduction of Perkins' influence in the party, was repudiated by Roosevelt. Pinchot replied bitterly, "The effect of your letter was to put Amos and me in a position which we did not occupy." They had not suggested that Perkins be eliminated from the party. "There is a notable difference," continued Pinchot, "between being in an army and being at the head of an army." He defended his position:

> I am still vigorously of the opinion that a bad mistake was made when Perkins failed to take the step [that of resigning the chairmanship of the Executive Committee] suggested to him by me in person, and by Amos and me in our letters to you, and in our talk with you. It was a mistake

because Perkins is not trusted by a very large number of Progressives, or by the general public because of his present connection with the Harvester and Steel Trusts and his past connections with Wall Street and New York Life Insurance Company, and to a much less degree because of his relations with Secretary Ballinger in the matter of Alaska.

Concluding that he felt as compelled to fight Perkins as in a previous period he had felt compelled to fight Taft, Pinchot made one thing clear: "Whatever differences of judgement I may have with you, they will not dim my affection for you, nor cloud the recollections of the good work we have done together."

As Gifford temporarily dropped the gauntlet, Amos picked it up. On December 3, 1912, he sent a long letter to Roosevelt, supplementing Gifford's position on Perkins and the United States Steel Corporation: "If we put every one of . . . [the Progressive] measures into practice and do not at the same time prevent the trusts from simply shifting the burden onto the shoulders of the people . . . we will accomplish little or nothing." Two days later Roosevelt replied in equally lengthy fashion, arguing that trusts did not account for higher prices and that the United States Steel Corporation had been less harmful than its competitors. At this time Roosevelt took an interesting position on the missing antitrust plank. He insisted that its elimination had been merely a matter of cutting "surplusages from the platform" and that, if Amos and Gifford desired, the plank should be restored. Roosevelt still insisted, however, that Perkins must retain the chairmanship of the Executive Committee.

It was obvious that Gifford and Amos and their forces were not satisfied with Roosevelt's answers. Gifford Pinchot foresaw that his suggestions about the Perkins leadership would not be accepted at a forthcoming December conference of Progressive leaders in Chicago. An attempt to eliminate Perkins by removing the national offices of the party to Washington, D.C., was defeated by a substantial majority. Perkins, of course, remained as chairman of the Executive Committee. Actually, Perkins' position in the party was strengthened at Chicago. Without question, he was second in command of the party; as chairman of the National Executive Committee, he was given authority to speak for the committee on any issue.

At the Chicago meeting Gifford's influence was confined to behind-the-scenes activity. He held frequent caucuses with Charles Merriam, the University of Chicago political scientist, Harold L. Ickes, future Secretary of the Interior, Jane Addams, of Hull House, and others, but to little avail. They did have the antitrust plank restored to the platform, but that had already been promised by Roosevelt.

That Pinchot had spoken truthfully when he said that he felt as compelled to fight Perkins as he had once felt obliged to fight Taft was borne out by continued attacks on the chairman of the Executive Committee, and Roosevelt continued to defend Perkins. By January, Roosevelt became exasperated. He asked Pinchot three blunt questions:

1. In just exactly what directions do you feel he [Perkins] is exercising or showing this preponderating influence?

2. Exactly what is he doing which is of damage that ought to be stopped?

3. What steps would you desire me to take in stopping it?

Pinchot, concluding that he and Roosevelt had come to an impasse, failed to reply for almost five months, although in the interim period he was a frequent visitor at Oyster Bay and worked closely with Roosevelt as the former President wrote his autobiography. At the same time, Pinchot conferred with his anti-Perkins group. On May 6, 1913 he answered the questions which Roosevelt had framed previously:

1. Perkins is and has been exercising such a preponderating influence first, as the heaviest contributor to the Progressive campaign fund; second, as chairman of the Executive Committee; third, as manager of the campaign and the decider of questions which arose in the campaign as far as they were not decided by you; and fourth, as the man to whom the omission of the Sherman Law plank of our Party was due. . . .

2. Perkins is constantly doing damage for the reason that his prominence in our council has impaired, and in the minds of many men has destroyed confidence in the sincerity of our Party and our platform; first, because of his position as a . . . trust magnate . . . second, because he stands for corporations which in their relations with their workmen are directly violating some of the most important planks of our platform; third, because . . . he represents to the labor unions the very organizations which have been and now are their most important opponents in American industry; fourth, because the country does not trust him.

3. It is perfectly obvious, to me at least, that Perkins should be replaced as chairman of the Executive Committee just as soon as possible. . . . I want to see the Bull Moose win next time, but I don't believe we can win under the present chairman.

Although disturbed by ideological differences within the Bull Moose Party, Pinchot must have received some consolation from similar differences within the Democratic ranks. "We are in the middle of a very vigorous fight here," he wrote to Lady Johnstone, "the outcome of which is likely to decide whether the controlling power in the Democratic party will be reactionary or progressive." Possibly overemphasizing his theme, Pinchot believed it not unlikely that the fight would center around conservation. After Wilson's inauguration, Pinchot still saw conflict within Democratic ranks, although he faintly praised the new administration:

> Wilson seems to have started off admirably. There is a lot of talk that he has succeeded in uniting the progressive and reactionary Democrats but in my judgement that is mere piffle. They put a reactionary Senator at the head of a committee, labeled him progressive, and then threw up their hands. Trouble is coming along later anyhow.

At the close of the year 1913, Pinchot was still suspending judgment about the Democrats: "We do not yet know where the Wilson administration will stand. . . . We are hopeful that its position will be wise." In truth, the record of the Wilson Presidency would prove to be quite progressive, although Pinchot seldom admitted it. History, of course, notes a gamut of progressive actions, including conservation of natural resources. More importantly, the Clayton Act, the Federal Trade Act, the Federal Reserve Act, the La Follette Seamen's Act, the Adamson Act, and sundry agricultural acts stand out.

CHAPTER V

1913

It is within the truth to say that Theodore Roosevelt is the best known and most widely respected personality in the whole world. . . . I have no hesitancy in calling him the first citizen of the Republic. Theodore Roosevelt began the national progressive movement while he was President. Without the foundations which he laid then, there would be no Progressive party today. [He] . . . has since done for that movement the greatest thing a great leader can do for a great cause. He has carried it to a point where it stands upon its own feet.

The above words were spoken by Gifford Pinchot in October of 1913 at a farewell dinner tendered Theodore Roosevelt prior to his trip into the South-American jungles. The speech does not reveal in the slightest the rather serious factional disputes in which the two men opposed each other in 1913; yet the warmth of Pinchot's words for Roosevelt manifested absolute sincerity. Pinchot adored Roosevelt and always would; differences between them would never dissuade him.

Even during the spring, when Pinchot struggled so hard against the Perkins leadership of the Progressive Party and when Roosevelt, just as adamantly, restrained Pinchot's influ ence in the party, Gifford was delighted to be a frequent guest at Oyster Bay. Work on the Roosevelt autobiography, particularly, drew the two men together. Pinchot aided Roosevelt considerably in the writing of the chapters on conservation. In certain sections Roosevelt paid glowing tribute to the former Chief Forester. Of course, extraordinary expression of mutual respect and kindness might well have been compensation for their political differences. "He is doing his best to be nice," Pinchot remarked privately of Roosevelt.

In 1913 Pinchot's activities were more diverse than during the previous year: He, of course, worked on the Roosevelt memoirs; he continued to oversee the work of the National Conservation Association; he fished; he pursued further the country-life problems he had begun to study in the Roosevelt administration; he wrote a great deal, and on various subjects; he found time to read *King Henry IV*. Without question, however, Gifford Pinchot's commitment to Progressive Party work was foremost among his activities.

In January of 1913, Frank A. Munsey, through his paper, the *New York Sun,* proposed amalgamation of the Progressive and Republican parties. When Roosevelt refused to accept the idea, the publisher turned on the Progressives: "This reform idea has so possessed the thought of the new party, and the spirit of uplift and idealism has so dominated it, that the bread and butter issue has been largely obscured." In effect, Munsey was asking how the party would be financed. Pinchot ignored the question; correspondence to a friend reflected his rejoicing over Munsey's defection:

I am especially delighted with the episode. Munsey has never been with us on principle in this fight, but only with us in some queer way of his own, while his convictions were mainly those of the most reactionary type of Republicanism. It will do us a lot of good if he is driven out of the party in spite of the loss of his papers.

"The [Progressive] movement is growing in the East," Pinchot reported optimistically sometime after the Munsey action. "I see no reason," he continued, "to fear fusion of any kind unless it should be fusion between the progressive Democrats and ourselves on the basis of our own platform or its equivalent differently stated. . . . I believe most heartily in the future of the party." Certainly, the thought of fusion with Republicans was anathema to Gifford Pinchot—ideologically and emotionally. On one occasion, in May, 1913, Pinchot shook hands with Elihu Root before he recognized the standpat Republican and former chairman of the 1912 Republican Convention, who was partly hidden by a wide-brimmed Panama hat. Upon recognizing him, Pinchot immediately dropped his hand and walked away. That night, Pinchot noted in his diary that he had debated whether or not he should go back to tell Root that he had shaken hands by mistake.

Fusion with Republicans was an equally repugnant thought to Amos. He would have welcomed a union with the progressives of the Democratic Party even more enthusiastically than Gifford; he would eventually join the Democratic ranks. Gifford would never be able to go that far, for he shared Roosevelt's loathing for the Democratic Party.

Although desertions from the Progressive ranks to the Republican Party continued throughout 1913, Pinchot, in a letter to Beveridge in late November, again reaffirmed his faith:

Fusion with the Republican party is impossible because it would amount to the sacrifice of our principles for the benefit of the very bosses out of whose ranks we came in order to get clean, and out of whose ranks we must stay in order to keep clean. All this goes without saying. We have other and greater things ahead. The greatest of all is to abolish privilege and the magnate system, so that every man shall get what he earns by service to the community, no more and no less.

The fight against fusion was, of course, a difficult one. The Bull Moose machine, built rapidly in 1912, appeared to be falling apart. Party positions and financial backing, both necessary to the life of a political organization, were lacking. In the hope of maintaining the Progressive crusade, the Executive Committee established the Progressive Service, under the supervision of a committee made up of the heads of departments in the new service. In addition to Gifford Pinchot, who managed the Department of Conservation, a list of illustrious members of the service includes William Draper Lewis, Jane Addams, and Charles Merriam.

Amos Pinchot was particularly happy about the service. First, he was pleased about Gifford's position. "You seem," he wrote to his brother, "to be on the Legislative Committee, to head the Conservation Committee, and I understand [you are] a member of the little committee of four which is practically the Board of Governors for the whole service." Also, Amos felt that the activity of the radical element at the December, 1912, Chicago meeting was paying off. "If we had not made our rumpus," he concluded, ". . . it would have been impossible to have got good committees at all."

In search of support for the Progressive Service, Gifford Pinchot explained:

The Progressive Service, under which is the Department of Conservation . . . is an organization of the Progressive party, but keeps as far from partisan politics as under the circumstances it possibly can. It receives contributions from people of other parties, and while its first task is to carry out the principles of the Progressive platform, it is not in the business of getting votes, except in that way.

The perpetuation of the crusade through the Progressive Service was theoretically a good idea. Obviously, there was room for activity in the departments set up by the service: social and industrial justice, conservation of natural resources, popular government, and business. Unfortunately, however, the service was having difficulty perpetuating itself. The problems that it faced after its first year of operation were discussed by Dean Lewis in a letter to Pinchot:

First, . . . few of us have any clear conception of the exact nature of the matters outside of the work falling to our committee.

Second, there is a wide-spread belief . . . that state social service organization work as undertaken by the national social service has hampered the political organization. . . .

Third, there may be a condition of discouragement in the office of the national service which impairs its efficiency. I know that there are a good many facts which indicate this condition. . . .

Fourth, it is practically certain that the Executive Committee of the National Committee will not continue its present support to our committee or to the work of the Speakers Bureau. . . .

Fifth, Miss Keller [the director] states that . . . no pledges have been secured for next year. She intends to start at once to try and secure contributions and pledges.

In view of these things I believe that the real facts as to the friction between the National Service and the state political organizations in the different states should be ascertained, and that the body ascertaining the facts should suggest a modification, if a modification seems to them desirable, in the present work of the Service in the states or in the plan of organization for state services being advocated by the national service.

Modification of the service was to prove impossible. By 1914 most of the services "so bravely proposed by the Chicago Conference had long since ceased to function." Even if the service had met all expectations, it had become quite apparent that the organization would not be enough to keep the crusade or the party alive. During its dismal year of existence, the primary interest of the leaders of state and local machines was to beseech the national party for nonexistent subsidies. The reply to such requests, that the National Service was keeping Progressive ideals alive and that the National Finance Committee expected each local unit of the party to finance itself, did not impress harassed local leaders. They saw little relationship between Progressive ideals and the local political machine. Politicos wanted money, with which they could create new positions to be filled in their organizations. When their national party and their leader at Oyster Bay were unable to lubricate the machinery in this manner, the organizations barely moved.

Almost as if to compensate for the lack of Bull Moose Party machinery and activity, Pinchot re-emphasized Progressive principles. An occasion for this emphasis was presented to Pinchot at a Progressive Party banquet at Asbury Park, New Jersey, on February 22, 1913:

> The Progressive party lost the election, it is true, but it lost nothing else. Its principles have a hold on the public

mind and conscience. . . . We have made it plain to the people of the United States that we propose to work for the principles embodied in our platform in defeat as in victory, in power or out of power, in season and out of season.

You cannot stop a man with a great purpose so long as he is alive. You cannot stop a party with a great purpose at all. . . . Just so long as the Progressive party holds to the cause of human rights and human welfare as against privilege, and sticks to its determination to apply its platform, its enthusiasm and vitality and standing . . . will get stronger.

We are not beating the air. We have declared our principles, and our highest duty is to get them applied. . . . The Republican party committed suicide when it said what it did—the party first, the people afterward. Our strength is that with us the public good comes first.

Already we have . . . made it certain that the principles for which we stand will be carried into effect. If the Democrats fail to enact the Progressive policies into law, then the Democrats will go out of power. After that we shall come in, and apply our platform ourselves. Either way our principals win, and that is the main thing.

That Progressive principles were as important to Pinchot as were Progressive politics is made evident by his insistence throughout 1913 that the Bull Moose Party accept the radicalism that he and his cohorts espoused. In fighting for the acceptance of such radicalism, the intense ideological struggle of the Pinchot wing with party leadership was generally unknown outside the party hierarchy.

The intraparty struggle continued to revolve around the trust influence on party principles, with the issues becoming more pronounced and clear cut in 1913. Perkins saw more clearly that the combination movement in industry was inevitable and beneficial; he was more intense in his belief that the Sherman Law must be replaced by a federal business commission with power to charter and investigate enterprises. Such, to him, was the New Nationalism.

Pinchot, a principal architect of the New Nationalism, continued to have misgivings about the Perkins interpretation. To Pinchot, Perkins and his corporate interests epitomized the principles of privilege and concentration of wealth that he was fighting. Pinchot believed sincerely that he was fighting the battle of most of the people. "Privilege," he wrote to Medill McCormick, "is the power to use wealth, or results in the power to use wealth. The continued concentration of privilege in the hands of a small fraction of our people is hostile to the welfare of all the rest. It must be stopped." Elaborating further, Pinchot continued:

> No man among us is so foolish as to propose the confiscation and division of property. Nevertheless, we must recognize that the work we are engaged upon is a class war, a war of the unprivileged classes against the privileged classes. . . .
>
> It is not right that through privilege such an undue proportion of the total wealth should be in so few hands. . . . We are fighting not so much to take it away from them now as to make it certain that the concentration of riches and opportunity which curses the nation today shall not curse the nation of the future.

Pinchot constantly reminded those around him of the class war and the reasons for its existence. He constantly badgered T.R. about Steel Trust abuses. When in April of 1913 Roosevelt was informed by Pinchot of the U.S. Steel Corporation's refusal to agree to the eight-hour day, the former President promised that he "would see Perkins about it."

In his fight against wealth and private monopoly, Pinchot was not as radical as his opponents pictured him. Certainly, he was not as radical as Amos, to whom he wrote:

> I am not ready to go so far as government ownership and operation of the railroads. Nor do I believe this country is anything like ready for that idea. . . . As Miss Tarbell said, you can always control the direction in which public thought will go.

Also, Gifford was not as convinced of the wisdom of adopting a single-tax scheme as was his brother.

During 1913 Amos worked hard for the Progressive cause. Active in the party and its New York Progressive Service, he championed a proliferation of liberal municipal causes: home rule; charter revision; responsible city administration; extended public utilities; rapid transit extension; dock and water-front development; and improved labor and industrial conditions. Amos Pinchot's manuscripts reveal numerous and diverse demands by radical organizations and troubled individuals upon his time and money. Once he gave $500 to a Patrick Quinlen to appeal what Amos agreed was a wrongful court conviction. Like Gifford, however, Amos' first concern was the fate of the Progressive Party.

By 1913 Amos' persistent anti-Perkins and antiregulatory position had made him *persona non grata* to T.R. Amos was openly in support of Wilson's ideas about trusts. He saw the Bull Moose Party dying unless "we can keep ourselves from being thrown, hog-tied, branded and delivered over to the government regulation of private monopoly." By the summer of 1913, Amos felt that the party had been indoctrinated and that the idea "that the Steel and Harvester Trusts are purely charitable institutions" had crept into the party ranks. Amos was so loud in his criticism of the situation that the party chairman of Idaho expressed the hope that these pronouncements would not wreck the Progressive Party. Amos defended his stand in replying that monopoly was "hostile to the fundamental idea of democracy."

By July of 1913, Gifford was closer to both the concept of regulation and Amos' theory on government control. He stated in a letter to Amos that all of the large enterprises could not possibly be abolished:

> We need an inter-state commerce commission, but we also need the Sherman Law. Our enemies probably try to twist what we say into an assertion that all regulation is futile, whereas what we mean as I understand it is that we must regulate all large business at the same time we break all monopolies or put them into public hands.

While Pinchot was on the Chautauqua stump calling for the dissolution of monopoly, Roosevelt, from South America, rebuked the radicals in the party. Amos was disturbed when he wrote Gifford:

> By the time he [Roosevelt] gets back he will have framed us up as a bunch of maniacs trying to tear down every factory larger than a corner grocery. He is putting this over, too, for people really do not understand the differences between fighting monopoly and fighting business on a large scale. They understand it less and less the more the Colonel talks. Somehow, I do not love him for his clever South American speeches.

Gifford, however, was less worried than was his brother. Having talked with the venerable Senator Moses Clapp, of Minnesota, he was happy to report that the Senator's ideas coincided with those of the Pinchots—"that any kind of a private monopoly is an outrage." "His view," continued Gifford, "is that regulation of private monopoly is almost a contradiction in terms. In fact, he said it was like a disreputable house kept by the YMCA."

By the end of 1913, Amos had distilled the argument of the radical element of the Progressive Party. The brief was submitted for Gifford's approval:

Behind this term of the abolition of private monopoly we will muster all our various social remedies: conservation, the land tax idea to a certain extent, tariff reform, patent reform, etc. Almost all the privileges flow from private monopoly of some kind, and practically every remedy for privilege is found in attacking private monopoly.

Here is our line, so plain that everybody can see it, between those who favor private monopoly, that is to say the water-power trust, private railroads, private municipal utilities, tariff privilege, the money trust, the industrial trust, etc., and those who are against these things. Under such a clarification we can make this fight perfectly simple. . . . We will have the monopolists on one side who wish to hog the wealth and the production of wealth and the people on the other side. We will make it perfectly plain, for it is easy to do, that "trust regulation" is a fake, and we will show up the conflict of interests between the people who are against monopoly, for it robs them, and the magnates who want to preserve monopoly and apply to it a regulation which will mean only the continuation of robbery. . . .

Throughout 1912 and 1913, few men were as wholeheartedly pledged to national progressivism as were Gifford and Amos Pinchot. Yet both were also attracted to Progressive activities in their respective home states, Pennsylvania and New York.

CHAPTER VI

The Washington Party

UPON LEAVING the Taft administration in 1910, Pinchot lost
no time in putting down political roots. "Please have my name
entered on tax list as resident," he wired his lawyer in Milford,
Pennsylvania.[1] A stillborn "Pinchot for Governor" movement
in the state had not gone unheeded. Pinchot worked hard at
becoming known in Pennsylvania, taking advantage of every
opportunity to speak in the state. It became his political home
and would remain so for the rest of his life. Seldom was his
political involvement more intense than during the years following the great 1912 crusade and, especially, during the 1914
United States senatorial campaign in Pennsylvania, when Pinchot ran against Boies Penrose.

Pennsylvania needed progressivism; it is paradoxical that a
state which had been exposed to a succession of "boss" rule—
Simon Cameron, J. Donald Cameron, Mathew S. Quay, and
Boies Penrose—should be one of the few states to support the
Progressive Party in 1912. Philadelphia's "Gas Ring" had typified the strangling effects of the unsavory political leadership
in that city. By charging exorbitant rates for inferior gas, the

---

[1] Quoted in M. Nelson McGeary, "Gifford Pinchot's 1914 Campaign,"
Pennsylvania Magazine of History and Biography, Vol. LXXXI, No. 3
(July, 1957), p. 305.

trustees of the gasworks had funds with which to set up and pull down mayors, treasurers, legislators, and councilmen. West of the mountains, William Flinn and Christopher Magee had divided Pittsburgh between them, Magee taking the financial and corporate interests, Flinn receiving the public construction contracts. Lincoln Steffens described the corruption of both cities in 1903 in *McClure's Magazine* and later in his provocative book *The Shame of the Cities*. Particularly interesting was his account of the sordid past of William Flinn, the champion of Pennsylvania progressivism in 1912. Of Pittsburgh Steffens wrote:

> Magee and Flinn were the government and the law. How could they commit a crime? If they wanted something from the city they passed an ordinance granting it, and if some other ordinance was in conflict it was repealed or amended. If the laws in the State stood in the way, so much the worse for the laws of the State; they were amended. If the constitution of the State proved a barrier . . . the Legislature enacted a law . . . and the courts upheld the Legislature.

In more recent years, however, the picture changed somewhat in Pittsburgh and Philadelphia. Flinn, having been driven from power in 1903, was converted to progressivism, and Philadelphia elected an independent reform mayor in 1910.

In 1910, when progressivism was struggling to gain control in Philadelphia, Boies Penrose, the Republican boss, still ran the state. He put over John K. Tener, a first-term Congressman, as the gubernatorial candidate at a time when Pennsylvania Republicans wanted the United States Secretary of State Philander Knox as the nominee. More importantly, Penrose succeeded in having Tener elected Governor over State Treasurer William H. Berry, the popular candidate of the independent

Keystone Party. It was believed by many Democrats that Penrose forced their leaders to run an unknown for Governor, State Senator Webster Grim. Penrose's complete manipulation of the 1910 election fitted exactly the Cameron-Quay boss-rule tradition.

Penrose had controlled Pennsylvania since Mathew Quay's death in 1904. It was Penrose who had decided that Quay's United States Senate seat would be dispensed by auction—at $500,000. Encountering difficulty in selling the seat at that price, Penrose hawked it in New York, informing the interests there that the Pennsylvania Legislature would await their orders. The interests paid the price, removed Philander Knox as Attorney General of the United States, and placed him in the Senate, where he would be made "safe" by a cautious Senate majority. Penrose also made Samuel W. Pennypacker Governor of the state, knowing that he would be quite unaware of any near-by racketeering.

Penrose's political orgies were legend. Although an accounting of them becomes repetitious and dull, they evidence great political skill—particularly by the fact that Penrose avoided censure. Once, when his bitter enemy Bill Flinn had absolute evidence that Penrose had accepted $25,000 from Standard Oil's John D. Archbold, Penrose deflated his enemy as he read on the Senate floor a telegram in which Flinn had also sought from Standard Oil comparable financial support for the same services which Penrose had rendered.

In 1912, however, Penrose met his match. Boss Flinn was making a comeback, as a leader of the Roosevelt movement. His cunning and skill must surely have been admired by Penrose. In that year Flinn was one of the first progressive Republicans in the state to drop La Follette in favor of Roosevelt. Then he drove through the Republican primary a slate of Roosevelt delegates to the National Republican Convention. To make sure that the Republican voters would recognize the Roosevelt delegates on the ballots, Flinn arranged for every Republican in the state to receive a postal card listing data concerning these delegates. Flinn was so successful in getting Roosevelt delegates elected that he replaced Penrose as the national Republican committeeman from Pennsylvania.

Flinn was loudly pro-Roosevelt at the Republican National Convention in 1912, frequently taunting the standpat temporary chairman, Elihu Root. When Root aided in the expulsion of more than enough Roosevelt delegates to assure Taft the nomination, Flinn led his Pennsylvanians from the hall and into the new third party. Again, Flinn outwitted Penrose by coming up with a "Washington Party" designation for the Pennsylvania Progressives after Penrose had pre-empted the Progressive Party label. At Harrisburg, the state capital, Penrose had filed pre-emptions for every sort of party title in which the word "Progressive" or "Roosevelt" could be utilized. The true Progressives were therefore barred from using any such names, for, if they had appropriated the title "Progressive," the Penrose machine could have put its candidates on the ticket and have had the advantage of the vote cast for the Roosevelt candidates.

The Washington Party of Pennsylvania won the state for Roosevelt in 1912. T.R. had 444,894 votes, compared with Wilson's 395,637 and Taft's 273,360. The reasons for the feat were manifold: Flinn's political *savoir-faire* was a factor; also, the Washington Party was supported by the *Philadelphia North American,* a leading eastern paper; Roosevelt and Pinchot campaigned hard in the state. Another factor was the considerable conservative support tendered the Progressives. Many conservative Republicans preferred Roosevelt to Wilson, sensing, of course, that Taft had no chance. Interestingly, the president of the silk-stocking Pennsylvania Manufacturers' Club supported Roosevelt.

Pinchot was identified closely with Pennsylvania Progressive politics. With Edwin A. Van Valkenberg, the editor of the *Philadelphia North American,* Flinn, and William Draper Lewis, Pinchot had been one of the four Pennsylvanians who signed the call for the national Bull Moose Party convention. Pinchot, however, was quick to credit Progressive success in Pennsylvania to state organization and leadership. He described Flinn as "one of the three men who impressed me most at the Chicago convention, especially as to his directness and common sense."

Roosevelt, too, was quick to pay homage to the Progressive state organization for what it had accomplished for the nation in the 1912 fight. "We have had great movements of righteousness," said Roosevelt to the first annual Progressive Conference of Pennsylvania on March 14, 1913, "great movements that stirred the souls of men in this country. The time when the country was founded; the time when it was saved; and now the time when it was dedicated to the lives of the average men and women who make it up." Roosevelt noted that in the third great movement of righteousness Pennsylvania had taken the lead. "It's the Keystone, among other things, of the Progressive party," he concluded. Roosevelt, like Pinchot, gave extravagant praise to Flinn, at least in public. "I never stood up more heartily," the former President said to the Pennsylvania Progressive Conference, "in honor of any one than I stood up tonight in honor of Senator Flinn." T.R. then became even more expansive and related Flinn's explanation to him, a year previously, of his reason for joining the Progressive ranks. Flinn had said:

I have gone into it because I want to see this country put in such shape that it will be a healthy country for my children to live in, and it won't be a healthy country for my children to live in if it is not a country in which substantial justice is done to the children of other men.[2]

Privately, Roosevelt spoke in a different tone about Flinn. As noted previously, he insisted to Pinchot that Flinn was a greater burden to the national Progressive Party than was Perkins. Indeed, as Pinchot was justified in seeing the new party stigmatized by Perkins' trust associations, Roosevelt was justified in fearing the stigma of Flinn's associations with the notorious Mayor Magee. The Flinn-Roosevelt relationship was paradoxical because Roosevelt was capable of expressing two opposing views at the same time.

The Pinchot-Flinn relationship also proved to be paradoxical, to a lesser degree. Pinchot was soon to learn that his faith in Flinn's conversion to the Progressive fight for social justice was not entirely justified. Although Flinn and Magee parted ways in 1912, the parting was only temporary. Flinn soon concluded that he could not carry the 1913 Pittsburgh mayoralty election without the old Flinn-Magee organization. It became evident to many that he had been interested in the 1912 Roosevelt movement more as a device to stop Penrose than as a movement for social justice. The renewal of the "unholy alliance" between Magee and Flinn in the seat of the state Progressive power almost lost for Flinn the support of the independent voters who followed him in 1912, although "they saved him from defeat for [his candidate's mayoralty] nomination in the

[2] George F. Holmes (ed.), *The Story of the Progressive Movement in Pennsylvania* (Philadelphia, Pa.: Council of the Progressive League of Pennsylvania, 1913), pp. 63–64.

1913 Pittsburgh primaries" and, in the election, from an even worse defeat.

The Progressives became particularly incensed when, after the 1913 defeat, Flinn proceeded to consult Magee about the 1914 fight against Boies Penrose. "Now there is a revolt in our lines," complained H. W. D. English, a Pittsburgh Progressive leader and Pinchot confidant. "The people here said very emphatically they want neither Magee nor Flinn." Specifically, English reported that the Progressives in western Pennsylvania were disturbed over conferences between the Flinn-Magee combination and Van Valkenberg, the Washington Party leader in the Philadelphia area. "We understand," wrote English on November 11, 1913, "that a deal is now being made by Flinn, Van Valkenberg and Magee, all of whom have gone East looking to a local politician for United States Senator and a Democrat for Governor." English noted further that, judging from conferences that he had held with Progressives, "they want to name you for United States Senator, claiming you represent the Progressive principles they stand for and come from the eastern part of the state." "I am told," he concluded, "such a program would meet with opposition from both Flinn and Van Valkenberg."

Pinchot was sufficiently alarmed by English's information concerning the Flinn–Van Valkenberg fusion attempts to question the Philadelphia leader. "The storm sent out from Pittsburgh concerning our conference was totally misleading," answered Van Valkenberg, summarizing that he only agreed to favor fusion if President Wilson and Roosevelt would so request it for purposes of defeating Penrose—a request that Van Valkenberg saw as being very unlikely. "Don't quote me, please," he hastened to add. "I must avoid seeming to act in bad faith toward our Pittsburgh friends." The latter statement revealed that English was substantially right about the fusion.

In December, Van Valkenberg again assured Pinchot that English's concern over a Magee-Flinn alliance was unnecessary: "The question raised by Mr. English is nothing you need be disturbed about. There can be no alliance with Magee because he will not support the Washington party candidate for United States Senator, or even candidates for state offices." He also told Pinchot that Flinn had not yet determined his course for the 1914 anti-Penrose campaign and that he would see Flinn before a decision was reached. Moreover, Van Valkenberg insisted that he would present to Flinn English's point of view—that Flinn should ally himself with English and his friends and that Pinchot should be the Progressive candidate for United States Senator—a view with which Van Valkenberg agreed substantially. Concerning Pinchot's candidacy, Van Valkenberg remarked, "Sentiment seems to be all one way concerning your nomination."

Throughout 1913 Progressive leaders other than English and Van Valkenberg were interested in a Pinchot candidacy for Governor or Senator in 1914. As early as March 24, 1913, the *Philadelphia Press* had sensed a pro-Pinchot feeling, foreseeing, however, certain obstacles to such a candidacy, especially from the Flinn quarters:

> Perhaps this is some reflex . . . having William Flinn, the angel of the Bull Moose in Pennsylvania, make the race against Penrose. In fact, shrewd politicians are inclined to the opinion that when Flinn's aspirations collide with the plans for that select group which is pushing Mr. Pinchot forward, that the first serious split may develop in the Washington party. . . . Certainly Flinn would like to see some-

one in the Senatorship whom he would have more hope of
guiding than he could expect to have were Mr. Pinchot the
man in the saddle.

Pinchot, in correspondence with his Progressive associates in
1913, disclosed little concern about Flinn opposition. Indeed,
he assumed that the senatorial nomination could be his for the
asking. His attitude is demonstrated in a letter to his friend
Plunkett:

> There seems to be a gradually crystallizing sentiment that
> there would be more chance to drive Penrose out of control in
> Pennsylvania and clean up the state if I made the race against
> him. . . . The decision I must make on this question in-
> volves the general direction of my work for the rest of my
> life, as I see it. Either I must decide to fight for conservation
> and country life in politics, or out of politics.

The fact that the personal decision appeared to Pinchot to be
the predominant issue did not lessen other considerations. In
addition to such issues as possible Flinn opposition, a prior
Pinchot commitment to the William Draper Lewis candidacy,
and questionable residence qualification, Plunkett, in his response to Pinchot, mentioned another: an open ideological
conflict between Pinchot and Roosevelt. "One reason," wrote
Plunkett, "I have urged you on several occasions to retire for
awhile from politics was, as you know, a feeling that there was
bound to be a painful conflict between yourself and one whom
you love and to whom you owed much in public life." Then
Plunkett suggested that in the Senate race Pinchot would be
operating at a state level and, thus, would be less likely to come
into conflict with the former President and the national leadership. Also, Plunkett saw that Pinchot's bent, temperament,

family, and friends favored his making the race. "So, go ahead, with the warmest good wishes from one more friend."

On December 8 Pinchot wrote to his sister in Holland:

> There is . . . nothing new yet about the Pennsylvania situation except that evidently the nomination is coming to me without contest. . . . I think the fight is well worth making, and I judge the right thing to do will be to go ahead with it but I don't want to decide for a couple of weeks.

During those two weeks Pinchot consulted many Bull Moose leaders, the outstanding one being, of course, Roosevelt. To Roosevelt, Beveridge, and Hiram Johnson, Pinchot indicated that he would make the race only on the condition of their active support. He wrote to Roosevelt:

> One of the strongest arguments in favor of going in is that Van Valkenberg tells me you have agreed to come into the state and help in the fight. That would make more difference to the result than any other possible thing. If I do go in I shall of course bank on your support in the fight and shall do my best to make it hot for Penrose and his gang.

"You are going to be nominated for Senator in Pennsylvania," assured Beveridge in response to Pinchot's request for advice, "so what is the use wasting any time thinking about it?" Writing again to his sister, Pinchot said, "I am getting more and more persuaded that the Pennsylvania senatorship is the thing for me to undertake. . . . I am more and more anxious to begin fixing plans for the coming summer."

Pinchot's decision to run was not based on only optimistic, and sometimes superficial, encouragement from state and national Progressive leaders. He was aware of adverse campaign conditions. T. R. Shipp, one of Pinchot's protégés in the National Conservation Association, made for Pinchot a thorough study of Pennsylvania's internal political conditions. In general, the report was unfavorable to Pinchot's candidacy. Shipp concluded principally that his mentor would have hard sledding; that, although Pinchot and the Progressives would make a good showing, Progressive strength had declined since 1912; and that Penrose, who would probably be the Republican candidate, would make the tariff the main issue. "He [Penrose] hopes to gain by the anticipated bad industrial conditions, which are already beginning to show in different parts of the state," wrote Shipp. Other salient factors that Shipp felt should be considered by Pinchot were: the "big interests" contributions going to Penrose; the manifest increased confidence of the Democrats; the Republican fear of Roosevelt's making Penrose the principal issue.

More specifically, Shipp analyzed the positions of political parties in Pennsylvania by sections. In the eastern part of the state, Penrose, William H. Berry, and Pinchot would be the choices for Republican, Democratic, and Progressive candidates. In predicting victory, Shipp favored the Democrats first, Penrose second, and the Progressives last. The following conclusions were drawn about political conditions in the east: great disintegration of Progressive strength; strong opposition to Penrose; solid Democratic front and strong candidates; large stay-at-home vote among Republicans; Progressive losses caused by lack of organization and lack of confidence in Boss Flinn and Van Valkenberg.

In Shipp's analysis of central Pennsylvania, the state capital of Harrisburg was described as a bad place to get a line on what the state was thinking, for every opinion there was tainted with strict partisanship. Newspapermen in the city, however,

confirmed, with little variation, the main points brought out
in reports from eastern and western Pennsylvania.

About western Pennsylvania, the Shipp Report stated:

> The impression is very strong . . . that the Democrats
> have a good fighting chance to win out in the fall election.
> The impression is equally strong that the Progressives can-
> not possibly hold their strength of last fall. It is reported that
> Progressives have been holding conferences, and apparently
> they are much more active in the western part of the state
> than in the eastern part of Pennsylvania.

The report also indicated that in western Pennsylvania Flinn
was "trying to run Gifford Pinchot with the view to demand
a big campaign fund, to which Pinchot will be the heaviest
contributor." Shipp continued about Flinn: "There are a good
many unkind things said of him by newspaper men—for in-
stance, the statement is made that he is thoroughly unscrupulous, and willing to sacrifice anything for his own gain." Also,
the report declared, "The Washington party is not in particularly good repute in Pittsburgh. . . . It is said that it has made
strange political bed fellows. The allegation is that a certain
element of it is pretty low grade, including gamblers and saloon
men." Further analysis of western Pennsylvania, the seat of
Pennsylvania progressivism, indicated that Penrose's representatives "are busy stirring up the discontent among the workingmen"; that Roosevelt and Pinchot, campaigning together,
would create a stir; that Republicans and Democrats were
returning to their party organizations; that Pinchot would
have to prove his Pennsylvania residence; that in Pittsburgh
certain politicians were attempting to ridicule the combination
of Pinchot, Flinn, and the Washington Party; and that Repub-

licans would gain strength through existing industrial conditions. Shipp concluded his report with a general summary of Penrose's plans:

> As indicated by the main body of the Report, the plan of Penrose and his associates is to begin early, and make hard times and the tariff the overshadowing issues. By this they hope to gain in two ways, by the vast number of workingmen in the state who will be immediately affected by hard times; and second, the big interests and large employers on whose support they are counting. The play they are making is that Penrose has always stood for high protection, and that the only hope of the big interests is through his re-election. They point out that the present Democratic administration is responsible for the hard times that are coming on and they declare that the Progressive party is as yet untried.
>
> .   .   .   .   .
>
> The Penrose machine is more confident since the city elections of this fall, which while not contributing much encouragement, have through an analysis of the vote, it is claimed, inspired the old leaders with a feeling that there is a good chance to regain strength, particularly if the tariff can be made the issue. They have not lost hope by any means. It is the uncertainty of the primaries that bothers them.

Pinchot's correspondence gives no indication of his being discouraged by the Shipp Report. If it did cause concern, Flinn's enthusiasm for Pinchot's candidacy might well have compensated for it. "Flinn," wrote Gifford Pinchot to Amos, "said I could be elected if the Progressive state ticket were beaten by fifty thousand. Afterward, he moved it up to 75,000 and it would probably have reached 100,000 if the talk . . . had continued."

On the day following the Flinn conference Pinchot decided to run. He asked the veteran Senator Albert Beveridge for specific instructions in organizing a senatorial campaign. "There is not a minute to spare," was Beveridge's first advice. "Perfect your organization. As a brass-tacks matter of getting votes into the ballot box, it is worth more than speeches."

Simultaneously with Pinchot's decision to make the race, Nevin Detrich, chairman of the Washington Party, called a state conference for January 14 and 15 for the purpose of crystallizing sentiment for the coming campaign. "STATE PRO-GRESSIVES RENEW THEIR BATTLE FOR SOCIAL REFORM" was the headline in the *Philadelphia North American,* with the subheading "TO BEAT PENROSE"—the theme of the conference. "We all hope," declared Flinn to the conference, "that he [Penrose] gets the nomination. He and all the other gentlemen concerned in the Chicago theft must go to the political block." Referring to proposals by supporters of Penrose and Barnes, New York Republican boss, for changes in the Republican rules as an inducement to bring Progressives into the Republican fold, Senator Clapp warned the conference, "It was the rulings, and not the rule, that wrecked the Republican party." James Garfield heaped venom on Penrose: "[He] . . . represents, symbolizes, typifies all that is bad in public life." Congressman Henry W. Temple, of Pennsylvania, hoped that the "big grizzly" of the Republican Party—Penrose, of course—would not die before the Washington Party got its shot at him in November. Temple pointed to "the Progressive duty of uprooting the political plant from which Penrose springs, so that it can never put forth another flower of his kind." Indeed, Progressive sentiment crystallized quickly at the conference. Optimism about a successful anti-Penrose campaign ran high.

Following the adjournment of the conference, state chairman Detrich, directed by the Resolutions Committee "to communicate with various county chairmen and state committeemen throughout the state as to the sentiment in the various counties in regard to the candidates for United States Senate and state offices," carried out his instructions and reported his findings to the reconvening conference on February 6. After hearing Detrich's statement, the conference resolved:

> that it is the sense of this Conference, based upon the reports of sentiment throughout the state that Gifford Pinchot be requested to submit his name for the consideration of the Washington party voters at the primary election on May 19, 1914, for the nomination for United States Senator.

The nomination, of course, was Pinchot's, with the blessing of his fellow Progressives and the special blessing of Flinn. Most importantly, Pinchot felt—probably with justification—that Roosevelt was exceedingly eager for him to make the race. Pinchot's election would give the former President an eastern spokesman in the Senate. Significant also to Pinchot's acceptance of the nomination was the fact that his friend Dean William Draper Lewis, to whose senatorial candidacy Pinchot had been pledged, stepped aside. Complete Progressive support, however, did not lessen extraparty opposition. The *Philadelphia Public Ledger* cried, on February 8:

> Where was Mr. Pinchot in the past quarter of a century of his adult life when Pennsylvania needed men of the qualifications his supporters claim for him today? Was he a volunteer? Did he assay to join the brave spirits who were contending against the overwhelming odds of a corrupt organization? . . . Not at all! He was . . . drawing a com-

fortable salary in some Federal position as a resident of another city! Born in another state, a citizen by legal fiction less than three years, a voter less than two years, and now a candidate for the highest office within the gift of the State! Mr. Pinchot should wait.

The intraparty unanimity that accompanied the selection of Pinchot as the Bull Moose candidate for the Senate was not expressed in the selection of a gubernatorial candidate. Six candidates were brought forward for that office: William Draper Lewis; H. W. D. English, president of the Pittsburgh Chamber of Commerce; Congressman M. Clyde Kelley, of Allegheny; State Treasurer Robert K. Young; Judge Charles Brumm; and William Wilhelm. When the February 6 Harrisburg conference which nominated Pinchot had reached an impasse over the question of a candidate for the Governorship, a subsequent conference was called in the hope that in the interim some of the aspirants would withdraw.

Of the six original candidates for the governorship, Wilhelm and Brumm were not serious contestants. Young, suspected of being backed by Flinn and Van Valkenberg, was ultimately described by Van Valkenberg as being unavailable, in which opinion Pinchot concurred. Concerning the remaining contenders—Lewis, Kelley, and English—Pinchot wrote to a Pittsburgh friend that for some time he had reduced the list to these three. "English tells me," he wrote, "that he intends to prevent consideration of his name. The sentiment I have met seems to be crystallizing rapidly around Dean Lewis and I am going to tell Clyde Kelley today of my having reached the same conclusion. This is nothing against English." Pinchot further explained his choice: "I would gladly make the race with him [English] as a running mate. Under all circumstances, however, I believe Dean Lewis will make the more available . . . [candidate]."

Although Kelley, a brilliant Congressman with more practical political experience than either Lewis or English, might have been the logical Pinchot running mate, especially as he represented western Pennsylvania, Pinchot was adamant in his position. "The strongest thing against Kelley is his youth," said Pinchot to a Pittsburgh friend, "a difficulty which time will cure but which in my judgement would be hard to meet this year." To Kelley Pinchot expressed a different objection—the fear that, inasmuch as he had stepped aside for Pinchot in the Senate candidacy, Progressives might feel that it was a bit peculiar if Kelley were now given the gubernatorial candidacy. Kelley, of course, was not impressed with Pinchot's line of reasoning and implied that he would make the race, assuring Pinchot, however, that he would support the winning nominee. Pinchot wrote, in the course of reporting this conversation to English, that Kelley had "in my judgement a completely mistaken idea of the course and extent of the demand for his candidacy in the state, and he evidently believed that he has a fair chance to win." Objecting to Kelley's nomination for still another reason, his tariff record, English, again disqualifying himself, suggested to Pinchot that he choose his own running mate on a purely political basis and that Lewis would then be the logical choice. Thanking English for his "fine spirit," Pinchot replied that he intended to think the matter over carefully before the new conference convened. Two days prior to the scheduled conference, Kelley finally acquiesced in Pinchot's support of Lewis; and, when the conference finally assembled on February 26, William Draper Lewis accepted the draft to "submit his candidacy for the Washington party nomination at the May primaries."

With a running mate finally selected to his satisfaction, on March 2 Pinchot presented to the press his formal acceptance of the Washington Party February 5 resoultion. He noted that he had to accept the nomination in order to have "a hand in the first great task now before the citizens of Pennsylvania,— namely, to drive out of power and destroy the bi-partisan political machine which has so long dominated and exploited the state in the interest of the privileged few and private monopoly." Only the Washington Party—a party without fusion, deal, or understanding with either of the old parties—was free to clean up the state. Pinchot, of course, could not resist noting that conservation of natural resources would be paramount in the campaign. "I believe," he concluded, ". . . that the people have the right and the duty to control and use the government, the laws, and the natural resources for their own benefit, and that the object of government is not great riches for the magnate but human welfare and justice between men and women." Pinchot was obviously committed to the Progressive cause in Pennsylvania. To him, 1914 was a repetition of 1912.

Reaction to the public announcement of Pinchot's candidacy was generally gratifying to his camp, with particular emphasis placed on the campaign's appeal to youth. "Your selection," said A. L. S. Rowe, president of the American Academy of Political and Social Science, "is a real inspiration to the younger men of the state to spare no effort in the struggle for better things." Said Francis Biddle of Philadelphia, the future Attorney General of the United States:

This is the first time for many years that at last the youth of Pennsylvania have a leader behind whom they can enlist. . . . You will, I am certain, have the support of the greater number of young men who believe that ideals are practical things, and that practical politics should mean making tangible the more just ideals.

The Pinchot candidacy did not enjoy absolute approval. The opposition had two ostensible reasons for being unhappy. They felt that Pinchot was not a true Pennsylvanian and that he was much too wealthy. To the former charge, which even the leading Democratic candidate for the Senate, A. Mitchell Palmer, dismissed, Pinchot replied that government service had required his Washington, D. C. residence from 1898 to 1910 but that "after the conclusion of the Ballinger episode, I went back to the region with which my people have been identified since Revolutionary days, and established a legal residence in Milford, Pike County, in December, 1910." Concerning the "silver spoon" charge, an Altoona *Times* editorial reflected the most able refutations. Recognizing that Pinchot might be assailed for some things, the newspaper did not believe that his wealth should be one of them. The *Times* listed questions which should be asked about Pinchot:

> Has he made proper use of the money that came to him? Have his activities been in the interest and for the welfare of his country and his countrymen? Has he frittered away his time in idle and vain glorious pursuits? Has he made a cheap and vulgar display of wealth, or has he applied himself to problems that have to do with the development of the nation, the preservation of its wonderful resources and the conservation of the people?

The *Times* concluded succinctly:

> It is entirely creditable to him that, during a period when rich men's sons have been making donkeys of themselves and doing much to bring wealth into disrepute, he has been

carrying a man's load, meeting his duty as a man and a citizen.

During the period between his March 2 announcement and the May 22 primary, Pinchot gained stature by stumping the state. Campaigning as if he were encountering opposition in the primary fight, Pinchot visited the most remote corners of the state. Also, he spent a two-week period in Chautauqua debating with Woodrow Wilson's Secretary of Labor, William B. Wilson, a fellow Pennsylvanian.

The most publicized of the addresses that Pinchot gave during his state tour was a speech to the exclusive Five O'Clock Club of Philadelphia, an organization of "privileged men." Having spoken just previously to mill hands in another part of the city, Pinchot showed considerable courage in his prefatory remarks:

> Coming here from the Light House I cannot help noticing the contrast between you and the men I just left. This contrast has impressed upon me the small chance the men in the Light House have compared with the such as you.
>
> And as I faced the other audience I could not help thinking that what would be bad luck for you would be great luxury for them. There is a good deal the matter with this country. And we can find the basis for it in just such gatherings as this tonight.
>
> The only possible way these men can meet with men like you on equal terms is for them to line up on common strength on their own side.

Indeed, such a remark made his audience visibly uncomfortable and incited a fair amount of heckling. After restoration of order, Pinchot concluded his speech and was followed in rebuttal by James M. Beck, of New York. Lauding the Constitution of the United States, Beck accused Pinchot of considering it obsolete. "If any class," countered Beck about the laws under the Constitution, "is favored it is the laboring class, because it is the only class exempt from the Sherman law."

Having expressed his anti-Republican beliefs on the state-wide campaign tour, Pinchot directed his platform planks against the Democratic forces represented by Secretary of Labor Wilson in the Chautauqua debate during the latter part of April. The debate centered mainly around the Democratic tariff bill, the administration banking bill, the repeal of the Panama Tolls Bill, and the administration's conservation policy. Although not lacking evidence, Pinchot's antiadministration arguments, with the exception of the tariff issue, were obviously less fervent than the anti-Penrose charges.

Pinchot sensed his success over both Republican and Democratic forces, and, as the day of the primary approached, he eagerly anticipated the commencement of the summer campaign. Certainly, forewarnings of the Shipp Report were not evidenced by Pinchot's behavior, although Van Valkenberg saw Pinchot doing poorly at this time. For the moment the Progressive senatorial candidate was encouraged by recent grassroots reports. He wrote to Beveridge:

> In two widely separated counties I talked recently with men who had been circulating petitions for candidates. One had spoken to about five hundred Washington party men, the other to something over 900, and the total number of men with us in 1912 who will not be with us this year out of the whole 900 was just exactly four. Accurate facts such as these speak far more convincingly than the claims of campaign orators ever can.

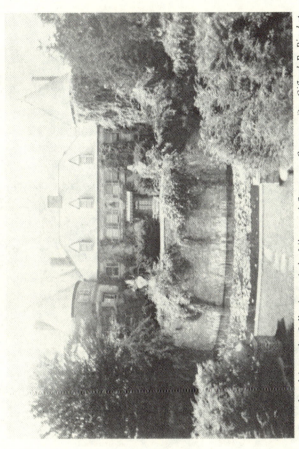

Fig. 1. "Grey Towers," the Pinchot family home, designed by Richard Morris Hunt and built by James W. Pinchot, in Milford, Pennsylvania.

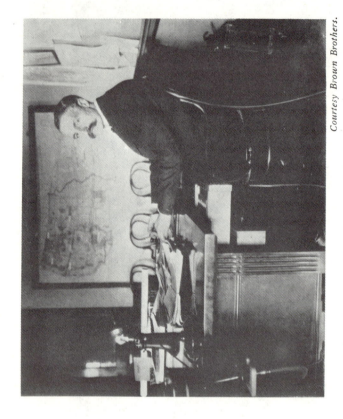

Fig. 2. Gifford Pinchot, as Chief Forester of the United States, seated at his desk in the Bureau of Forestry of the Department of Agriculture.

Fig. 3. Theodore Roosevelt after his Presidency, during the period in which he and Gifford Pinchot were closely associated in national political activities.

Fig. 5. James R. Garfield (left) and Gifford Pinchot at the 1912 National Republican Convention in Chicago. Garfield was Secretary of the Interior in the Roosevelt administration and subsequently became a Pinchot confidant in Progressive Party activities.

Fig. 4. Gifford Pinchot.

Fig. 7. Gifford Pinchot stumping Pennsylvania during the 1914
U.S. senatorial campaign.

Fig. 6. Amos R. E. Pinchot, Gifford's brother, in 1914. During this year Amos served as an adviser to Gifford in the U.S. senatorial campaign in Pennsylvania and as a severe critic of George W. Perkins, chairman of the Progressive Party Executive Committee.

Fig. 8. Robert M. La Follette, fighting progressive U.S. Senator from Wisconsin, was backed by Gifford Pinchot for the 1912 Republican presidential nomination prior to Pinchot's shifting his support to Theodore Roosevelt.

"GO BEAT THE FACE OFF HIM, GIFFORD."

Fig. 9. This cartoon was printed on May 24, 1914, during Gifford Pinchot's U.S. senatorial campaign in Pennsylvania as a Progressive candidate, against the incumbent, Republican Boies Penrose.

Fig. 10. In this cartoon, printed on Thursday morning, June 16, 1910, two days prior to Theodore Roosevelt's return from an African-European tour, Gifford Pinchot's happy expression reflects his confidence that Roosevelt and the court of public opinion would support his position in the Ballinger controversy.

Fig. 11. Gifford Pinchot addressing a street-corner crowd during his 1914 campaign for U.S. Senator from Pennsylvania.

Primary statistics, however, were to support Van Valkenberg's point of view. Of the total primary vote for the senatorial nomination, the Republican, Democratic, and Progressive parties polled 92,168, 24,366, and 15,447 votes, respectively. The fact that there were contests in the Republican and Democratic primaries partially explains the wide variance in the voting, but in general the vote did not bode well for the Pinchot campaign.

The struggle actually commenced with the primary. In reporting the primary vote, the *Philadelphia North American* attacked Penrose: "Backed by the gang elements, the liquor interests and business-tories, Penrose had an easy time of it in his party. He carried with him Mr. Martin Brumbaugh, his choice for governor." Editor Van Valkenberg then prophesied that "the majority of the army of Progressive voters . . . within the Republican party . . . will line up in the fall behind Gifford Pinchot and William Draper Lewis." The *North American* editor also remarked happily that the Democrats were so split internally that Pinchot's Democratic counterpart, A. Mitchell Palmer, national committeeman and chief dispenser of federal patronage in the state, would encounter little support in the November election. In this statement, Van Valkenberg was grasping only an element of truth. Although Palmer and Vance McCormick, the Democratic candidate for Governor, had only recently seized from their party's old guard the reins of the organization, Democrats were fast reuniting and were becoming respectable for the first time in fifty years. Under Palmer's and McCormick's leadership, the Democratic Party was no longer only a second Republican Party in the state; it no longer subsisted on only Republican patronage crumbs; now it was seeking public office in its own right. Furthermore, it had a President in the White House—a President who was sympathetic to its new endeavors.

In a sense, the *Philadelphia North American* editorial marked the real beginning of Pinchot's senatorial campaign. Ideologically, of course, the campaign had been many months in the making. The senatorial platform had evolved painstakingly.

CHAPTER VII

A Senatorial Race

THROUGHOUT PINCHOT'S 1914 campaign activities, his great concern over Bull Moose principles continued. Indeed, the prospect of issuing a platform upon which to stand against the notorious standpatter Boies Penrose stimulated Pinchot to sharpen the Progressive issues. As might be expected, such a sharpening renewed intraparty conflict. Pinchot, of course, was still quite conscious of the dilemma: How could he best represent the Progressive Party in this test case if national party leadership opposed his stand on the vital trust question—Pinchot demanding dissolution, and Perkins advocating regulation? Amos prodded his brother to fight the Perkins influence.

The early months of 1914 saw Pinchot airing his views in two documents which he prepared for publication: an article for issuance in a national periodical, repudiating the conservative stand of the Perkins element of the Progressive Party; and a senatorial platform to be published in late April, about two months after the announcement of his candidacy, "as a second strong bid for public attention." The magazine article, tentatively scheduled for publication in the *Saturday Evening Post,* was to preface Pinchot's April platform and the Washington Party platform that would be published in June. "The platform of the Pennsylvania Progressives," elaborated Pinchot, "will be made some time in June. In other words, there will be the best kind of a good chance to write into our platform just exactly what we think it ought to contain. This . . . makes it all essential that our [radical Progressive] statement should get out [in the *Saturday Evening Post*] not later than the first of March."

Looking to the publication of his statement and platform, early in January Pinchot contacted state and national political leaders about their Progressive slant on various issues. Concerning the sharpest area of controversy, private monopoly, Pinchot sounded out his Pittsburgh friend H. W. D. English:

> Amos and I, with George Record [a New Jersey reformer], have been talking over the following tentative plan, about which I should like to get your judgement:
> We are all agreed that private monopoly is the source from which our political evils come. . . . Why not then go straight to the bottom, and begin, for example, by proposing that the United States Government shall take possession of sufficient anthracite coal land to break down the anthracite monopoly, and supply coal to the consumer at a reasonable price? If this cannot be done without owning a coal road like the Lackawanna, then we will take the railroad. In other words, we will go at this question of coal monopoly, and do whatever may be necessary to put an end to it, and to reduce the price of coal to the consumer. Such a program ought to appeal very powerfully to the coal miners . . . and to the consumer. It would be a really fundamental reform, and would differentiate our program very sharply from the real mean tap on the wrist which Wilson proposes to administer to the monopolies.

Pinchot felt that the proposal that he presented to English would serve two purposes: it would eliminate abuses originating in a coal and railroad monopoly and, at the same time, would improve the Democrats' plan of trying to curb such abuses through regulation. Interestingly, the Wilson administration, under the influence of Pinchot's close friend Louis Brandeis, was abandoning the New Freedom concept of competition for the Roosevelt-Perkins New Nationalism concept of monopoly regulation.

Pinchot and his friends still felt that regulation of monopoly by a commission such as the Interstate Commerce Commission was not practical. "It has been a grotesque failure," insisted George Record, "and as to the point of fixing rates [of railroads], which the Democratic administration has scarcely attempted to do . . . it will be unable to do in the future because of the monumental task of first valuating the physical worth of the roads." Pinchot wrote to the renowned national Progressive and publisher E. W. Scripps seeking advice on the monopoly problem:

> I believe we shall not reach a thorough solution of the problem of private monopoly until the monopolies are destroyed by the destruction of special privileges which have created, and now maintain them. For example, I look forward to the time when we shall have government ownership of the railroads in this country, and when certain of the great basic resources like coal, iron, copper, lead, timber, and water power, will all be held and administered by the public. . . . How fast is it wise and practicable in the present state of public opinion in this country to bring such a program before the people?

Scripps responded, "I applaud your platform—the abolishment of special privileges and the destruction of fortunes resting on the same." He continued:

> But, Mr. Pinchot, I do not believe that special privileges will ever be abolished by men like yourself. You are too clean minded, too much of that gentleman I accused you of being; too self respecting in fact to ever be a demagogue . . . [and to arouse the millions of exploited people] to action and votes will require something more than even the splendid reputation of Gifford Pinchot, and far more than the preachment of Pinchot ethics. . . .

Few Progressives were as sympathetic to Pinchot's public-ownership ideas as was Scripps, and, needless to say, Pennsylvania Progressive politicians were openly unsympathetic. As one person who was more interested in votes than in political ideologies, P. Stephen Stahlnecker, Pinchot's secretary, quite agreed with Pinchot's confidant Overton Price. Price suggested that someone ought to give George Record, whose influence on Pinchot's thinking had been great, a dose of chloroform. After a Philadelphia conference of Progressive leaders, Stahlnecker wrote comfortingly to Price, "Mr. Pinchot came to realize the impracticability of advocating that scheme of taking over coal mines and railroads. . . . He will not include that matter in his platform."

Gifford tried to explain to Amos the reason for dropping the government-ownership idea: "The more I think of the condemnation or purchase plan of coal lands . . . [before squeezing out monopoly profits by regulation], the more I am satisfied it is *not* the right thing to do." Then Gifford outlined his reasoning:

First, we stand for the abolition of all private monopoly.

Second, that abolition must be carried out in a way to relieve the public, whether directly or through the government, from paying the cost of monopolization just so far as we can bring it about.

Third, price regulation and rate regulation both inevitably lead to government ownership.

Fourth, rate regulation . . . is a strong weapon (a) to reduce injustice, and (b) to bring about government ownership.

Fifth, price regulation is obviously impracticable as to commodities delivered to the public in multitudinous forms, such as shoes, clothes, hardware, etc.

Sixth, price regulation of the products of natural monopolies, as a means to reduce injustice and to bring about government ownership, is practicable in commodities sold in recognized units . . . [such as] hydroelectric power . . . [and] transportation. . . .

As far as I can see now, I am inclined to believe that this is on the whole the shortest practicable way, and for the public the cheapest way to control the basic natural resources now in monopolistic hands. It is perfectly evident that to take control of them under a plan which will compel the public to pay the monopoly profit [government purchase via public taxation] on any considerable portion of them involves a hardship which we ought to avoid if we can.

Amos balked, and he protested immediately that Gifford's new stand would be of no service to himself or to his party. Criticizing Gifford for not settling down "to quiet and unhurried study of the situation," Amos reviewed his own conclusions, made after ten days of careful study of the monopoly question: Regulation by price-fixing will not work, for the power to determine prices rests with control and ownership of the avenues of commerce and of natural resources. If we are really going to preach abolition of private monopoly, continued Amos, we must "tell how we are going to abolish it and we cannot stop at merely saying that sometime in the future we are going to abolish monopoly by this means or that." Specifically, said Amos, "the first step should be along the line of opening the avenue of commerce to everybody on equal terms, and the only way to do this is government ownership of railways. Should we merely advocate government ownership of railways at some future time and not tell when, where, and how?" Amos was not impressed by Gifford's concern for squeezing out the profit of the monopoly before public purchase. He wrote to Gifford:

> You fear that our plan contemplated taking over the railroads at a price which will include the inflated value. We have never contemplated anything like that, so far as I know. What we want to do is to get one road into government ownership and use it as a club to make other roads come and ask to be bought at the government's terms.

Amos also impressed upon his brother the importance of the issue at stake. Aside from the need to aid exploited peoples, Pinchot's stand on public ownership was vital to surpassing Wilson in his relentless antitrust fight and to smashing the Roosevelt-Perkins element within the Progressive Party. About the former point, Amos Pinchot wrote:

> I do not think you ought to go into a campaign with the abolition of monopoly as the issue unless you have convinced

yourself of the feasibility of some one definite measure beyond and in advance of Wilson's anti-trust measures. This
is a matter that no one can work out but himself, and you
cannot work it out while on the stump.

Amos concluded that Gifford's new position would do more
than place him in the regulation camp—it could make him
look foolish: "The idea of freeing Pennsylvania without defi-
nitely attacking the source of monopoly [the railroads] which
has enslaved Pennsylvania is an impracticable idea." He then
admitted that he was not acquainted with the situation in
Pennsylvania; that perhaps Gifford's record and character
might afford him a victory; and that perhaps a radical campaign would not be wise in the state. Amos closed on a dramatic
and important note:

> I know this, however, that unless we are able to draw an
> issue with the reactionary group in the Progressive party,
> Roosevelt will be tied to that group. . . .
> Unless the Colonel can be made to see this too—unless we
> can get him to use his power on the right side instead of
> the wrong side, as he is doing it now, the party is on the
> edge of natural decline.

Although Amos and George Record were disappointed in
Gifford's final stand on the monopoly quetsion, many of Gifford Pinchot's associates agreed with his new position on regulation. Said Garfield:

> I think the statement that regulation means license of
> monopoly is not true, as it involves confusion of ideas. If I
> am right regarding the results of thorough-going regula-
> tion, then the evils of monopoly are prevented, and the evils
> are what we are seeking to destroy.

The monopoly-plank problem being resolved, at least to Gifford's temporary satisfaction, the senatorial platform was presented to the public on April 14, 1914. Although radical in advocating dissolution—this being more than the national Progressives had advocated in 1912—the platform did not mention government ownership as a means of carrying out the measure. Regulation was emphasized, of course, as noted in the following planks:

> The destruction of private monopoly in natural resources or the products of industry. To end their power to raise the cost of living, their exclusive privileges must be destroyed. That is our greatest task.
>
> The regulation of all large corporations not monopolies. Honest competition and fair dealing with the public must be assured.
>
> A law giving to a national commission the power to limit wholesale prices charged by the anthracite monopoly or its agents in interstate commerce. . . . The saving to the public should be applied in part to greater safety for miners, and in part to lower the cost of living by reducing the price of coal.

For the same political reasons which had prompted Pinchot to decide against incorporating a government-ownership plank in his senatorial platform, he decided against publishing the article which presented the radical viewpoint of the national Progressive Party. This resolution disturbed Amos, who pleaded with Gifford:

> Before finally deciding against publishing the article in question, please consider these points:
>
> 1. Norman Hapgood [of the *Saturday Evening Post*] says the article will force Roosevelt to come out on our side of this issue because it will be the popular side.

2. . . . If the article is published and you OK it, Roosevelt won't dare not shout hard for you, for both the Progressives and the public are sick of Perkins and will be sicker after the article is published. And if Roosevelt doesn't stand by you he will be in very bad [trouble]. . . .

3. How are we going to find the nerve to claim we are the party of the small men,—the weak, the oppressed majority, while we allow our party to be led by an individual who is one of the chief exploiters of the small men, the weak, the oppressed majority?

4. Your taking the leadership in the fight against money domination in our party will be proof that you mean business.

5. What would be your and my comment if Brandeis and Colonel House should approve or tolerate the selection of Mr. J. G. Duke or Mr. Henry C. Frick as Chairman of the Executive Committee of the Democratic party.

"I believe absolutely with you," Gifford replied to Amos, "that unless the Progressive party rids itself of Perkins . . . it cannot reasonably expect to get and hold the confidence of earnest and public-spirited Americans. I do not agree with you that now is the time to begin the fight on Perkins." Convinced that, ultimately, the fight had to be made, Gifford Pinchot concluded that it should be waged according to a deliberate plan of action on the part of all Progressive leaders and that concerted effort should be taken to impress upon Roosevelt the fact that Perkins was not a true Progressive. Gifford continued the letter to Amos: "I would rather see the Progressive party win with Mr. Perkins still a member of it, next November, than to see it lose with Mr. Perkins outside of it." Believing that the following November might be the time to move against Perkins, Pinchot stated, "I believe, Perkins or no Perkins, that the Progressive party can help American more by winning in November than by losing in November."

Concurrence by Van Valkenberg, state Progressive Chairman Nevin Detrich, and Flinn in Pinchot's decision not to publish the anti-Perkins article increased rather than lessened Amos' wrath. He wrote to Gifford:

> I think the trouble about the whole situation is that everybody is afraid; they all seem to think the party is a mere shell, which will crumble into dust if anyone jars it a little. I think it is becoming more and more a shell for the lack of a little vigorous action. . . . I do not see how we are going to qualify as the party of industrial justice, standing at Armageddon with our leadership largely in the hands of a group, whose ideas on industry are the same as J. D. Rockefeller's.

Although Gifford's refusal to discuss public ownership or "real" dissolution of trusts in either his platform or a national periodical disturbed Amos, the brothers generally agreed on other issues.

On the tariff issue, Pinchot had little compunction about standing opposite the Wilson progressives and advocating protection. He did hope that such protection would find its way into the pay envelope of the wage earner and seemed to believe honestly that Pennsylvania industry demanded such protection to shore up employment. Pinchot insisted that such a tariff should "equalize the condition of competition between the United States and foreign countries and . . . [should] be based upon the findings of a non-partisan scientific commission." Rather innocuously, he suggested that "The Tariff must be taken out of politics."

Another important national issue in 1914 was that of tolls. In

1912 Congress had enacted legislation fixing the tolls for the Panama Canal when it opened. The act stipulated that American ships engaged in coastwise trade should be permitted to use the waterway without charge. The British government protested against this legislation on the grounds that it violated the Hay-Pauncefote Treaty of 1901, which provided that the canal would be open to all nations on equal terms. Although many Democrats, eventually including the President; Republicans, such as Henry Cabot Lodge, one of the authors of the Hay-Pauncefote Treaty; and Progressives, such as Amos Pinchot, agreed with the British point of view, Gifford was adamant in his disagreement. He said to his good friend Plunkett, "It seems to be perfectly clear that under the terms of the Treaty . . . 'Vessels of commerce' does not include coastwise shipping, and we are not among the 'nations observing these rules,' and it is clear that the Senators who confirmed the Treaty did not believe that it referred to our coastwise trade." To another party, Pinchot stated, "Also, free tolls through the Panama Canal is no more a subsidy than free tolls through the Suez Canal, or indeed free passage over any waterway or any road in the country." Pinchot, in his senatorial platform, took the position that the Progressive candidate had expressed frequently to his friends: "The right to secure sovereignty over the Panama Canal, and . . . free tolls for coastwise trade. Cheap transportation in American coastwise ships will break down the present monopoly of the transcontinental railroads. That monopoly must be destroyed."

In the area of labor legislation, Pinchot's views were entirely sympathetic to the employee. Influenced particularly by John Mitchell, president of the United Mine Workers, who demanded an adequate workingmen's compensation law as one of the most important requirements of workingmen in the state, Pinchot's platform gave emphasis to such a law and to other measures for alleviating industrial conditions.

A workingman's compensation law. The great transportation, manufacturing, and building industries, and not the wage earners and their families, should bear the burden of industrial accidents. Farmers and domestic employers should be excluded.

A workman's insurance law. The dread of poverty from accident should be removed.

Standards of safety, health and employment in mines, railroads, mills and factories. The welfare of the workers comes first.

. . . . .

A national child-labor law. The exploitation of childhood for profit must cease.

An effective mine-cave law effectively enforced. It is outrageous that men and property should be engulfed without notice and without redress.

. . . . .

The right of workmen to organize in unions, and by every fair means to compel recognition of such unions by employers. Only through their unions can the workmen meet the employers on equal terms.

Pinchot further qualified his position on labor. To the Pennsylvania Federation of Labor, he expressed his belief that the state constabulary should not be abolished but that, "like any other force contracted by the State, it should be completely impartial in labor disputes, as in all other disputes." In addition, Pinchot advocated the requirement of safety measures such as abolition of electricity in gaseous mines, obligatory certification of competency for miners, and washing facilities for all manufacturing, railroad, and mining establishments.

In the area of taxation, Pinchot came close to supporting the single tax. Pinchot wrote to a Progressive candidate in Nebraska concerning this issue:

> Personally, I am not a single-taxer. Still, I believe most heartily that the unearned increment should go to the public and not to private individuals. I believe also that other kinds of taxation are necessary. . . . Unless your situation in Nebraska is different, the effect of defending the single tax as a whole would be to jeopardize your candidacy without corresponding gain in forwarding the principle for which you stand. . . . My own intention is to stand for taxing the improvements less and the land more. Even the single taxers in Pennsylvania, or at least a number of them, with whom I have come in contact, do not suggest anything further. They say it is useless to talk the single tax just now.

In accordance with the advisability of not advocating a single tax, Pinchot generalized in the area of taxation, setting down two aims:

> A constitutional convention in Pennsylvania, so that our constitution may be adjusted to the needs of our time, and our system of taxation may be thoroughly revised.
>
> A sharply graduated inheritance tax. Swollen taxes drain the people.

When Amos warned, in connection with another platform area, that the Standard Oil Company usually started a prohibition campaign as a feint in any state where issues adversely affected them, Gifford replied, "The prohibition matter has reached the state of a movement of the whole people of Pennsylvania, and that I think will control the makers of platforms this year. I don't believe there is anything not genuine about it." In the subsequent campaigning, Penrose came to be bitterly assailed as being tied to Pennsylvania liquor interests. In his April platform, Pinchot defined his stand on prohibition:

Local option as to the liquor traffic. Each county and large city should decide for itself.

National option as to the liquor traffic, through constitutional amendment giving the people of the Nation the right to decide for themselves.

Also included in Pinchot's platform were a miscellany of planks:

A law to prevent fraud in clothing. Honest clothes are more needed than undoctored whiskey.

. . . . .

The protecting of our forests in Pennsylvania.

. . . . .

A law to limit franchise and require compensation from water power companies.

. . . . .

State and National laws to promote cooperation among farmers.

. . . . .

Equal suffrage for men and women. The women are needed in public affairs.

. . . . .

The spread of knowledge by the State to all citizens, old and young, to help them in solving their private and public problems, and opening the school buildings to the people.

As planned, the platform was published on April 14, bringing Pinchot before the people at a time about midway between the announcement of his candidacy and the May 22 primary. "While I do not place much faith in platforms," wrote Senator Clapp, "still I do not know of a suggestion I would make as an additional commitment to the one you have prepared either as to spirit or form of expression."

Three days after the publication of Pinchot's platform, Amos expressed consternation over the absence of a genuine dissolution and public-ownership plank and Gifford's failure to publish his article in the *Saturday Evening Post*. Amos threatened to run for the United States senatorial nomination in New York State. In such a campaign he would most certainly not hide his feelings about trust dissolution and public ownership. He was aware of the possible consequences as he wrote to Gifford:

> If I should run . . . I don't see how I can make this issue very well without accomplishing the harm which you fear the present publication of the *Saturday Evening Post* article would effect, that is to say, without making some kind of a split in the party. If I publish it later during the campaign, as a result of controversy in New York State, it will be right in the middle of the campaign, and perhaps very much more harmful than now. So I don't know what to do about the Senatorial business. It looks as if I ought to drop it. I certainly must drop it, unless I can come out and fight hard and savagely against the steel trust influence in the party.

Most Pennsylvania politicians quite agreed with Amos that he ought to drop the New York senatorial candidacy. Aside from the fact that Amos would have to split openly with the national Bull Moose organization, Nevin Detrich based his opposition to Amos' candidacy on the complications that might be added to Gifford's residence qualification problem and on a waste of "printer's ink on the 'Pinchot twins and their hurdle race towards the Senate.'" Detrich concluded:

> To state it bluntly I feel . . . that there are numerous reasons why your candidacy at this time would be a serious handicap to the candidacy of Gifford Pinchot in Pennsylvania and if my advice is worth anything—and I trust you will take it for exactly what it is worth—it would be, that you refrain from being a candidate and assist us, as I know it is your desire to do, in putting Gifford across.

Admitting that he appreciated Detrich's reasons for opposing Amos' Senate race and that Stahlnecker was in complete agreement with Detrich, Gifford also confessed to Amos, "The other side is that you ought to have the right and opportunity to express your views on all these matters, and it does not seem to me fair to let my own fight stand in the way." Gifford's suspicion, however, that his own election might be jeopardized by Amos' plans and a letter from Mamee, their mother, opposing the idea, resulted in Amos' abandonment of the New York contest.

Amos continued, however, to differ with his brother about the ideological course on monopolization that the Progressive Party should follow; and Gifford continued to refute the concept of public ownership. He likened his position to that of Lincoln. As Lincoln had to proceed slowly on abolition, contenting himself for a time with nonextension of slavery, so Pinchot must proceed slowly on ownership of trusts. Gifford wrote to his brother:

> I do not know whether this analogy will appeal to you or not. It does to me, and I think it may be explained further by

saying that Lincoln's statement that "This country cannot endure half slave, or half free," although it contained no suggestion of a remedy, is strategically parallel—to compare great things with small,—without preachment that the destruction of monopoly depends on taking away its exclusive privileges.

Amos' acquiescence was ominous. Could he continue to restrain himself? Reluctantly, he had subscribed to his brother's decision: that Gifford should not advocate public ownership in his Pennsylvania platform or in a national periodical and that Amos should not run for the United States Senate in New York. Finally, Amos remonstrated, and in a confidential letter to the national party chairman, Senator Dixon, copies of which were sent to every member of the National Committee of the Progressive Party, he charged that Perkins' actions had been contrary to the original purpose of the Progressive Party and that Perkins was a friend of the trusts and a foe of unorganized labor. Amos continued:

> To talk against monopoly, to place the words "social and industrial justice" on our banner, and then to hand over this banner to a man who has been monopoly's ardent supporter and one of the most distinguished opponents of social industrial justice . . . is in my opinion, a handicap to the party, and a fraud on the public.

Amos concluded from these facts that for the good of the party Perkins' resignation was necessary.

"I have sent out the letter to the National Committee and to a number of prominent Progressives who are friends of ours," wrote Amos to Gifford, "and have had quite a number of responses so far—most of them rather guarded in tone." The guarded tones that Amos referred to became roars when, three days later, the letter found its way into public print, and the whole country was apprised of the Progressive family quarrel. Gifford bore the brunt of quick and harsh reaction. Faithful Albert Beveridge wrote, "I was dumbfounded to read that Amos had made his public attack on George Perkins." Beveridge wrote further that Amos might as well have attacked T.R., whose economic views were the same as Perkins'. "But this is beside the point. . . . The point is the injury Amos has tried to do me and you and the party." Then Beveridge asked Gifford "whether you knew that Amos was going to do this before he did it."

Medill McCormick was more moderate than was Beveridge. In a letter to Gifford he agreed that Perkins should have resigned from either the Board of Directors of the International Harvester Corporation or the chairmanship of the Progressive Party's Executive Committee. "But," added McCormick, "I share the opinion, which I find is held by the leaders of the party all over Northern Illinois, as well as in Chicago, of whom Merriam is the most conspicuous, that Amos's publication of his letter was folly."

"I regret he sent it," wrote James Garfield to Pinchot, "for I do not see how it can do any good at this time; and I greatly fear it is going to hurt in Pennsylvania. . . . Outside of Pennsylvania there is much the same feeling toward Flinn . . . as that felt by Amos and you toward Perkins."

Gifford answered his many correspondents who wrote about Amos' letter:

> I did not want Amos to make public this letter. He sent
> it to members of the National Committee, and from some

source which has not been identified, garbled portions of it were then made public. Under the circumstances there was only one thing for Amos to do and that was to print the letter as it actually was. The responsibility for the publication of it, therefore, does not rest with Amos, but with the man who broke confidence, for every copy was marked as confidential and not for publication.

Publicly, Pinchot defended his brother. To the press he said:

> My brother is right. I am in hearty agreement with his desire that the Progressive party should be free from the burden of Perkins' chairmanship. Perkins has had, and will have nothing whatever to do with my fight against Penrose in Pennsylvania. The people of our state appear to take little interest in Perkins.

Roosevelt, as would be expected, was in complete disagreement with Amos. "Mr. Perkins has been, on the whole, the most useful member of the Progressive party," T.R. said to the press upon his arrival in the United States after a trip abroad. "No man has served with greater zeal and disinterestedness. As for reading him out of the party, when that is done they will have to read me out too."

Amos, of course, had a case—at least so his recent biographer thinks. Helene Maxwell Hooker notes that Progressive fortunes in 1914 were indeed limited but agrees with Amos that, with Perkins gone, Progressives would have had "something left to continue fighting for." [1] Perkins, however, is treated more kindly by his recent biographer John Garraty. After explaining that Perkins' Progressive activity was largely motivated by Taft's attack on the United States Steel Corporation

[1] Quoted in Amos Pinchot, *The History of the Progressive Party, 1912–1916*, pp. 58–59.

and the International Harvester Corporation and by a fervent desire to replace the Sherman Law concept of dissolution with federal regulation, Professor Garraty concludes with a truism: "His basic political idea about the relation of government and big business, if still challenged, comes every year closer to acceptance in the modern world." [2] In 1914, however, the public image of Perkins was that of adulator of trusts; the public image of Amos Pinchot was that of reformer in his own right, as evidenced by a poem, published in the nation's Associated Press newspapers:

> Who stands at Armageddon as a battler for the Lord
> And calls on heads of soulless trusts for epaulets and
>   sword?
> Who boosts R-E-F-O-R-M of every blend and sort
> And finds in bull moose politics a most engaging sport?
> Who made page one not long ago by somewhat pointedly
> Suggesting to George Perkins that he quit the Bull Moose
>   party?
> Who got a jolt when one T.R. his scheme would not O.K.
> But gave for Mr. Perkins a loud hip-hip-hooray?
> Who made it plain, at any rate, that Brother Giff, by gad,
> Is not the whole darned family. That Amos Pinchot lad.

*   *   *

The anti-Perkins letter gave Amos an unusual amount of space in the newspapers of 1914, but Gifford, as always, received even more. "PENNSYLVANIA SHOULD UNITE ON PINCHOT TO DEFEAT PENROSEISM" was the *New York Tribune*'s headline for its May 22 editorial. In commenting on the Pennsylvania primary, the Republican organ ad-

---

[2] Garraty, *Right-Hand Man: The Life of George W. Perkins*, p. 391.

mitted unhesitatingly that Penrose's election would hinder American public life and that the Republican Party would be far stronger without him. "The issue is so big," declared the *Tribune,* "so vitally important to the country and to the party, that the *Tribune* has no sympathy with the cowardly counsels that have prevailed in Pennsylvania and that have enabled Penrose to win his victory at the primaries." Concluding that only selfish interests could gain by Penrose's election, the newspaper turned to Pinchot:

> He is a worthier candidate than the man chosen at the Democratic primaries [A. Mitchell Palmer]. The necessity of defeating Penroseism transcends all partisan considerations. Opposition to it should not be divided. The Democratic candidate ought to withdraw. All citizens, irrespective of party affiliations, should unite in support of Mr. Pinchot.

The *Tribune* editorial reflected national interest in the Pennsylvania campaign. Its comment was more conspicuous because of relative Bull Moose Party inactivity throughout the country. Only a handful of states put up Progressive tickets, most of which were headed, however, by illustrious persons: Albert Beveridge, of Indiana; Hiram Johnson, of California; James R. Garfield, of Ohio; and Victor Murdock and Henry J. Allen, of Kansas. Many states had fusion tickets; Roosevelt's home state had some fusion tickets, which did not particularly disturb the former President. In fact, at one point in the New York pre-primary activity, Roosevelt suggested that Progressives combine with the progressive Republican element in the state. He thought both parties might support Harvey D. Hinman, a former Charles E. Hughes supporter, for Governor. Only when it became definite that such combination would not materialize did the New York Progressives select their own candidate for Governor. The Progressive situation in New York State reflected the general lassitude of the party's titular leader, of the party's national headquarters, and of many Progressives around the country. Recognition of this inactivity makes more understandable the *New York Tribune*'s interest in Pinchot's vigorous Pennsylvania campaign.

In his campaign, Pinchot capitalized on the aura of public support which he enjoyed. He gathered together an impressive array of campaign statements from outstanding Americans. "I saw him," said Judge Lindsey, "standing in our national capital championing the rights of our people in the face of the threats of . . . great privileged interests." "I have hardly met a man who combines in one person in such measure the qualities of a lofty and uncompromising idealism with the energy and ability of a successful administrator," wrote Henry Stimson. Said Harvey Wiley, "With his record . . . and devotion . . . the people of the State could do no better." From the Senate Chamber came the testimony of Senator Clapp: "There are few men, even in Congress, who have to their credit so large an achievement in bringing about constructive legislation in the public interest as Gifford Pinchot may justly claim." Henry Wallace praised, "I know of no man who has a clearer vision of the wants of humanity, and particularly of the people living in the open country, or a better way of realizing this vision." "A man of sublime unselfishness," wrote Congressman William Kent, of California. Indeed, there seemed to be no end of public praise, and in subsequent months Pennsylvanians were to be exposed to it as sympathetic newspapers throughout the state printed the tributes as they came from Washington Party headquarters.

Next, Pinchot urged impressive figures to come into Pennsylvania to speak on his behalf. Among those scheduled for appearances were Charles Merriam, Harvey Wiley, Senator Poindexter, Jane Addams, Senator Clapp, Judge Lindsey, George Pardee, and former Senator Beveridge. The most outstanding speaker was, of course, Theodore Roosevelt.

On May 21, the day after Roosevelt's return from South America, Pinchot spent the afternoon and night at Sagamore Hill, "devoting a large part of the evening to a recital of the outlook in his state." The political session, stated the *Philadelphia North American,* "removed all doubts whether he, Roosevelt, would take an active part in the campaign this year. It is known that he expects to make one of the most arduous fights of his career." Doubt on the part of the Washington Party committee that Roosevelt was anxious to throw himself vigorously into the campaign was dispelled by a letter which Roosevelt wrote to Chairman Detrich:

> A sufficient answer is the fact that on the 30th of June I come to the second Annual Pennsylvania Progressive Conference at Pittsburgh, and I shall come again and take all the part I can in the campaign for Messrs. Lewis and Pinchot and their associates. This has been announced by me publicly again and again. Good luck to the Progressives in Pennsylvania.

Pinchot badgered successful politicians in various states for advice about campaign techniques. "Take two automobiles," wrote Governor Bird of Massachusetts, "one to carry literature, the American flag and a first class bugler." Bird also recommended emphasizing street rallies. His advice continued: "Don't spent much time trying to convert Democrats"; "Talk the social welfare planks" and the vacillating policy in Mexico; "Of course, you will also talk about the bosses of to-day who control the Republican party as they have in the past." Other voices suggested covering only fifty miles each day and arranging routes to arrive in mills and factories at noon or closing time. "Also, stay out of private homes. . . . The essential object of the trip is to meet and shake hands with just as large a part of the voters of Pennsylvania as possible." Details were not lacking:

You should never go through any room in any mill, factory, or shop, without meeting two or three of the men (this does not refer to the foreman) in that room even if time or circumstances do not permit meeting them all.

We cannot expect to reach every voter in the State with literature, not having money enough. The advance car should distribute a few copies of each document to each local committeeman asking him to put two in each room of the mill.

Take an hour and a half off for supper free from all interruptions. Then you will be free for the evening speech. . . .

There should be held without fail a meeting of the county committee with the candidate at the county seat. . . .

Tobacco stores, fire companies, backrooms of tailor shops, drug stores, or other similar gathering places should be visited to shake hands where practicable during a stop. . . .

The advance agent should meet all newspapermen in each town he visits impressing on our friends the need for publicity.

Pinchot seems to have heeded much of the advice given him. His organization communicated constantly with county committeemen in the state, requesting lists of factories, shops, and yards employing more than one hundred men; locations of gates; and opening and closing hours. Committeemen were also asked to advertise Pinchot's itinerary. County chairmen assumed responsibility for assessing the general county situations and reported to Pinchot prior to his entrance into the county. "Dauphen County in a fairly good shape," stated one memorandum. It continued: "Men to whom an extra hand shake should be given are. . . ." "Centre County is a part of the Senatorial District which Maulthrop of Du Bois hopes to represent in the Senate, but organization there is not strong," reported another memorandum. "When you get to Bradford," said another report, "you will find some excellent material, but that county [McKean] has been suffering from lack of attention on the part of our leaders."

Commencing his campaign in earnest in June, Pinchot spent the month touring the southeastern part of the state, traveling twelve hundred miles during the first two weeks, meeting some twenty thousand people, speaking briefly, and distributing forty thousand copies of his platform. "In some counties as high as forty scheduled stops were made and some days as many as fifteen or eighteen stops were made." In line with his platform, Pinchot particularly sought out the laborers and the farmers.

"You made a splendid impression among the men you stopped to greet," reported Senator Clapp, who had passed through the territory which Pinchot had toured. Also enthusiastic about the first campaign circuit, Stahlnecker reported that an opposition newspaper reporter had confidently expressed the belief that Pinchot was gaining strength daily. "Penrose is licked already," concluded Stahlnecker. Pinchot admitted that his secretary was correct. "I believe we have our friend, Mr. Penrose, beaten," he wrote optimistically to a friend.

Concluding what he felt had been a successful first circuit through southeastern Pennsylvania, Pinchot had his morale bolstered further by Roosevelt's first appearance in the state on June 30 at Pittsburgh. In his speech Roosevelt attacked

Democratic foreign and domestic policies and denounced Republican bosses for placing the Democratic Party in national control. His attack on the administration's domestic policy confirmed Amos' avowal of Roosevelt's conservatism and of Perkins' influence on him. The former President stressed the dangers of the administration's economic program. He argued that its antitrust policy was discouraging industrial development and threatening the nation's economic prosperity. He accused the Wilson administration of indiscriminately attacking honest and efficient corporations. Roosevelt, however, saved his strongest barbs for Pinchot's opponent: "It is of vital consequence to drive from public life all men whose political activities in state and nation have been such as that of Senator Penrose."

Pinchot, of course, was honored by Roosevelt's presence in Pittsburgh. The former President chose Pennsylvania as the state in which to make his first major political speech since the crusade of 1912. In such a setting Pinchot advertised his campaign's success to date:

> In spite of the fact that we are only at the beginning of the summer, the people in the counties I have visited are already deeply interested in this fight. They come to see the candidates—twenty at a cross-road, fifty at a little village, a hundred at a way station—far more in many towns than there are voters, the farmers, the mechanics, the workers come to see the candidates and size them up. There is interest, and real interest already. What it will be before the campaign ends, I hesitate to prophesy.
>
> The men who voted for Roosevelt are going to vote the Washington party ticket this year. . . .
>
> Everywhere throughout the counties which I have already

visited by automobile, Democrats, dissatisfied with Wilson, and the Republicans . . . disgusted with Penrose, are coming to us. . . .

Best of all, there is everywhere apparent the feeling that the Washington party, and the Washington party alone, can clean house in Pennsylvania this year.

During July Pinchot continued his campaign in the east, swinging northward into the vital hard-coal region. In that area Pinchot was not without friends. Robert D. Towne, editor of the *Scranton Daily News,* found a new brand of politics at work in the state. Towne noted that, unlike the old type "that plans to win by deception and fraud," and is characterized by "gansters . . . [who] look at you in every crowd, who leer at you cynically," the new politics was in favor of ". . . making Pennsylvania a better place for all the men, women, and children who live in it." Although he wished to avoid the appearance of flattering Pinchot, the editor could not restrain himself:

. . . Pinchot has more horse sense than any one of the fifty men I have heard repeat the inane statement that he isn't big enough for Senator. He has courage of the fearless kind without vanity. He is one of the best informed men I know. He is honest and sincere as all clear, wholesome men and women are honest. He has accomplished more in a big public way than almost any other man in our public life. And Pinchot is able, a far stronger man in every way than Boies Penrose.

I saw something else new and strange yesterday. Pinchot stood in the middle of the road at Mayfield talking with two men just out of the mines. He was telling them that if they voted for him for United States Senator they could trust him to stick to his principles. No man in Pennsylvania ever voted for a United States Senator until this year. The rule of the people is already here. And so I saw a man aspiring to the highest office in the government, not down in Philadelphia hanging around the boss, not buzzing round the legislators to see how many votes he could control, but up in the street in Mayfield talking to his political masters, two miners. The people is now the boss.

Optimism pervaded the Pinchot campaign at its mid-point in July. Add to the above type of commentary the facts that Roosevelt and the Progressives had carried the state in 1912 and that Penroseism epitomized the element that progressivism everywhere stood solidly against, and Pinchot's feeling of assurance can be appreciated. Also, Pinchot was a national figure, the manifestation of what the great bulk of the nation's Progressives represented. Indeed, many Americans viewed the Pinchot-Penrose state campaign as they had the Roosevelt-Taft 1912 campaign: the 1914 version of Bull Moose Progressive versus standpat Republican.

The 1912–1914 analogy was a dangerous assumption. Roosevelt's 1912 success could be at least partially explained by the fact that Penrose had drawn the former President into Pennsylvania so that he would do less damage elsewhere. In 1912 Penrose also stumped hard in the state to keep the Republican organization intact, although admitting defeat for its slate. Actually, he was not too concerned about Republicans voting for Roosevelt in 1912. He had written to a county leader:

> You and your people are very tired of the Republican party, . . . and most likely will vote for Theodore. . . . Between you and me, I would not care if Theodore did carry Pennsylvania. The only thing you and I have to worry about is who is to save the great Republican party in Pennsylvania. It would be something awful if this man Pin-Shot was to be

the leader. We can't allow that. And Bill Flinn can't control himself, much less the rest of us.[3]

Walter Davenport, a Penrose biographer, insists that Roosevelt's 1912 Pennsylvania victory was futile, for two reasons: He lost the national election by concentrating so much time in Pennsylvania; and Penrose kept his Republican state organization intact. "Therefore," concluded Davenport about the 1914 senatorial campaign, "Mr. Pinchot labored under the delusion that Roosevelt's victory in Pennsylvania meant something."

In 1914, Penrose again worked hard at holding the Republican organization together. With his own candidacy at stake he was strongly motivated to action—to "deals." He was willing to give the state house, or governorship, to the Vares of Philadelphia in exchange for their support of him for the U.S. Senate. The Vares had been sulking since Penrose had refused to allow William Vare to run for mayor of Philadelphia in 1911. Now Penrose accepted their candidate for Governor, Martin G. Brumbaugh, a distinguished educator. For the moment, Penrose shared control of the Republican Party in Pennsylvania.

Although many Pennsylvanians might not have understood the subtleties of Penrose's political behavior in 1912 and the reason for his alliance with the Vare Philadelphia organization in 1914, it was obvious that the Republican machine could hardly be smashed with the anti-Penrose forces split between the Progressives and the Democrats. One interested anti-Penrosean wrote:

I cannot for one moment think of the deplorable thing it would be to see the good citizens of Pennsylvania dividing

[3] Quoted in Walter Davenport, *Power and Glory: The Life of Boies Penrose* (New York: G. P. Putnam's Sons, 1931), pp. 205–206.

their votes among four candidates, and the special interests, the rum soaked gang, going together, and voting together . . . and giving Penrose's discredited machine a new lease on life. . . . Cannot a combination be formed dropping one candidate for Senator and one candidate for governor in each of the two parties named, and make success certain?

Pinchot responded adamantly:

> I shall not have time to answer you further than to say that I entered into this campaign with the definite statement that I should make the fight as a straight Washington party candidate without fusion, combination, deal, or understanding with either of the old parties and that I propose to go through on that line.

Pinchot's antifusion feeling was not shared by his running mate, William Draper Lewis. On the contrary, Lewis came to favor fusion enough to withdraw in favor of the Democratic candidate, Vance C. McCormick. The Progressive candidate stated that, in actuality, he and McCormick stood for the same progressive measures and that inasmuch as "the forces making for evil are united, those making for good should not be divided." Lewis also pointed out that his decision was not the result of any agreement with the Democrats in respect to other candidates on the ticket, implying that no arrangement had been made to have the Democratic candidate for the Senate withdraw in Pinchot's favor.

Lewis, of course, did not make an independent decision to leave the race. There is considerable evidence that Flinn and perhaps Roosevelt were behind the move. Throughout the campaign, Flinn had worked closely with Democratic candidates. After Roosevelt had made his anti-Wilson Pittsburgh speech on June 30, Flinn asked the former President to modify his criticism of the Democrats. T.R. spoke immediately to Lewis about Flinn's criticism: "Wilson I attack because his principles are all wrong." [4] Roosevelt, however, soon came around to Flinn's point of view. When he next came into the state he concentrated his fire on Penrose. He even shared his speaking platform with Democratic candidates—not an easy task for T.R.

With Lewis' withdrawal, Pinchot, though always the opponent of fusion, sensed an obligation on the part of the Democratic organization. He wrote Amos:

> So far as I can figure it out, Lewis's withdrawal will help me much more than I at first supposed. There is a good deal of feeling, even among the Democrats, that Lewis's action ought to be met by a corresponding withdrawal on the Democratic ticket, and Palmer's refusal to withdraw will lead a good many of them, I think, to vote for me.

In a public statement he gave his reasons for remaining in the race:

> In protectionist Pennsylvania the surest way to elect Penrose would be for the other protectionist candidate to withdraw. Pennsylvania must have a Senator in Washington who stands also for the protective tariff principle on which the prosperity of our great state is based. . . . The Washington party is the majority party in Pennsylvania. . . . The temperance and moral forces of the state in representative conventions have given to me, and not to Mr. Palmer, their powerful support. . . . Finally, Colonel Roosevelt, the na-

[4] Elting E. Morison (ed.), *The Letters of Theodore Roosevelt* (8 vols.; Cambridge, Mass.: Harvard University Press, 1954), VII, 777.

tional leader of my party, is coming into Pennsylvania, while President Wilson has made public announcement that he will not come to Pennsylvania during this campaign. . . .

Pinchot's late summer campaigning was made particularly difficult by concern for his mother, who had been in poor health since the first of the year and who became seriously ill in August. Her death on August 25 was a severe loss to Gifford, who had been her favorite. The loss, however, was modified by the new Mrs. Gifford Pinchot. Pinchot and Cornelia Bryce, the daughter of the former United States Minister to the Netherlands, were married on August 15. The marriage event, coming earlier than originally planned, was in compliance with Mamee's wish to know of her son's happiness. Cornelia shortly proved to be an avid campaigner on the stump.

On Labor Day Pinchot began his campaign in the western part of the state. Avoiding for the most part the issues that he had so carefully thought out in the spring, Pinchot put his campaign on a personal basis. It became easier for Pinchot to point to Penrose as "the villain" when the Republican platform, released on August 27, 1914, ignored the issues of local option, workmen's compensation, and child labor. Pushing hard at Penrose for his lack of concern with the moral issues, Pinchot anticipated getting votes as a consequence of endorsement by such bodies as the East Pennsylvania Conference of the United Brethren Church, the North Philadelphia Baptist Association, the Pittsburgh Conference of the M.E. Church, the Philadelphia Methodist Preachers Meeting, the "Billy Sunday" Anti-liquor Association of Cambria County, the Anti-Saloon League of Cambria County, and the Ministerial Association of Centre County.

Encouraging also to Pinchot was Republican organization

concern about Penrose's attitude toward moral issues. Indeed, by mid-October Pinchot was able to tell his good friend James Garfield, "So far as we are able to judge, the thing we most desired in the campaign has happened—that is, an impression swinging my way as the man who can beat Penrose. If we are right about it, and I think we are, I ought to win rather handsomely."

Perhaps Pinchot was whistling to keep up his courage. Certainly, friends had indicated a truer picture than the one that he had been painting. A New York friend, who attempted to discover trends from influential persons in various parts of Pennsylvania, reported to Pinchot: "The general trend of the letters is that Penrose has a good lead over you." The leading issue, continued his friend, which was seemingly overcoming Pinchot's moral one, was business conditions. Indeed, as Progressives feared, many Pennsylvanians came to be influenced by a stereotype that only the Republicans could bring the economic stability that industrial Pennsylvania needed so desperately. Francis Biddle, of Philadelphia, also recognizing a shift in sentiment to the prosperity issue, urged Pinchot, in view of certain well-founded bribery charges against Penrose, to push the moral issue even harder. Biddle pleaded with Pinchot to call Penrose "a briber, a liar, and a debaucher of public officials, and challenge him to answer you." Pinchot did not call Penrose a "liar . . . and a debaucher," although he came close to it. Only the Democratic candidate for Senator, A. Mitchell Palmer, was more critical than Gifford, promising to prove one charge per day against Penrose.

Pinchot seemed not to be concerned by the pessimistic reports. Perhaps his confidence can be explained in his unbridled faith in the appeal that Roosevelt's tour would make. Roosevelt would not spend the weeks in Pennsylvania that Pinchot had anticipated, but he was coming. When reports were circulated that Pinchot could not be sure of a Roosevelt tour, T.R. insisted to the press that he would certainly campaign in Pennsylvania. "I shall stand by whatever Mr. Pinchot will say and do. I consider that the issue—the great issue—is to eliminate Mr. Penrose and the things Penrose represents, and I shall back up Mr. Pinchot to the last in his efforts to accomplish that result."

Behind the scenes, Roosevelt's enthusiasm for the Pennsylvania tour was less pronounced. Pinchot had been making exasperating demands on Roosevelt's time for late October, insisting upon the stumping which Roosevelt's physicians had warned against. In addition to the former President's physical condition as a reason for cutting short the Pennsylvania tour, New York and West Virginia were also demanding his presence. Pinchot, asserting that he had never asked Roosevelt for personal favors, continued to beg for more time. "You make it very hard," wired Roosevelt. ". . . I am exceedingly sorry." [5]

On October 25 Roosevelt departed for Pennsylvania, speaking first in Pottsville. On the following morning he moved into Williamsport, in the near center of the state, where 100,000 people wildly cheered the former President. He said all he could for Pinchot: "Pennsylvania must stay in the van of the great movement and keep the place it had two years ago. . . . If you don't vote for Gifford Pinchot you either give a full vote to Penrose or you give a half a vote to Penrose." By half a vote Roosevelt was referring to a vote for Palmer, the Democratic candidate. On this trip, however, Roosevelt played down the criticism of Democrats.

From Williamsport, Roosevelt traveled to the northwestern part of the state, then down to the southwest where he began

[5] *Ibid.,* VIII, 825.

the second day of the tour in the industrial region south of Pittsburgh. Talking to Charleroi citizens, he was sure that the crowds were bigger than they had been two years before. "I really believe," he said, "that Gifford Pinchot will do better than I did in Pennsylvania in 1912." Throughout the second day Roosevelt and Pinchot stumped the steel area, heading eastward, through Johnstown, to reach Altoona in south central Pennsylvania for an evening meeting. "Pinchot," reported an optimistic party press release, "was called on to speak at every stop and it was evident from the demeanor of the crowd everywhere that Pinchot was the favorite candidate in the Senatorial race."

On the third day Roosevelt continued his remarkable pace, starting at York and moving northeastward into the hard-coal region for a rally at Scranton. Everywhere Roosevelt attacked Penrose, stumping his way to the state capital of Harrisburg and then to Philadelphia, where he wished Pinchot good luck and left the state.

Pinchot and his followers felt that a great deal had been accomplished by Roosevelt's appearances. "We needed Mr. Roosevelt to draw the crowd," said a friend to Pinchot, adding, "Let me tell you that it was your own personality that impressed the people more than anything that Mr. Roosevelt said for you."

Continuing his campaigning until the night before the election, Pinchot, during the last days, gave particular attention to meetings in the Philadelphia and Pittsburgh areas, returning to Milford on election day. Supplementing his final drive were numerous state-committee press releases for partisan Pinchot newspapers. Again presenting endorsements from outstanding Americans, last-hour bulletins also emphasized predictions of anti-Penrose Republicans from representative sections of the state: from Towanda, "Although the Republican leaders are working here for Penrose . . . I believe Pinchot will beat him in this county by at least two to one"; from Lycoming County, "I believe Mr. Pinchot will be high man in this county by 5,000 votes"; from Du Bois, "The progressive thinking Democrat says Pinchot is stronger than Palmer, therefore to beat Penroseism will vote Pinchot"; from Armstrong County, "Mr. Pinchot will carry Armstrong County by one thousand majority . . . this a most conservative estimation, basing it on the vote of two years ago"; from Somerset County, "I have been unable to find any of the old Roosevelt vote of 1912 but what will be on the firing line for Pinchot"; from Clarion County, "I find quite a number of Democrats who will vote for Pinchot because they think he is the stronger of the two"; from Elk County, "Pinchot has behind him practically all the enlightened public sentiment and the better class of the citizenship of the County." In a similar vein Washington Party releases went through the gamut of anti-Penrose county reports.

Last-minute party press releases, however, were not consistent with reports from the more reliable and objective *New York Times,* which saw strong Pinchot support in western Pennsylvania but predicted that Penrose would generally be supported on the culminating central issue: prosperity and the tariff. Republicans took the opportunity to close the campaign on this issue. They ignored Pinchot and his protectionist doctrines; to the end, Penrose acted as if Pinchot did not exist. He concluded:

With the close of the campaign Republicans throughout Pennsylvania are more than ever confident of victory next Tuesday. After a tour, including every section of the state,

I will say that I believe the Republican ticket will win in counties heretofore considered safely Democratic.

Dissatisfaction over the legislation on the tariff and other issues by the Democratic party and resentment over the leadership of Palmer and McCormick will bring to the support of the Republican candidates a large element of the Democratic party.

On November 4, 1914, Pennsylvania went to the polls to elect, for the first time, a United States Senator.

*   *   *

Penrose and the *New York Times* had been right. "NATION WIDE ANTI-WILSON REVOLT CARRIED REPUBLICANS TO VICTORY," interpreted the *Philadelphia North American*. Particularly notable were Republican sweeps in the great industrial states of Pennsylvania, Illinois, and New York. "I attribute the vote," said the chairman of the Washington Party, "to a revulsion against the Democratic administration, and a belief on the part of the electorate that the Republican party is the instrument of prosperity."

In the U.S. senatorial race in Pennsylvania Penrose received 518,810 votes, compared to Pinchot's 269,265 and Palmer's 266,436. Pinchot's support came generally from the hinterland between the heavily populated Pittsburgh and Philadelphia areas. He carried the counties of Bradford, Cambria, Clearfield, Jefferson, McKean, Potter, Somerset, Tioga, Warren, and Wayne. These areas were apparently less disciplined by the Republican organization than the urban areas, where a heavy Penrose vote was corralled. Pinchot was also hurt in the urban areas when many laborers who had supported T.R. in 1912 saw progressivism in the Wilson administration and thus supported Palmer. Then, too, the Democratic state organization, under McCormick and Palmer, was no longer a tool of the Republican Party. It demonstrated considerable independence and vigor.

Van Valkenberg, in an editorial in the *Philadelphia North American,* attributed Washington Party defeat to what the public conceived to be the Democratic peril. He took the easy way out, not being able to note that progressivism was dying. Specifically, he wrote:

> Opposition to the Democratic policies on the tariff, business and foreign relations were the chief factors in giving the pendulum of sentiment such a tremendous swing against the party in power.
>
> In Pennsylvania the same deduction is inevitable. After taking into account every factor which contributed to the result, the magnitude of the Republican gains can be explained only as an effect of the irresistible ground swell against the Democratic administration and the Wilson policies.
>
> That Penrose would have the solid support of the liquor interests . . . was fully understood in advance, and the turning to him of a large body of Democrats opposed to the Wilson-Palmer combination was likewise discounted.
>
> But . . . his [Penrose's] plurality of more than 200,000 cannot be accounted for merely by the rum vote and the Democratic losses due to factionalism.
>
> . . . It was plainly a manifestation of a widespread, deep rooted discontent with the Democratic administration.
>
> Nothing less than deep seated revolt against Democratic politics could carry for Penrose the State and every one of the forty-eight wards of Philadelphia, including districts that have been resolutely independent for twenty years, or

could have induced tens of thousands of working men to support the machine which has knifed every measure for the benefit and protection of labor.

Pinchot, of course, was not alone in defeat. Of the strong Progressives running for office throughout the country, only Hiram Johnson, of California, won. Besides Pinchot, Beveridge, Garfield, Victor Murdock, and Henry J. Allen were defeated. Many conservative Republicans, defeated in 1912, returned to office. For example, Joseph Cannon and Nicholas Longworth returned to the Congress. The Bull Moose Progressives now had only one of their party in the House of Representatives.[6]

Of the fact that Pinchot had fought hard, national Progressive leaders were fully appreciative. "Our exultation in victory," wrote Hiram Johnson, "has been tempered by the loss of our friends in the East." "I am tremendously disappointed," said James Garfield, "however, you have no cause to regret." Warmest sympathy came from the Democratic ranks; Louis Brandeis, an intimate of Ballinger controversy days, wrote: "Your campaign, what you said, and particularly what you are, must have made a deep impression on Pennsylvanians. The State and the country will be much better for it."

In a similar vein state leaders expressed themselves, adding their own post-mortems. Interestingly enough, however, their comments on the cause of Washington Party defeat frequently differed. Faithful H. W. D. English of Pittsburgh laid the defeat to the conservative state and national leadership of the Flinn and Perkins element. Other Pennsylvanians saw weakness in lack of newspaper support. A Washington and Jefferson College professor explained, "A people who have shown their

---

[6] The total Progressive vote in the nation fell under two million, as campared to six million each for Democrats and Republicans.

god is in their belly are not moved by reason or by appeal to honorable motive." Agreeing with the professor, one state Progressive saw the struggle as a class war: men who vote as they eat and drink simply outnumbered those who vote as they pray. Then there were those who criticized Lewis for withdrawing from the campaign. "I told . . . him," wrote W. Frank Garrecht of Lancaster, "it would injure the Progressive cause, give no material support to McCormick, and absolutely insure the election of Penrose." General Progressive comment from within the state, however, centered around the point that Pinchot had lost because of the prosperity issue. All party workers in the state were agreed that Pinchot's fight had been a gallant one.

Pinchot's reaction is best gleaned from his correspondence with his sister, Lady Johnstone, in Holland. Expressing no regrets about having made the race, he thought it a scandal that Penrose had won. Like so many others, he thought the vote was a direct condemnation of the Democratic tariff and the Wilson administration. He continued:

No one seems to have come through of our people except Hiram Johnson, who is Governor again in California. My own showing was apparently next best to his. I ran second in Pennsylvania, and none of our other candidates for Senator ran better than third. The wave of the "stomach" vote swept practically every state, and I take it that nothing we could have done would have been effective against it. The serious part is that no one seemed to know in advance that we were to be beaten, and certainly no one thought the defeat would be so complete. There is a general feeling that the church people threw us down by voting for Penrose and "pros-

perity" where they voted at all, which most of them did
not do. They are a lot of weak sisters, and no mistake. Even
if Palmer had drawn out, I do not believe we could have
won, although this is not sure. Neither do I believe that the
withdrawal of Lewis in favor of McCormick from the Governorship made any real difference one way or the other.
This was not our year, and that is all there is about it.

Although admitting that 1914 was not a good year for Progressives, Pinchot held his faith not only in the Bull Moose
Party but also in the principles he felt that it should espouse.
"I hasten to say," he wrote to William Allen White, "that in
my judgement the Progressive party ought to go straight ahead
but that in order to do so we must absolutely have issues that
will differentiate us more than has been the case in the past
from the progressive Democrats and progressive Republicans."
Indeed, the point that Pinchot raised was as old as the party.
"Amos believes strongly that government ownership of the
railroads is this issue," continued Pinchot, "and I am inclined
to agree with him. . . . I see nothing to be gained by abandoning our organization and much to be lost by failing to
keep up the fight for our principles." Concluding that Progressives, from the writing of the 1912 platform up to the
defeat of 1914, had not gone far enough in attacking privilege,
Gifford Pinchot looked forward to taking up his brother's
contention at a December conference in Chicago. By that time,
however, T.R. thought Amos' attitude "preposterous." "He
says," wrote the former President to his friend Perkins, "that
we lost by not being radical enough. As we have lost not to
the Democrats but to Penrose and Barnes, this statement is
equivalent to saying that people, because they thought we

were not radical enough, turned and voted for Penrose, for Barnes and for the ultraconservatives, and reactionaries everywhere. Such a statement is too nonsensical to discuss and we dignify Amos Pinchot needlessly by giving the slightest heed to his antics." Roosevelt saw Amos as no longer being a Progressive. He "is writing in a Socialist paper, attacking the Progressive party. . . ." [7]

Gifford was, of course, still *persona grata* in national party circles and intended to continue pursuing a radical course there, although he and fellow radicals were unsuccessful in overriding Perkins' objections to the establishment of a new policy committee to be headed by men like Beveridge, White, and Pinchot. Pinchot's national interests did not lessen his interests in the Washington Party. Indeed, his fight for the national or state Progressive Party and its principles was unaffected by defeat. This he told his workers on the last day of December in 1914:

> I have waited purposely to write this letter until we can see where we stand. It is clear today that the result in Pennsylvania gives no reason for depression, but on the contrary for encouragement. We lost this battle, but we are not beaten. In the face of a landslide which swept every state in the Union except California, the Washington party polled 270,-000 votes in Pennsylvania and held its organization unbroken. . . .
>
> Our people are far from being discouraged. In all the letters and interviews I have had since election there has not been a single suggestion to quit.
>
> Of course the Washington party is going ahead. . . . Our

[7] Quoted in Morison (ed.), *The Letters of Theodore Roosevelt,* VIII, 849.

time is coming. When it does come it must not find us un-
prepared. The essential thing now is to keep our organization
effective and in touch with men who believe as we do.

This is the kind of fight that can never be lost unless
we quit fighting. I have been at it for fifteen years. I propose
to keep on, and I count on your help. . . .

Pinchot kept his word; during the next year he kept on with
the fight.

CHAPTER VIII

1915

THE GREAT European war had its effect on American progressivism; its effect on Pinchot's progressivism was peculiar. Active in the cause of radical progressivism, Pinchot was even more fervent in the Allied cause abroad. Paradoxically, radical Bull Moose Progressives most generally took a weak preparedness and an anti–Allied aid stand. Many either were midwesterners, prone to isolationism, or feared that involvement in war would threaten democracy at home. In 1915 Pinchot proved adept at squaring radicalism and preparedness.

There can be little doubt that Pinchot's feeling for the Allied cause can be largely explained by his sister's closeness to the European conflict and by the deprivation experienced by the French people in those areas of France in which Pinchot received much of his early forestry education—areas that he had come to love. Pinchot was so interested in the many problems created by the German invasion that, during the early months of 1915, he aided his sister, Lady Johnstone, in her British hospital activities and, more importantly, as a member of the American Commission for Relief in Belgium, was "given charge of the feeding of the French inside the German lines in Northern France." Concerning these activities, Pinchot wrote to Stahlnecker on March 1:

This will be a large job, and will take a number of months, —depending, of course, on the length of the war,—to carry through. The first task will be to organize it. Food is landed in Rotterdam in the ships of the Commission, of which about forty to sixty are at sea all the time. For the Belgians, 4,000 tons of food are required every day. The food for the French will, like the Belgium food, be landed at Rotterdam, then transferred by canal south through Belgium (all the railroads are used by the Germans) and into Northern France, where it will be distributed under a very close system of inspection by the heads of the municipalities. All this is done so that there may be no question of the food intended for the local inhabitants being used to supply the German army.

Pinchot was obviously committed to the Allied cause. More important than the commitment was the intensity with which he felt and expressed it. "I want to say right here," he reported, "I have never seen anything finer in my life than the attitude of the women in England, those I mean, with whom I have come in touch, who have either lost, or may lose their menfolks because of the war; it is superb beyond anything." Such feeling would color Pinchot's actions during the remaining Progressive years.

Further indication of his feeling was his concern about British irritation over the American attitude: "There is a very strong, and I think a growing feeling of resentment over the failure of the United States to understand what is actually at stake. . . . The feeling is that the English are fighting the fight of liberty, democracy, and civilization, against military autocracy; that it is our fight in the last analysis, almost as much as it is their fight." In writing to T.R. about the situation, Pinchot was happy to note that the attitude toward Roosevelt was "wonderfully warm." Pinchot and Roosevelt were of a like mind in their affinity for the British and the French.

Pinchot had planned to spend several months carrying out his new assignment in the American Commission for Relief in Belgium. He had wangled an appointment as a special agent of the Department of State, hoping that such an appointment would expedite his work. In early April, however, his services were abruptly terminated. "The Germans objected," he wrote to Henry Wallace, "to my going into that part of France which is under their control on the ground that my sister married an Englishman. . . . I have succeeded in finding nothing else where I could make myself useful in any effective way, and so I am coming home."

The fact that Pinchot was returning to the United States certainly did not mean that he would be any less interested in the European conflict. On the contrary, he was even more convinced of the rightness of the English and French cause than he had been before his trip. Upon arriving in America he instantly threw himself into a campaign to enlighten the American people about their pro-Allied responsibilities. Of the letters which he wrote furiously, one was addressed to former Governor Pardee, of California:

> You ask what can we do if we should get embroiled in the war. In the first place, we can throw our moral influence on the side of righteousness. . . . In the second place, our Navy could be of real value. In the third place, we could to some extent add to the difficulties of the Germans by refusing to allow any of our trade to go to them. Fourth, and most important of all, we could increase the supply of ammunition of the Allies in a most vital way.

Pinchot took to the stump in favor of the Allied cause. At a time when the President called for neutrality in thought as

well as in action, Pinchot dramatically incited his audiences.
Before one group he cited "an incident of a German soldier in
a hospital, who told his nurse he could not sleep because he
had shot a woman and child while a pistol of his commanding
officer was held at his head to see that he did his duty." Pinchot
described even more gruesome instances of Germans killing
Belgian priests and nuns. "You lie," screamed one listener; it
was no lie to Pinchot. If the Germans were to win, he believed
such cruel deeds might well be perpetrated on American soil.
"The only subject upon which I am willing to speak," wrote
Pinchot to a Cleveland, Ohio, civic organization in late 1915,
"because it seems to me the paramount question now, is the
interest of the United States in the war. The talk . . . will not
be relished by any pro-Germans in my audience. On that basis,
do you want to have me come?"

The intensity of Pinchot's sympathy with the Allies was
reflected in his antiadministration position. His position gathered strength in direct proportion to the growing tenuousness
of Britain's military forces. Pinchot also had a natural tendency to be anti-Democratic. On February 1, 1916, he wrote to
his sister:

> So far as I can judge, Wilson's method seems to be this:
> He proclaims loudly his stand on a certain matter. So long
> as it costs him nothing he stands by that proclamation. The
> moment the contrary stand becomes more profitable he pro-
> ceeds to do the very opposite of what he said, trusting, and
> so far often with success, that the men who read his promise
> will not learn of its less vociferous repudiation. . . .

Pinchot's pro-Allied efforts had an anomalous effect. He
found himself embracing the Roosevelt faction of the Progressive Party. Although that faction's stand on preparedness coincided with Pinchot's, its view of domestic issues was becom-

ing increasingly conservative. Forgetting for the moment the great intraparty difference, Pinchot had only praise for Roosevelt's strong stand against Wilson's "soft" foreign policy. Both Pinchot and Roosevelt despised the administration for the weak diplomatic notes sent to the Imperial Government of Germany in regard to the sinking of the Lusitania. "I think T.R. has performed a great service," Pinchot wrote to Lady Johnstone. He noted further that T.R.'s forthright position would certainly make the former President a "big factor" on the national political scene in 1915.

*   *   *

In 1915 the Bull Moose Party was in a state of disintegration. Pinchot was certainly not oblivious to this fact; he devoted much time to stemming the process. Although he did not devote all of his time to the great "aid for the Allies" problem, it is significant that his relationship to domestic politics and to the Progressive Party was constantly slanted by his aid and preparedness points of view.

Amos had hopes in 1915 that Gifford would direct more time than he did to Progressive politics, especially to the fight for government ownership of monopoly. Amos had written to Gifford in England noting considerable Progressive interest in politics, particularly in preparation for the 1916 campaign, "with government ownership as the main plank in the platform. They seem to think, I am told, that you ought to lead the fight. I hope you will." As if wondering about his own influence on Gifford, Amos spoke to Stahlnecker two weeks later:

> I wish you would begin to think over the proposition of getting my brother to lead the fight for government ownership when he gets back. He ought to be at the head of a live

movement. There is nothing alive in the Progressive party, and the conservation work does not furnish the kind of issue that he ought to be embracing.

Amos was not alone in his evaluation of the Progressive Party. "In the present state of affairs," wrote Progressive Congressman William Kent to Gifford, "it looks as though there would be no Progressive party in the field." Kent, however, had resolved the problem to his own satisfaction. "I shall," he continued, "probably support Wilson as being the first choice to make [in 1916], and shall do so with heartiness." Kent had been particularly disturbed to see Roosevelt shaking hands with Taft, with a seeming determination "to stand for the Republican party whoever the nominee may be."

It is not difficult to understand Kent's shift of support. By the spring of 1915 it was quite apparent to him and to many Progressives that, while leading the drive for national preparedness and friendship with the Allies, Roosevelt had unhesitatingly joined his one-time conservative foes. Many Progressives thought Roosevelt rather enjoyed a new association with Perry Belmont, Henry Clay Frick, and other tycoons. The "malefactors of great wealth" seemed to be becoming "great benefactors."

Roosevelt apparently wanted to retain the Progressive Party but only for bargaining purposes in the 1916 Republican Convention. At the same time the former President felt he must show publicly a willingness to co-operate with Republicans; therefore he did not criticize those who had returned to the Republican fold. Those who had not re-entered were encouraged to remain Progressive. The former could be Roosevelt forces within the Republican Party; the latter could be used for bargaining power.

Certainly all the subtleties of Roosevelt's movements could not be perceived by Progressives. Enough was seen, however, to create rumblings and confusion within the party. "PINCHOT RENOUNCES ALLEGIANCE TO TR SAYS AMOS, WITH GIFFORD AND WILLIAM ALLEN WHITE," misquoted the *New York Times* headline about an address given by Amos at the East Side Forum in New York. Of course, Gifford was quick to correct the error and in the process probably revealed more about his state of mind than he had expected. First, he insisted that Roosevelt was the leader of his party and represented "my own precise position on public questions." Almost seeming to have confessed to "guilt by association" with conservative T.R., Pinchot hastily added that he still thought "George W. Perkins to be entirely unfit to lead in any movement undertaken in the interest of the people." Rather peculiarly, he also noted that the churches would not always "be found opposed to democracy in the world of industry." This reference apparently stemmed from his still being rankled by the lack of church support in his Penrose fight. Next in his retort to the *Times* Pinchot indicated that, while the Progressive platform omitted many things which should be incorporated, "I do not propose to join the Socialist." He then returned to the great public question of "whether we shall condone the crime of irresponsible murderers, and allow the German government to nibble away the dignity, honor and safety of the American people." He thought it was the paramount issue, implying that it necessitated his allegiance to T.R.

Amos did not bother to refute the *New York Times;* it reported correctly his renunciation of T.R. Unlike Gifford, Amos was not so exercised by Britain's plight and Wilson's foreign policy. His concern was revival of a Progressive Party

to agitate for various radical causes, such as government ownership of the railroads. Municipal ownership of public utilities
and federal land programs to provide jobs and food for idle
men were also important to Amos.

The ideological gap between Amos and Gifford was a wide
one. Amos recognized this fact when he wrote:

> Gifford has the handicap of having worked during a long
> period with the hearty and useful cooperation of a lot of
> men who are not now standing for real progress and de-
> mocracy . . . but he cannot now work with this same crowd
> and lead anything that is worthwhile because Roosevelt,
> Garfield . . . and the rest are no longer headed the right
> way.

Amos was sorry about the turn of events; he had wanted so
much to bring Gifford to his point of view: "Gifford is too fine
a citizen to be hamstrung by people of this kind, and he is too
loyal and unselfish about things to break away. I cannot make
him see the situation as I do without hurting his feelings."

More than ever now the Progressives reflected divergent
points of view, ranging from Amos' radicalism to T.R.'s conservatism. Gifford stood somewhere at the mid-point, perhaps
closer to Amos than to T.R. In such a contest the party was
leaderless. "We are more or less at sea," wrote William Allen
White to Gifford in June of 1915. Although optimistic about
progressivism in Kansas, as White looked around the nation
he saw Progressives posing to throw Progressive strength
with "the party which gives us the most in its platform and
candidacy." White, however, thought it "hopeless to go into
the Republican party and folly to go into the Democratic
party." In regard to the preparedness issue, on which Pro-

gressives also reflected divergent opinions, White, as a westerner, took a strong antimilitarist position.

"The more I see of the situation," responded Pinchot to White, "the more I am satisfied that I cannot have anything to do with the Republican party in Pennsylvania" or in the nation. Although Pinchot, like White, was adamant in seeing no future in the Republican Party, it is interesting to note that his agreement with White was not conclusive. Indeed, in his reply to White, Pinchot failed to comment on his correspondent's criticism of Roosevelt's militarism. It is obvious that Pinchot was facing a dilemma. He admired Roosevelt for his militarism but frowned upon his fusion and conservative tendencies.

Moses Clapp, another radical Progressive, had adopted a wait-and-see policy. "I hardly know what to say," he wrote, ". . . the 'indivisible government' has a grip that I doubt if it had when the struggle began in 1909, because now I think it has woven its tentacles into the Democratic party as it had not at that time." Seeing a "plague" on both Democratic and Republican houses, Clapp, like so many Progressives, waited for some direction from their party leadership. What he sought was not forthcoming from T.R., their titular leader.

Victor Murdock, of Kansas, one of the few remaining Bull Moose leaders in Congress, also saw Progressives, in their bewilderment, "sitting tight." Like Pinchot, he felt the Progressives were "not strong enough to win—and unable to form a consistent and contented alliance." Specifically, he concluded:

I have mulled a lot over the problem and this is what I get: everywhere a lot of individual Progressives who are stubbornly and heroically hanging on to their principles with a grim and mostly silent belief that the country cannot get

along without the Progressive party. So they are sitting tight
—aggressively hopeful that some turn in events will whirl
them to the top.

Murdock hoped for a Democratic split which would catapult
the Progressives into a winning, or at least a strong bargaining, position.

Another report, that of Raymond Robins, of Illinois, followed a traditional midwestern isolationist viewpoint: "All
domestic interests suffer in the racial, national and emotional
obsessions growing out of the great war." Indeed, Pinchot
might well have represented the problem referred to by Robins.
Certainly, Pinchot's domestic interests were suffering, although
he still fought for social justice. Tenuousness of Progressive
lines was also seen in another of Robins' statements. Not unlike
Kent, of California, he said, "I can see myself working for the
re-election of Woodrow Wilson, if a Republican reactionary
is named and the Progressive position is negligible." To en-
vision such Wilson support on Pinchot's part is rather difficult.

Publicly, Progressives did not evidence the insecurity and
divergence of opinion that was rampant in the party. "PRO-
GRESSIVES TO BE IN FIELD SAYS PINCHOT," head-
lined a Michigan newspaper which explained further that
Pinchot had received reports and resolutions from Pennsylvania areas refusing overtures from Pennsylvania Republicans
for amalgamation and that grassroots reports indicated that
Hiram Johnson was being considered as a possible Progressive
presidential candidate. "The Progressives," Pinchot was quoted
as saying, "are a great potentiality. It is really not of very great
importance that the party is not organized thoroughly in many
states. It is organized sufficiently to name a candidate who will
respond to Progressive ideas and ideals."

In mid-summer of 1915, Pinchot was still against fusion, although his position was less firm than previously. This weakening was indicated in a letter which he wrote to Hiram Johnson:

> I should immensely prefer to have us nominate a good man and help him make the best fight possible rather than to support Wilson, whose attitude toward the war seems to me absolutely inexcusable, or back a Republican who was not exactly the right type. Even if such a man were nominated, I am not sure but that it would be better for us to make our own fight.

Although the war issues had colored his point of view and brought him closer to T.R., Pinchot's long and consistent fight for social justice could not be rapidly dissipated. In spite of attempts to talk only of the war situation, Pinchot occasionally but adamantly spoke and wrote about the need for government ownership of railroads and coal mines. In December of 1915 he refused to believe that the national party was dying. Pinchot felt that the party still had a crusade to lead—a fight for social justice.

*   *   *

In 1915 Pinchot would not allow the Progressive Party in Pennsylvania to die. He successfully fought Flinn's fusion attempts.

Although the Washington Party was comparable to the national Progressive Party in its state of disorganization during 1915, there were perceptible differences. Whereas grassroots responses to Pinchot's December, 1914 letter to his workers in the senatorial campaign revealed a rather intense loyalty to Pinchot, many segments of the national Progressive ranks were not comparably loyal to Roosevelt. Many suspected Roosevelt, and justly so, of disloyalty to Progressive principles. In addition, differences between the state and national organizations were seen in the intent of the leaders. While Roosevelt was anxious to lead his party back into the Republican fold in 1915, the Washington Party leadership, under Pinchot's influence, was less anxious to return. Also, Pinchot seemed to be more cognizant of the wishes of the ranks of the Washington Party than Roosevelt was of the feeling within ·the national Progressive Party.

Although Pinchot's interests in early 1915 were tied to his work in Europe, Pennsylvania political conditions were known to Gifford. Stahlnecker had described for Pinchot Governor Brumbaugh's surprisingly liberal stand on state legislation and a Flinn-Detrich-Lewis decision not to push Progressive legislation, fearing that "it might have a tendency to throw the Republican political machine and Brumbaugh together against the . . . [Progressives]." On April 31 Stahlnecker again reported favorably on Brumbaugh's efforts in obtaining legislative action on a child-labor law, compensation bills, and a local-option bill.

In view of Brumbaugh's progressive program, Stahlnecker anticipated a Brumbaugh-Penrose split within state Republican ranks. However, he added in his letter to Pinchot, "the break may not come because Brumbaugh has the Presidential bee buzzing as a favorite-son candidate for trading purposes at the Convention." In the event of such a split within the Republican organization, "there are a number of rumors," continued Stahlnecker, "of an attempt by Flinn to deliver over the Progressive vote . . . if Brumbaugh tries to build up his own organization in the Republican party." Stahlnecker was right about Flinn, who was ready to support Brumbaugh.

In writing to Pinchot, William Draper Lewis enclosed copies of letters from a western Pennsylvania party leader, who had quoted Flinn as stating that "possibly our place is back in the Republican Party." Lewis suggested to Pinchot that he refute Flinn's statements about fusion in a message that should be submitted shortly to the Washington Party workers. He also said, "I think your presence in this part of the world by the first of June is of very great importance to us and to you." He continued, "On receipt of this letter I would suggest a cable [to Progressive state leaders] requesting that nothing be done until your return. . . . Such a request would have to be heeded."

It was not difficult for those Washington Party leaders who were inclined to return to the Republican Party to respect Pinchot's request "that nothing be done." Progressives such as Flinn and Van Valkenberg needed time to determine how they should re-enter the old party. Pinchot wrote to Roosevelt, summing up the Pennsylvania situation:

> Flinn has evidently made up his mind to return to the Republican party. Dean Lewis, I judge, is less inclined in that direction. I personally do not see how it is possible for me to belong to a party in Pennsylvania in which Penrose is the dominant force. However well Brumbaugh may be doing in certain respects, I am unable to see that he is sufficient to disinfect the whole organization.

Pinchot still maintained such a stand upon his return to Pennsylvania in late May—with, however, qualifications hinging on the war situation. For the first time Pinchot entertained the idea of the possibility of fusion. Reporting a Roosevelt conference to E. A. Hempstead, a western Pennsylvania Progressive, he wrote:

His [Roosevelt's] feelings about Wilson, with which I fully sympathize, may draw him to supporting a Progressive Republican, if such a man is nominated, in order to prevent the re-election of Wilson. Personally I should be disposed to sink questions of partisanship before the questions of National preparedness and National honor, but we have not reached that point yet.

On June 1 Roosevelt expressed himself very strongly about fusion in Pennsylvania. Reporting to Pinchot on his correspondence from Flinn, Roosevelt agreed with Flinn that Governor Brumbaugh should be favored "but that the men in Pennsylvania should decide." Seeming anxious for fusion, T.R. wrote to Pinchot that "if Flinn and Van Valkenberg favor that course I should of course back them."

Obviously, Roosevelt's letter reflected his confidence in Flinn's judgment. Inasmuch as Flinn was holding conferences throughout the state, apparently to prepare for the transition of the state Progressives into the Republican Party, Pinchot, not ready for fusion, felt compelled to act.

He wrote to Lewis:

What would you think of our preparing a short joint statement, to be issued to the Progressives of Pennsylvania, saying that we believe the organization of the party ought to be maintained with a possible view of 1916. . . . What would you think of asking Flinn to join us in signing such a statement after we had agreed on its form. If he did, then [Chairman] Detrich would, of course, sign it also. If so, we would have the two heads of the tickets [Pinchot and Lewis] and the two heads of the organization [Flinn and Detrich].

Lewis liked the idea of the statement; but he also envisioned obstacles growing out of the complex political situation. Flinn was not the only Progressive among the Pennsylvania leaders who was looking to the Republicans. Lewis questioned:

> Have you heard from Van Valkenberg? I think, though it is only a guess, that he wants Vare nominated for Mayor and will then, if he can, try to swing the Progressive organization for Vare to down McNichol [a Penrose man] and his crowd —thus . . . getting the support of the Governor—all of which will have an important bearing on the immediate future of the Progressive organization in the state.

Van Valkenberg, seeing that Vare had supported Brumbaugh in his progressive state administration, might well have hoped to effect a similar cleanup in Philadelphia by supporting Vare in a fight against the machine influence in the mayoralty race. Van Valkenberg had been impressed not only by the Governor's legislative program but also by his open warfare against Joseph Grundy, the vocal leader of the GOP organization. Though sympathetic to a possible co-operative arrangement between the Progressive Party and a Brumbaugh Republican Party, Van Valkenberg's newspaper reported favorably on the Pinchot-Lewis statement. Flinn did not support the statement; in answer to Pinchot's letter of August 7, asking him to place his name on a forthcoming public statement urging state Progressives to "sit tight," Flinn wired: "Cannot agree to sign statement. . . . I do not agree with your criticism of Governor Brumbaugh." "LEWIS AND PINCHOT URGE PROGRESSIVES TO STAND BY CAUSE" was the *Philadelphia North American* headline over the Pinchot-Lewis statement—a vigorous statement reminiscent of the Progressive Party's early days. It noted that Progressive principles were as necessary in 1915 as they had been when the party was first organized. Also, it stated, "The Republican party today is as reactionary in its leadership as it was in 1912," and the Democratic Party "failed to secure the safety, honor or welfare of our people, either at home or abroad." In reference to Pennsylvania, Pinchot and Lewis objected strongly to fusion with Republicans:

> In our own state of Pennsylvania, however praiseworthy much of Governor Brumbaugh's record has been, he cannot if he would, rescue the Republican party from the Penrose-McNichol-Vare control. For Progressives to return to the Republican party would simply strengthen the hands of Penrose and his allies, . . . and make sure the nomination of a SERVANT of special privilege for President in 1916.

Pinchot and Lewis concluded their statement with a declaration of party independence in the forthcoming 1916 presidential race:

> Accordingly, we shall register and enroll as members of the Washington party, and we urge all Progressives to do the same, to maintain their party organization, and to be ready to support Progressive party candidates for President and other national offices in 1916.

Pinchot was not disturbed by Flinn's rejection of the statement: "I think there are times when we are just as well off without his concurrence." Lewis agreed, writing to Pinchot, "With the diminishing strength, of our Party organization, whatever personal influence we may have is not strengthened, at least, in Eastern Pennsylvania, by being associated in publication with William [Flinn]."

Van Valkenberg's support of the Pinchot-Lewis statement in his paper was not incongruous with his personal support of a possible Progressive coalition with a Brumbaugh-dominated Republican Party. Though impressed by Brumbaugh, he was still suspicious of the old-guard element of the GOP; and, as Pinchot and Lewis suggested in their statement, it was possible that even Brumbaugh could not rescue the Republican Party from boss control. It appeared that Pinchot and Lewis had been correct when Governor Brumbaugh threw his weight to a Penrose choice, Thomas B. Smith, for the Philadelphia mayoralty race. Van Valkenberg and many other Progressives became disillusioned with Brumbaugh, for Smith looked like another contractor-politician.

Now Van Valkenberg was opposed to Flinn's pro-Brumbaugh and fusion positions. "The Senator seems to be dead set on a course of action which is most unwise for his own good, and which will be decidedly hurtful to the Progressive cause," Van Valkenberg wrote to Pinchot. "I have very decided views now which can only be changed by convincing arguments as to their unsoundness." Anticipating trouble with the Senator, Van Valkenberg insisted that Pinchot aid him in restraining Flinn's fusion attempts.

Expressing appreciation to Van Valkenberg for a bold anti-Brumbaugh editorial, Pinchot indicated doubts that Flinn would ever call a state Progressive Committee meeting:

> In that case I wonder if it would not be wise for Dean Lewis and me to ask the Progressives to come together. The more I think about it, the more advantage such a course seems to have. I don't believe it should be undertaken hastily—I mean until the Senator has fully made up his mind,—but it does seem to me that such a meeting ought to be called between now and the first week of October.

On the same day Pinchot also explained his idea to Lewis. He prefaced his letter: "It is beginning to look to me as if you and I would have to break with Flinn."

Flinn's ideas of fusion cooled perceptibly, as did Van Valkenberg's, when Brumbaugh threw his support to the Philadelphia "spoils crowd." "The political suicide," said Van Valkenberg to Pinchot, "of the Dunkard, preacher Governor has caused the Senator to forego his plans to have our friends endorse Brumbaugh for President." We have tentatively agreed, concluded Van Valkenberg, "that a meeting should be held sometime around October 20 for the purpose of frankly giving our views to our friends before the election." Van Valkenberg's revelations about Flinn were confirmed two days later, by Flinn himself. Flinn made it clear to Pinchot that, although a meeting would be called in October, it should consist only of "our associates," not the state committee: "Just what a State Committee should meet for now I do not know." The state committee should be called to consider some proposition, Flinn wrote to Pinchot, and "I haven't any idea as to what that would be. . . . If you have any [suggestions] I would be glad for them."

Pinchot had no suggestions; his principal reason for urging the meeting—to block Flinn from having Progressives follow Brumbaugh back into the Republican Party—was now much less immediate. "Now that Brumbaugh has blown up completely I can conceive of no reason why even Flinn should be anxious for us to return to the Republican party," wrote Pinchot to Hempstead.

Pinchot, however, soon returned to his skepticism about Flinn. Like Lewis, he saw "that a decided parting from Flinn is inevitable"; both men were right. Hempstead reported that, although Flinn had been disillusioned with Brumbaugh, he was again warming up to him.

Flinn once more attempted to return Bull Moose Progressives to the Republican fold, but as an effective segment in the state Republican Party and with himself as their leader. With the accomplishment of this task, he might again replace Penrose as the power in the Republican state organization. With this goal in mind, Flinn proposed the organization of a Dry League to break the Penrose machine's hold on 100,000 to 200,-000 votes. Two weeks after its inception, however, the Dry League was abandoned. "It did not last through the second meeting," reported Hempstead to Pinchot. "Really, it was never received by any of us with very much favor. Now, instead we have a 'Progressive Republican' organization." The ostensible purpose of the organization, continued Hempstead, was to accomplish through the medium of the Republican Party certain gains in areas such as prohibition, local option, and economy.

Hempstead asked Pinchot what he thought of the "Progressive Republican" organization. Pinchot replied immediately: "I have just finished looking over the proposed Progressive Republican organization. What I think about it is simply unfit to print." He noted that Flinn was merely reaching for devices to return the Progressive organization to the Republican Party. "Now, as for me," he continued, "I am not a Republican of any kind, progressive or otherwise, and do not propose to become one." Pinchot concluded that he would fight Flinn's progressive Republican organization.

In mid-October Pinchot was still disturbed by Flinn's attempts at merging the parties. "I am thinking of sending out a letter to a lot of about 3,000 Pennsylvania Progressives," he wrote to Lewis, after describing the proposed league as Flinn's "new way of getting around the Brumbaugh situation." Action by Pinchot, however, was not forthcoming, for two good reasons: Pinchot could not act effectively without the support of the Washington Party's Executive Committee, which Flinn dominated. More importantly, Pinchot was beginning to have serious doubts about whether or not the Washington Party should prepare a slate for the 1916 election.

By late 1915 even Pinchot was faltering about Bull Moose Party direction in 1916. He was now aware that independent Progressive action in the 1916 presidential election would be fruitless. He was willing, however, for the sake of principles, to place a Progressive candidate in the field. More realistically, he considered the idea of maintaining a vigorous Progressive organization which would have to be recognized by the Republicans. "I am more and more confident," he told Washington Party Chairman Detrich, "that the Progressives hold the balance of power, and that what the Republicans do will be almost entirely determined by their realization of the fact that they cannot win without Progressive support."

Detrich agreed with Pinchot; but, because he was a Flinn lieutenant, his sentiments had a hollow ring. Although Detrich and Flinn were preparing plans for the 1916 Progressive National Convention, Pinchot felt that they were waiting for the earliest propitious moment to join the Republican organization. At this time Pinchot noted that Brumbaugh was back in Flinn's good graces: "Brumbaugh has completely hypnotized him [Flinn]."

In December of 1915, Pinchot informed Flinn of what he thought of the progressive Republican League. He reviewed a Washington Party meeting held in Philadelphia, at which the plans for a progressive Republican League within the Washington Party were presented. "The proposed Constitution of this League enumerated a series of principles, closely resembling those of the Washington party, which the League undertook to promote through the Republican party instead of through our own organization." Pinchot then restated an opinion which he had expressed previously.

That the proposed plan was both unwise and unfair; that if adopted it would amount to a declaration by the leaders of the Washington party that it was moribund and negligible; that it would be in effect notice that the enemies of the Washington party need not fear it because its friends had no faith in it; that wherever the plan became known either to our friends or to our enemies it would do harm; that it was utterly unfair to the men, still numerous, who believe in and cling to the Washington party, to abandon them in this way; and that I personally would have nothing whatever to do with it.

Pinchot wrote further that he would fight publicly any effort to put through the proposed progressive Republican League before the Progressive National Convention met in 1916: "I will not sit quiet while the influence of the Washington party is thrown away." Pinchot was agitated; few realized that his mind was occupied with matters aside from Progressive politics. On the same day he wrote to Flinn, three days before Christmas, 1915, his son Gifford Bryce Pinchot was born.

Flinn responded calmly to Gifford's letter: "I think you are giving too much importance to the organization of which we talked in Philadelphia." Adding that he and his associates had agreed to "postpone the formation of the Progressive Republican League until after the National Convention was held," Flinn saw no disagreement between them. As for Pinchot's threat to attack the league publicly, Flinn could see nothing to attack: "You are only fighting a shadow." Insisting that he would do nothing behind Pinchot's back, Flinn assumed a heroic air: "I must be like the captain of a ship, the last to leave."

"I am greatly pleased," answered Pinchot, "to learn not only that the proposed Progressive Republican League has been dropped for the present, but also to be assured by your letter that we shall have no trouble in agreeing when the time comes."

While Flinn seemed almost condescending in his attitude toward Pinchot, the latter undoubtedly impressed his progressivism upon Flinn. An editor of the *Philadelphia Public Ledger* gave clairvoyant testimony to the fact that Pinchot was an important force:

> Nobody need be surprised, least of all the politicians, that so progressive a Progressive as Gifford Pinchot is unwilling to entertain the idea that Republicans and Progressives of Pennsylvania should unite in the support of Governor Brumbaugh as a Presidential candidate. . . . Republican Pennsylvania cannot afford to go before the Nation as the champion of a politician so shortsighted, nor could conscientious Progressives be expected to give their allegiance to a candidate who has shown himself willing to sneeze whenever a boss takes snuff.
>
> Mr. Pinchot says that to follow Brumbaugh would be the same thing as following Penrose. . . . Mr. Pinchot represents a type of insurgent against the old regime in State and National politics that is still a formidable factor to be reckoned with. Extreme though he may be in his insurgency, his attitude will be that of many others, even among voters who since 1912 have nominally returned to the ranks of the old party. If a nation-wide union of the forces opposed to the Wilson Administration is to be brought about; if the battle

for preparedness, the maintenance of the national honor, and the adoption of a sound economic policy as the basis of permanent national prosperity is to be won, and if the voice of Pennsylvania is to have weight in the councils of national Republicanism, the Pinchot forces must be recognized.

The year 1916 would determine the strength of Pinchot's insurgency.

CHAPTER IX

"What Shall We Do with the Party?"

ALL BULL MOOSE PROGRESSIVES were in favor of Roosevelt for President in 1916; his party adulated him. Again they nominated him as their standard-bearer for the high office. When, however, Roosevelt turned his back and refused the nomination, dissension racked the party and brought it down. No one was more closely involved in these events than was Gifford Pinchot; his role as a tenacious Progressive was unique. Having been devoted for years to nurturing the Progressive Party in state and nation, he was among the most reluctant to leave it— even in ruins.

In early 1916 Pinchot was pleased that William Flinn had given up the idea of establishing a progressive Republican League as a means of fusing the Progressives and Republicans in Pennsylvania; but Flinn had obviously not given up the idea. Again, he merely changed tactics; now he thought of supporting the eminent Republican Philander Knox as a candidate for the United States Senate. "It is stated," wrote a Philadelphia newspaperman to Pinchot, "that he [Knox] will have the support of Penrose, Governor Brumbaugh, and William Flinn. He will, of course, run on the Republican ticket and if Flinn intends to support him, it will have to be done in the Republican party. . . . The whole situation looks very strange." The reporter noted that the rank-and-file Progressives in Philadelphia were "in the dark."

In Chicago on January 11, national Progressives attempted to match Flinn's accomplishments in Pennsylvania. At this meeting of the Progressive National Committee, strange efforts were made to expedite fusion. A declaration of principles, calling for simultaneous meetings of the national Progressive and Republican conventions during the following summer, was adopted. It called for a "consideration of the issues involved in such an effort without any desire to revive partisan bitterness." [1] George W. Perkins seemed particularly eager for fusion. He went out of his way to indicate that Progressives and Republicans could agree on a candidate, "and it will not necessarily have to be Colonel Roosevelt." [2]

Perkins' idea of fusing the Republican and Progressive parties by "taking anybody" as a candidate who would be agreeable to both parties was hardly universal among Progressives. Many were sufficiently loyal to stand again with Roosevelt, as in 1912 —to "stand at Armageddon." Harold Ickes, Jane Addams' proxy on the National Executive Committee of the Progressive Party, typified the solid core of Progressives who wanted the party to carry on in 1916 as a truly independent party. He felt that, even if the Progressives would not win in that year— "and I never fooled myself that we could"—they could "at least help administer another thorough licking to the reactionary Republican party." [3] Ickes believed that the Republican Party

---

[1] Quoted in Harold L. Ickes, "Who Killed the Progressive Party?" *American Historical Review*, Vol. XLVI, No. 2 (January, 1941), p. 314.
[2] Quoted in *ibid.*, p. 315.
[3] *Ibid.*, p. 312.

could not stand another defeat, that if it again trailed the Progressives it would be relegated to minor-party status.

Some Progressives, like Amos Pinchot, were practically out of the party. They no longer saw it espousing the great liberal causes that it had in 1912. Amos certainly was greatly disillusioned. He and Gifford had little to talk about these days; they seldom corresponded. Amos perceived that by this time—late 1915 and early 1916—Roosevelt was a complete captive of business, especially of the United States Steel Corporation. In his *History of the Progressive Party, 1912–1916,* Amos notes that, on December 17, 1915, T.R. was a guest at a secret dinner given by U.S. Steel's board chairman, Judge Elbert Gary, the purpose of which was to again make Roosevelt President of the United States—a "safe" President. To Amos, such manipulation by a great steel magnate was merely a culmination of many Roosevelt–U.S. Steel relationships. Amos had known of numerous such associations with steel people: As President, Roosevelt placed Morgan men in his cabinet. In 1904 he accepted financial assistance from Gary and Henry C. Frick in his campaign against Alton Parker. He made a Presidential demand for repeal of the Sherman Antitrust Act. The 1906 congressional investigation of the Steel Trust was steered into "safe channels." Roosevelt suppressed an adverse report on the Harvester Trust, a Morgan interest, and prevented its indictment in 1907. During the same year he permitted the United States Steel Corporation to purchase the Tennessee Coal and Iron Company. As former President, Roosevelt violently criticized the Taft administration for permitting trust prosecution of the United States Steel Corporation. Also, of course, Amos would never forget that Roosevelt had deleted the antitrust plank from the 1912 Progressive Party platform.

Many ardent rural Progressives, like E. A. Hempstead, were

most desirous of continued Progressive action in 1916 but were fearful of Roosevelt's preparedness stand. Hempstead wondered if the policy might not hurt Roosevelt's candidacy. Gifford Pinchot disagreed; he set Hempstead straight, passing on to the western Pennsylvania Progressive Roosevelt's reaction to criticism of his militarist position. Roosevelt agreed with Hempstead that his preparedness stand might be harmful but added, "We should act as Americans and nothing else—and prepare in advance, so as to safeguard this Republic against foreign attack." Furthermore, said T.R., "It would be an entirely unwise thing to nominate me, unless the country is in something of the heroic mood that it was in the time of the Revolution and again in the time of the Civil War." Pinchot, of course, was emphatic in concurring with Roosevelt's patriotic beliefs.

In January of 1916 Gifford Pinchot favored Roosevelt as both the Bull Moose and the Republican nominee for the Presidency. He was dissatisfied, however, with Perkins' handling of the January 11 meeting of the Progressive National Committee. He thought Perkins appeared entirely too pleased with his announcement that the conventions would be held simultaneously, too anxious for both parties to agree on a candidate, and too presumptuous in saying that the candidate would not necessarily be T.R. "I repeated," wrote Pinchot about his conversation with Perkins, "very strongly that nothing ought to be said which would put the Progressive party in a position of wearing a sign 'Price 99 cents' on its chest."

Pinchot, like Roosevelt, was extremely conscious of the preparedness issue—preparedness to aid the Allies. As stated previously, Pinchot's reasons for a pro-Allied bias were manifold. Ironically, the issue of preparedness was so important to Pinchot that, despite his protestations against Perkins' fusion activity, he, too, noted—though more quietly—that the need to defeat Wilson might preclude Roosevelt's nomination. "Personally," he wrote, "I should be very glad indeed to join with the Republicans in trying to elect Hughes if necessary, and Roosevelt if possible, as against Wilson, whose policy in Mexico and as to Germany seems to me to have reached the final limit of cowardice and dishonor." He added, "But I see no reason why we should advertise ourselves as being for sale, and that, it seems to me, is what Perkins' statement has done."

On January 28, 1916, Francis Biddle wrote to Pinchot, stating that he was as much a Progressive as he had been in 1912. He wondered if Pinchot thought that an instrument perpetuating Progressive principles could be built on the broken structure of progressivism. Pinchot's reply was quite consistent with responses to other recent and similar queries made of him, especially consistent in its largely unfounded anti-Wilson bias.

Yes, like you I am just as earnestly Progressive as ever, but I see the principal issue of the thing somewhat differently. To my mind, everything else must during this election be subordinate to the question of the honor and safety of the United States. . . . Wilson, in my view, has disgraced this country to a degree which I for one can never forgive. I have come to have not only a complete disbelief in his sincerity, but a more bitter contempt for him than I have ever had for any other man in public life. There is not a policy, so far as I am able to discover, that he has not changed face on at least once, and if anything is made obvious by his political career it is that what he stands for today is not the slightest indication of what we will stand for tomorrow.

Until we can get rid of Wilson, it seems to me everything

else must wait. For that purpose, I hope and expect Progressives will join with Republicans this year, and my own fairly confident belief is that Colonel Roosevelt will be nominated. I am sure he will unless Hughes runs, and I don't believe the latter will."

Although generally silent on domestic policy in 1916, on occasion Pinchot could not resist addressing himself to the evil trust influence in his party. He had been doing it so long that he found restraint difficult—even for the sake of the preparedness issue. At the same time Roosevelt unashamedly defended the large munitions makers on the ground that they were aiding their country more than their critics were, "and that the men calling for government ownership were not in earnest but were merely seeking an excuse to divert the controversy from preparedness." Pinchot, however, seemed little concerned about his differences with T.R. over domestic policies. They were inconsequential, compared to the impassioned agreement of Pinchot and Roosevelt on foreign policy.

In the spring Pinchot was still in favor of maintaining his party—a party ready to co-operate with Republicans in defeating Wilson. He thought Roosevelt was still with him when he wrote to a friend, "[T.R.] . . . is strong for maintaining the Progressive party organization not merely until the Party Convention." Pinchot also felt that Roosevelt had agreed with his suggestion that "the Progressive platform should be separate and distinct from the Republican platform at Chicago." While seeing the two parties uniting on a presidential candidate, Pinchot held out for a separate "statement of principles."

In April Pinchot was optimistic about Roosevelt's chances. On April 9, he wrote to his sister:

As to politics it looks to us here more and more clear that the Republicans are going to be obliged to name Roosevelt. In spite of the opposition of local and even national leaders, he is getting stronger with immense rapidity. Where we read a little while ago that the Republicans wanted Hughes if they could get him, now it is doubtful whether they would nominate him if they could, and every change works to the Colonel's advantage. It certainly would be a blessing to get a real live man back in the White House, and I believe we have better than an even chance to see it happen.

At the state level Pinchot also perceived favorably Progressive-Republican co-operation. He was not even too discouraged about Washington Party endorsement of a Brumbaugh state slate. He was consoled by grassroots Progressive reports from the counties which indicated favorable reaction to the Governor, especially in preference to the Penrose machine. A typical report to Pinchot was this account from Towanda:

> These men will support Governor Brumbaugh, but the district is strong for Roosevelt, and I believe that the chief aim of Governor Brumbaugh at this time is to overthrow those who would ride into power by trampling on the right and liberties of the State and Nation. In other words, his aim seems to be to put politics in Pennsylvania on a higher plane than they have been in the memory of the present generation.

Although the patriotism issue carried Pinchot far in seeking Progressive support of Republican candidates in 1916, his radical spirit in regard to domestic policy was not easily dissipated. Whereas Roosevelt was insisting that "new times demand new ideas and new men," no longer seeing "the evil deeds of the malefactors of great wealth," Pinchot was still conscious of the need for social justice and a permanent Progressive organization. In a May magazine article, he made clear to the public that Progressives would one day return to the "good" domestic fight:

> But when our foreign relations have been adjusted once more to our own self-respect, and have thereby secured the respect of other nations, when through preparedness we have supplied ourselves with reasonable insurance against the danger of aggressions from abroad, when we have made it certain that the opportunity to work out our internal problems in peace has been assured us, then these internal problems will come once more to the front, and the issues which have been temporarily laid aside will press for attention and decision. Then we Progressives must be ready.

In preparation for return to concern about domestic issues, Pinchot continued to insist on a Progressive platform in 1916. Pinchot did not want to "leave . . . Progressives powerless if it should hereafter appear that the reactionary and not the progressive elements of the Republican party are in control."

Through a last-minute preconvention communication to Roosevelt on June 4, Pinchot manifested his concern for Progressive principles. Recognizing the possibility of Charles E. Hughes, Supreme Court Justice, receiving the Republican nomination, Pinchot believed that Progressives should support him "if he makes a proper declaration of . . . [Progressive principles] before the convention." Pinchot continued, "But I don't see how you or any of us can accept him blindfold [*sic*]. I personally will not accept any cat in a bag, and I am saying so to everybody who will listen—reporter or delegate. . . . I don't see how you can accept him unless he . . . [properly declares his position]. I don't see how we can nominate him unless he does so before the nomination." Apparently, Pinchot envisioned the possibility of the Progressive

Party being used improperly. In language far harsher than any he had used previously in communicating with Roosevelt, even during the Pinchot-Perkins conflicts, Pinchot wrote: If Hughes does not properly declare himself, "you are the only man we can nominate, of course, and we ought not to nominate you unless you are fully prepared to make the race, and that is hard saying. You cannot bluff in that, and neither can the convention."

Subsequent convention activities confirmed Pinchot's concern about Roosevelt's position. Indeed, at the Progressive Convention the radical Pinchot-Johnson-Parker-Murdock leadership seemingly bowed to the Perkins faction when it permitted the adoption of a platform suitable to both parties. The few social reforms which the radical Progressives insisted upon were condensed and buried in one rather insignificant paragraph. Most generally, the Bull Moose platform, like its Republican counterpart, demanded a high tariff and more national defense and criticized the Democrats particularly for their foreign policy.

The sacrifice on the platform was in vain. The double nomination of Roosevelt was impossible. Republican delegates would nominate only a tried Republican. On the first ballot Republican Roosevelt had 65 votes to 253½ for Charles E. Hughes. On the second ballot he had only 81 to Hughes's 328½.

The Progressives, meeting simultaneously at the auditorium in which they had crusaded four years previously, were restless. Suspicious that Perkins was "selling them out," most of them sympathized with calls for immediate Progressive nomination, regardless of Republican action. They waited, however, while from Oyster Bay Roosevelt engaged in feverish telephone conversations with Pinchot and other Progressive leaders—in particular, with Perkins. In conversation with

Pinchot, T.R. refused Gifford's request that Roosevelt wire the conference committees of the two conventions about his intent to run on the Progressive ticket if the Republicans nominated an unsatisfactory candidate. Pinchot obviously feared that Hughes, whom Pinchot felt had not yet declared himself on the great issues of the day, might be nominated by the Republicans, leaving the Progressives no choice except to nominate him also. Prophetically, Pinchot replied to Roosevelt, "Your refusal to run would kill the Progressive Party entirely." Roosevelt at least assured Pinchot that he would not "support Hughes until I know where he stands." [4] On the same telephone, in Perkins' suite, Roosevelt talked with Republican Nicholas Murray Butler. Realizing that Republicans would not nominate Roosevelt, he and Butler discussed a compromise candidate acceptable to both conventions. Butler mentioned Elihu Root, Philander Knox, and Charles Fairbanks; Roosevelt objected to each. He then suggested Major General Leonard Wood and Henry Cabot Lodge. Butler objected to Wood but agreed to discuss the possibility of Lodge with other Republican leaders. On the day after his conversation with Butler, Roosevelt publicly revealed his conservatism when he suggested Lodge to both conventions as the nominee—as the man of "broadest national spirit." Progressives, of course, were aware that for a quarter of a century the Senator from Massachusetts had been fighting against important progressive measures.

Angered and frustrated by Roosevelt's proposal and by Perkins' apparent determination to deal with the Republicans at all costs, the Progressive Convention procrastinated no longer. It nominated Theodore Roosevelt for President, faintly hoping to force a Republican nomination of Roosevelt. Three

[4] Quoted in Garraty, *Right-Hand Man: The Life of George W. Perkins,* pp. 343–44.

minutes previously the Republicans had nominated Charles
E. Hughes.

In short order the Progressive Convention nominated John
Parker of Louisiana as a candidate for Vice President. The
same day that the Progressives made their decision, Roosevelt
subdued his followers again by declining the nomination. He
wired the convention:

> I am very grateful for the honor you confer upon me. I
> cannot accept it at this time. I do not know the attitude of
> the candidate of the Republican party toward the vital ques-
> tions of the day. Therefore, if you desire an immediate de-
> cision I must decline the nomination; but if you prefer, I
> suggest that my conditional refusal be placed in the hands
> of the Progressive National Committee.

Actually, Roosevelt did "not intend to accept" the Progressive
nomination, but his followers were unaware of such a firm
intention. They sensed, however, the Roosevelt mood. Quite
in contrast to the enthusiastic conclusion of the 1912 convention, Progressives now went home dejectedly, feeling betrayed.

*   *   *

Following the betrayal, Progressives from many sections of
the country vented their feelings to Pinchot. The variety of
reactions marked a state of utter frustration, especially among
the party's more radical element. John Houck, of Tennessee,
suggested to Pinchot that radical leaders send the following
wire to Roosevelt, demanding his nomination:

> We cannot understand how the "Confession of Faith" and
> "the Charter of the New Democracy," the principles upon
> which Progressivism must live, can be suddenly set aside over
> the protest of one thousand delegates, true to the faith, in

favor of a Republican nominee who is the creation of the same leaders who robbed us in 1912. Have you more faith in this nominee than you have in one thousand Progressive delegates who have declared they do not want him? . . . As I understand it those who stand at Armageddon and battle for the Lord, battle unto the death. . . .

"Let's have a real Progressive party now," remonstrated E. A. Hempstead, the Pennsylvania Progressive. "If T.R. will not lead us, you are my first choice for President, Murdock [Victor Murdock, of Kansas] second." Hempstead wanted state as well as national Progressive candidates. "I had Detrich come to lunch with me," he wrote Pinchot. ". . . He said he would turn the Pennsylvania organization to you if you wanted it."

Pennsylvania State Treasurer Robert Young also had misgivings about the Roosevelt action but maintained his political composure better than most Pinchot correspondents. He played the role of the disciplined follower. Recognizing that Roosevelt no longer headed the Progressive movement, he concluded, "If I can best serve my country by falling in line behind this 'tribute to the Arctic Circle' [Hughes], and I get the word of command, . . . I shall swallow my disappointment and make the best . . . of it."

Professor Irving Fisher, of Yale University, was as bitter as Houck. "The . . . 'preparedness' issue," he wrote, "really obscures the fundamental Progressive issues and I cannot but feel that Mr. Roosevelt, in pressing this issue, was doing so largely to overtly force the Progressives back into the Republican ranks." Fisher wanted to hold the party together so that "four years from now it may be possible to resume the radical issues which the party started."

William Allen White, concerned about the vacuum created
by the elimination of the Bull Moose Party, wrote to Pinchot
a few days before the June 26 meeting of the Progressive National Committee, suggesting a number of alternatives:

> Shall we try to function as a party; or second,
>
> Shall we try to organize as a League of agitators who shall
> present a platform every biennium . . . holding ourselves
> willing to vote for the candidates of either party . . .
>
> Shall we go into our respective parties and there make the
> fight for the adoption of our state party organization [of
> Progressive principles] . . .
>
> Shall we be a sort of exalted National Voters League,
> devoting ourselves to recording the acts of men and passing
> upon what they have done in order to prevent misdeeds from
> recurring?
>
> .   .   .   .   .
>
> I stand ready to enlist in this cause and to follow the ma-
> jority wherever that majority may lead. . . . I am . . .
> mightily saddened. . . . We have the selfish material forces
> of our politics to fight. It is the same old fight. The question
> before us is merely choosing a place of battle and a line of
> attack. I shall be glad to meet with you or any men interested
> in this cause, for a conference.

Pinchot digested the Progressive reactions and passed on the
following word to the Pennsylvania Washington Party: "There
appears to be a widespread demand . . . that we should go
on, and it is evident that to let our party die would be to dissi-
pate a greatly needed force in American life." Although favoring continuation, Pinchot realistically pointed out the obvious
difficulties that the party would encounter.

In his letter to the Washington Party, Pinchot returned again, as if prodded by his conscience, to the theme of radicalism. Noting that Republican and Democratic platforms called for "Americanism" and "Preparedness," he saw the only chance for Progressive existence in adding "to these two issues a platform of thorough-going democracy, not merely including the planks in our 1912 platform, but going beyond that. Such a platform should include government ownership of telegraph and telephone lines, government ownership of railways, a heavy tax on profits from the manufacture of munitions, a considerable increase in the income tax on large incomes." Pinchot seemed as radical as ever.

As the time for the meeting of the National Committee approached, Pinchot wavered in his demand for radicalism. "I want to keep our party alive but I don't want to help Wilson," he wrote. "It is getting more and more evident to me that the only thing we can do is get behind Hughes." Again, Pinchot was faced with the old dilemma of wanting to fight hard for principles of social justice but recognizing that only Progressive co-operation with Republicans could defeat Wilson, who "has played fast and loose with the safety, honor and welfare of this country." Pinchot's fear of the consequences of maintaining the Progressive organization was not uncommon among Progressives; yet he saw himself as being almost alone in what feeling he did possess for the party's perpetuation. "I have talked with a lot of the Progressive party leaders," he wrote to a friend two days before the committee meeting, "and have succeeded in finding no one but myself really determined that it should be done and unless some of the other fellows feel as I do there is, of course, no chance."

Pinchot was unable to attend the June 26 National Committee meeting to decide what should be done about the Progressive nomination. "I have seldom missed any meeting which I wanted to attend as badly as I did that." Thus the position which Pinchot would have taken in that fateful meeting at the Blackstone Hotel is unknown. Emotionally, he would probably have been allied with dissenters who rejected Roosevelt's reasons for supporting the Hughes candidacy and who moved to substitute Victor Murdock for Roosevelt as the Progressive nominee. Practically, his distrust of the Wilson foreign policy would probably have placed him in the majority, of 33 to 15, which defeated the motion for independence and which pledged the Progressive Party to Hughes.

Only after this committee meeting did Pinchot express clearly his sentiment toward Roosevelt's behavior. To his sister, Lady Johnstone, Pinchot described Roosevelt's actions with some bitterness. His affection for T.R., however, restrained his comment:

> The failure to nominate T.R. at Chicago was, of course, a great disappointment. Leila [Pinchot's wife] and I went out there, and did what we could to have the Progressive campaign managed differently. Of course, as we all understand, the object of the Progressive Convention was not so much to nominate T.R. himself as to bring about his nomination by the Republicans. I thought from the beginning bad tactics were being used, but it is too late to groan over that now. Some of us did what we could to have the thing run differently. I, personally, have never seen anything more cruel and unnecessary than the way T.R. turned down the Progressive nomination. I quite believe that his object was patriotic in the highest sense, and like him I believe the first thing is to beat Wilson. But you never saw a madder lot of men in your life than the Progressives were when his mes-

sage reached them, for almost without exception they believed that T.R. was a bona fide candidate before the Progressive convention and would run if nominated.

As a result, thousands of men, who would not have voted for Wilson had the matter been handled more considerately, will now do so, and although I believe Wilson will be beaten it will be a very hard fight.

Pinchot was correct in assuming that Wilson would gain by Roosevelt's strategy. Indeed, some Progressives had begun to favor Wilson even before the Progressive Convention. Ironically, Amos Pinchot was a representative of that element. By July 6 he was completely disillusioned with progressivism, berating Gifford for ignominiously following T.R. Amos discussed the Roosevelt–Gifford Pinchot relationship in a letter to William Kent, the Progressive Congressman:

Needless to say, I agree with you that Gifford has made a vital mistake and wasted useful years following the oyster man—to nowhere. Now he has got to make a start along an entirely different line of thought and action. I feel very sorry about the whole thing, for Gifford clung faithfully to the illusion that Teddy, who really did fine work in supporting the conservation movement, would come out all right on other questions. But T.R. has proved himself only the captive balloon of undesirable citizens, who pull him down to earth or let him blow around up on the air, according to the needs of the time. The fact that T.R. himself has been one of the gentlemen manipulating the balloon does not make the situation at all better. His complicity in his own disaster has been one of the most unattractive elements in the game.

Of course, no one ought to really pity the Colonel, because whatever has happened to his devoted followers, he himself, by his last glorious manipulation, has succeeded in getting back home. He is now just where he has wanted to be all along—back in the stronghold of respectable, benevolent plutocracy. Nothing could be more desirable for the oyster man. Having eaten his oysters, he is now resting comfortably with a full belly.

Reluctantly, most Progressives supported the National Committee's action to back Hughes. William Draper Lewis represented their point of view: "To insure the re-election of a President by refusing to unit to secure the President's defeat would have been not only foolish, but morally unjustifiable."

A dwindling body of Progressives held out against both Hughes and Wilson. Harold Ickes wrote, "There is enough of the fanatic in me to have preferred to have gone straight down the road with a third party ticket and taken the terrific punishment that would have resulted from such a course." Since there was no such ticket, Ickes thought in terms of a national Progressive League with state and local organizations. He felt that such an organization could support Hughes if he lived up to the hopes of Progressives. "If Hughes," concluded Ickes, "should not be elected the League could then set to work actively if it thought it wise, to try to get control of the Republican organization and drive the old guard from control of that organization."

Pinchot expressed approval of the idea:

I don't know whether a Progressive League will answer but no other better way has suggested itself as yet. Such a League might well include a membership covering both parties, and if it were run by men who would see that it took a strong position on the big questions as they come up, and work for what it stood for, then we might at least achieve a condition of semi-preparedness which would enable us to mobilize without too much waste of time when the occasion demanded it.

To William Allen White, Pinchot said, "We must keep our people together."

Pinchot attempted to organize a league in Pennsylvania, but most Progressives were uninterested. Flinn was again a solid Republican; even ardent Pinchot supporters were not interested. E. A. Hempstead would not attend a league conference, writing to Pinchot, "The Progressive Party is dead so far as Pennsylvania is concerned." The *Philadelphia North American* did not even mention Pinchot's authorization to form a committee for organization of a league. "MOOSE PARTY OF STATE DIES 'NATURAL DEATH' " was the headline for a July 12 story:

> The State Committee of the Washington Party and the Washington Party of Pennsylvania died simultaneously this afternoon at 4:30. Gifford Pinchot, William Flinn, State Treasurer Young and State Chairman Detrich and a few others declared the death a natural one.

On the same day, however, the *New York Times* reported that the same meeting "authorized Gifford Pinchot to name a Committee for the Pennsylvania League."

"The object of the League is to keep the Progressives together as a fighting force," Pinchot wrote to Samuel Crothers in Philadelphia, pleading with him to serve on an organization committee of five members. He continued:

> My own idea is that the League should not pretend to dictate the immediate political action of its members but that pending the campaign it should adopt its constitution and thus

assure its existence, and as soon as the campaign is over, or possibly before, depending on how things develop, should proceed to get and keep in active touch with every Progressive in every county in Pennsylvania, call a meeting at which a constitution and set of principles previously prepared by the Committee, on which I hope you will serve, shall be discussed, amended if desired, and adopted; and that we shall then proceed to form local organizations in each county, and get together a membership.

Although Pinchot thought it "intolerable that the Progressives of the state should not have an organization devoted to the promotion of their principles," he faced the political facts and veered to Republicanism.

CHAPTER X

The Curtain

"MY IMPRESSION of Hughes is decidedly better than yours," wrote Pinchot to fellow Pennsylvanian E. A. Hempstead on July 6, 1916. The letter succinctly presented Pinchot's position: ". . . While I realize fully that he is not a radical, at the same time, it seems to me that he is far from being of the old breed." Admitting that Hughes fell below his and Hempstead's standards, Pinchot pointed out that the 1916 Bull Moose platform had also fallen below their standards. Next, Pinchot explained why he certainly could not follow Hempstead into the Wilson camp: "The President . . . has done things to this country for which I feel as if I could never forgive him." One month later, Pinchot was still recommending to Hempstead an anti-Wilson position: "The support of him after what he has done in our foreign relations . . . is utterly impossible." As the time for Pinchot's public reckoning approached, he demonstrated his pro-Allied bias even more acutely. "No man, in our time," he wrote, "has hurt this country in its prestige, in its military enthusiasm for readiness . . . as much as Wilson."

For reasons cited previously, Pinchot was rather overwrought in his criticism of President Wilson. History records that Wilson did talk of maintaining neutrality in thought and deed and that he did send notes to Germany rather than war over submarine attacks on ships carrying Americans. Also, however, history records that, by 1915 Wilson had shifted his prepared- ness position and had given Congress the go-ahead signal for armament legislation. At the very time that Pinchot was writ- ing to Hempstead, the Congress was passing such legislation.

Hempstead received a different picture of Wilson from Amos Pinchot, who wrote in late July that Wilson "speaks as if he had a real idea of democracy," and that Hughes was a "socially uneducated man with a set mind—old fashioned, un- compromising, with no idea of the real economic issues." Amos did not share Gifford's fear or concern about Wilson's foreign policy and thus scarcely mentioned that aspect of the campaign. Amos also felt that Hughes "like T.R. . . . believes in govern- ment by supermen, . . . [and] does not stand for the slow, inefficient progress of democracy." In this opinion, Amos was clinging to a New Freedom concept of minimum government interference which even Wilson had largely abandoned.

Gifford's defense of Hughes lacked enthusiasm. At best, his choice of supporting Hughes was a poor one but was made less difficult by the Wilson preparedness stand. He wrote his sister in England:

I am planning . . . personally . . . to make a statement which will appear in the first half of September . . . show- ing why I am against Wilson and incidentally why I am for Hughes and then do whatever campaigning the Republican Progressive Committee wants me to do. I feel like working my head off to beat Wilson, but much less enthusiasm about electing Hughes.

Pinchot's interest in only "incidentally" campaigning for Hughes became more pronounced upon his hearing of the Republican Progressive Committee's fate. Although Hughes placed the actual management of the campaign in this special campaign committee of twelve Republicans and six Progressives, the committee did not function. Instead, the Republican element ran the campaign with little thought of consulting with or recognizing Progressives. One severe consequence was a Republican snub of California Progressives when Hughes and his entourage shunned Governor Hiram Johnson, although both men were at the Victoria Hotel in Long Beach. Pinchot asked former Governor George Pardee, of California, "Why on Earth didn't . . . [Hughes] break his neck to meet and confer with Johnson? Is he a real man, or only just what I have always thought him."

In early September Gifford made a last vain attempt at influencing his brother. Noting, of course, the inadequacies of Wilson's foreign policy, Gifford Pinchot seemed almost to sense that Amos would be unimpressed with that argument, adding quickly that "his conservation record is decidedly unsatisfactory." Recognizing again that Hughes left much to be desired, Gifford believed he would "stand up as President as he did as Governor of New York against the grabbers." Gifford's hopes of influencing his brother were soon to be dispelled, however. Shortly, he would confess to a friend, "I wish that Amos were not taking the [Wilson] side but there isn't a thing in the world I can do about it."

By September 16, Amos was thoroughly pledged to the Wilson cause. Although in many ways he represented the Progressive element that favored Wilson, his support reflected a peculiar anti-Roosevelt, anti–Steel Trust bias. In a long outpouring to Samuel Seabury, the Democratic mayoralty candidate in New York City, Amos elaborated on his stand: "It has been fairly clear to most of us that Roosevelt, Perkins and the Steel Trust, old guard group around them have not been interested

in the things which the Progressive party stood for." In a bill
of particulars submitted by Amos, the following high points
evolved: "Colonel Roosevelt . . . promptly changed back to
the Republican craft . . . when . . . the Progressive ship . . .
got into rough water." Roosevelt's escape from the Progressive
ship was made possible by his discovering a "paramount issue"
of "Americanism," which was, in reality, "the patriotism of
Wall Street." "Some of us feel," continued Amos, ". . . that a
good deal of this so-called 'Americanism' is in reality not so
much a paramount issue as a paramount gangplank to get [the
Progressives] back without loss of face into old-guard Republicanism." Wilson "has embraced and put into execution progressive principles just as fast or a little faster than Mr. Roosevelt dropped them." "The Republicans, as a whole, stand for
the idea that the country should be governed by a small group
. . . [whereas] men like President Wilson and yourself . . .
stand for the opposite idea." "Nothing but a very skillful and
patriotic handling of the [international] situation by Mr. Wilson could have kept us out of most serious implications." "The
sabre rattling conception of national honor that Mr. Roosevelt
advances . . . is the dying idea of trial by violence." "The war
party [Republican] in the United States is also essentially a
moneyed, or leisure-class party. . . . Ordinary people have too
little, if any, margin above what is necessary to live, and are
too near to the realities of life to be anxious to make the sacri-
fices of war, or to indulge in international strutting."

On September 8, at almost the same moment that Amos
Pinchot wrote to Seabury, the Republican National Committee
issued a lengthy statement from Gifford in support of Hughes.
Gifford related that, after Wilson's first inauguration, he had
thought well of the President. "It was only," he added, "when
I began to check up on what he said by what he did that I was

forced to change my view." Wilson's vacillation became particularly disturbing to Gifford when Wilson publicly held Germany to strict accountability for the Lusitania affair but "let her know secretly . . . that what he said he did not mean." Worse yet, said Pinchot, under such conditions which only brought the country closer to war "Wilson did not raise a finger to put us in a condition of defense." Wilson ridiculed "the idea of a greater Navy."

Gifford Pinchot continued his list of Wilson's inconsistencies: The President ran on a platform which "pledged him to a single term . . . and then became a candidate for another term." He declared for conservation and then neglected the policy. He declared for efficiency in government and then gave way to the pork barrel. He called for civil-service reform and then became a spoilsman. He asked for "pitiless publicity" in government and then conducted a secret administration. He announced himself as a President of and for the people and then became a partisan President.

Gifford returned to the Americanism theme: "When every principle of freedom and equality for which our fathers fought was at stake in the great war, when our country eagerly awaited the leadership of the President, Wilson dodged." In three lengthy paragraphs, he pursued this subject. Whereas Amos saw Wall Street Republicans exploiting the war issue for financial gain, Gifford blamed the administration: "The ignoble stand of profit over principle which Mr. Wilson forced upon this country in our foreign relations, he has applied to himself as President. . . ."

Turning to Hughes's virtues, Gifford announced, "Hughes . . . is a man of his word—he proved it as Governor of New York, in conservation matters, on moral issues, [etc.]. . . . He will give us an honest and an efficient administration. . . . The safety, honor and welfare of the country will be in immeasurably surer hands."

Two weeks following his September 8 statement, Pinchot issued a second statement against the Wilson candidacy, capitalizing more on the issue with which he attracted much attention—the conservation of natural resources. After discussing a series of things that Wilson might have done about conservation, Pinchot concluded rather vaguely:

> To sum up, as in many other matters, the promise made was not performed. Instead of progress in conserving our resources, the last two years have seen a bitter and often a losing fight to hold what we had. Wilson talked well, began to act well, and then, yielding to the political pressure of special interests, went back on conservation.

Pinchot's criticism of Wilson's conservation policy was somewhat harsh, but it probably reflected an element of truth. In his acceptance speech six days previously, Wilson expressed "a wish [that] we could have made more progress than we have in this vital matter." [1]

Pinchot admitted privately that meeting anti-Hughes arguments was not easy. He said to Pardee:

> The only way to meet them . . . is to say what it is extremely difficult to say at this stage of the game, but true nevertheless —that Hughes, when elected, will have no more to do with Barnes, Penrose, and the rest of the gang than when he was Governor. I am proposing to say it myself on the stump and I believe it is good politics to do so because any man whose

---

[1] *A Compilation of the Messages and Papers of the Presidents,* prepared under the direction of the Joint Committee on Printing of the House and Senate (20 vols.; New York: Bureau of National Literature, Inc., 1917), XVII, 8159.

feelings would be hurt by an assault on Penrose would vote the Republican ticket anyhow.

Throughout October Pinchot was on the stump. Generally, he repeated what he had said in his September 8 National Committee release, adding what he told Pardee he would use to meet Democratic arguments about Republican bossdom as represented by Penrose, Barnes, and Smoot. On October 19, he told a Wabasha, Minnesota audience:

> I reply, how about Sullivan, Murphy, and Taggart [Democratic bosses]? The truth is that corrupt politicians are found in both parties, always have been, and doubtless always will be. The essential fact about Hughes is that he has made it clear as daylight that the bosses cannot control him. I have not one word to take back that I have ever said concerning Penrose, Barnes, Crane and their like. If I did not believe Hughes would be wholly independent of this control while he is in the White House, I should not be on the stump for him today.

To a Fargo, North Dakota audience on the following night Pinchot said that Wilson possessed the most dangerous quality that a man could have: "He says one thing and does another. His whole record is proof that what he says is no indication of what he has done or what he will do." On October 31, in Los Angeles, Pinchot continued unenthusiastically on the stump, relating a parable he had used previously to illustrate Wilson's weakness of misusing words:

> Wilson reminded me of a man who went into a grocery store and asked the storekeeper for a jar of pickles. When it was handed him he said, "Come to think of it, I don't want pickles after all. I'll take a pound of coffee instead."

But when the coffee was wrapped up and laid on the counter he picked up a broom and said, "By George, my wife wants a broom. I'll take this in place of the coffee," and then he started out of the door with the broom.

But the storekeeper called after him, "Hold on, my friend, you haven't paid me for that broom."

"Yes I did," said the man, "I gave you the coffee for it.'"

"But you never paid me for the coffee."

"I did too," said the man, "I gave you the pickles for it."

"But you haven't paid for the pickles."

"Of course I haven't," said the man, "I didn't take the pickles." And away he went with the broom, leaving the storekeeper scratching his head.

As if Gifford Pinchot's campaign for Hughes was not difficult enough, Amos worked hard at embarrassing the Republican campaigners, though exercising extreme care in not attacking Gifford, "for family reasons." Once, in a letter to Thomas J. Walsh, the Democratic western campaign manager, Amos suggested a plan for forcing Roosevelt into demonstrating that in 1912 he had been "bought" by the "Steel and Harvester Trusts": Amos had a typewritten letter from Roosevelt, dated December 5, 1912, in which the Colonel interlined a sentence, admitting that he had personally removed the antitrust plank from the Progressive platform, presumably at the behest of Perkins and Munsey, who would not subsidize the party unless it was "sound" on the trust question. "If," suggested Amos, "the Colonel's copy of this letter does not also contain a copy of his interlineations, I think the chances are that he will deny that he ever told Davis [O. K. Davis, Progressive national executive committeeman] to kill the endorsement of the Sherman law. . . . I have Roosevelt's letter in my safe . . . if a showdown comes." To Amos' disappointment, the Democrats did not use the letter.

In late October Pinchot wound up his campaign in California and awaited the election results. The preference of California voters was decisive. Prior to the late counting of votes in that state, Hughes was ahead in the national contest. When the Republicans lost California by 4,000 popular votes, however, Wilson's electoral college vote put him over, 277 to 254. Wilson had needed California after having lost the important eastern states of Massachusetts, New Jersey, New York, and Pennsylvania, upon which victory for the Presidency had usually depended.

California was too Progressive to go Republican in 1916. Hiram Johnson, the 1912 Bull Moose vice-presidential candidate and successful 1914 Progressive candidate for Governor, had entrenched Progressives too solidly to hastily move them into the Republican camp in 1916—even though he loyally supported Hughes. Of course, the Republican snub of Johnson in Long Beach was viewed coolly by Progressives throughout the state. Certainly, Johnson did everything he could for Hughes —contrary to many historical interpretations. Johnson wrote to Pinchot:

> Every night I would sit down with fifty or a hundred of our Progressives. . . . I talked . . . of the patriotic duty that was ours; of how none of us should permit resentments; . . . of the necessity for maintaining the moral fiber of our nation and of the obligation that rested upon us to support Hughes.

"We have met the enemy and they have eaten us up," wrote Gifford Pinchot to his sister, shortly after the election. "Why?" Pinchot asked himself. "Peace at any price" he felt to be the

principal reason, more than the idea that Wilson "kept us out
of war." Also, said Pinchot, the campaign was managed badly;
Hughes was tagged as a Wall Street candidate; and hundreds
of thousands "voted for Wilson on the ground that a vote for
Hughes was a vote for Penrose, Barnes, and Crane." Pinchot
also alluded to the California situation: "As they told me when
I was out there, he [Hughes] had the state by 100,000 when he
came, and when he left he didn't have it at all." Pinchot complained that much of Hughes's defeat was attributable to "the
attitude of state and county Republican organizations toward
the Progressives—they weren't recognized." He listed other
reasons for the Hughes defeat; but "one thing is sure," he said,
". . . if T.R. had been nominated, he would have been elected
with a whoop."

Strangely, in the immediate postelection period, Gifford in
no way sensed that Wilson's victory in 1916 was even in part
attributable to Democratic espousal of Progressive Party principles. Although his own brother, to whom he had listened so
frequently in the past, saw Wilson rightly affirming that Democrats were leading the fight for social justice, Gifford could not
agree. As seen previously, Wilson's foreign policy largely affected Gifford's view of the administration's domestic policy.
Ironically, much of the Democratic commitment to Progressive
principles in 1916 was for the purpose of appealing to radical
Progressives like Pinchot. Indeed, Pinchot's consistent advocacy
of domestic radicalism since 1912 played a decided role in pushing Wilson considerably to the left in 1916 and thus, with Progressive support, back into the Presidency.

By December, Pinchot grudgingly read in the election results
a certain amount of Progressive support for Wilson. He and
most of the remaining leaders of the Progressive Party, however, could not think in Democratic terms. December 5, 1916,

marked the final exodus from the party and their return to Republicanism. At a Chicago conference of Progressive hold-outs, Pinchot, Harold Ickes, William Allen White, James Garfield, Chester Rowell, and Raymond Robins issued the following statement:

> The result of the election has shown that the only hope of victory for any political party in America lies in securing and retaining the support of the progressive voters. In spite of certain progressive achievements, the merit of which we do not question, it is clear to us that permanent progressive advance through the Democratic party is impossible. We welcome the enactment of progressive measures by any party. But we are firm in the conviction that in the existing two party system constructive progressivism may be best achieved through the Republican party. But to gain either of these ends, the Republican party must be thoroughly progressive in organization, leadership and principles.

Pinchot and his cohorts did not capitulate easily. They meant to make the Republican Party thoroughly progressive, con-cluding their statement with a call for a national conference of Progressives and progressive Republicans "to take steps toward reformatory progressive principles as applied to present needs and consider how to put them into effect." Also, a last plea was made for giving Progressives stronger representation on the National Republican Committee.

"I am more and more impressed," wrote Gifford Pinchot to Harold Ickes on December 10, "with the idea that we need to get out the call for the conference at the earliest possible date." On the next day he wrote again to Ickes, his sole corre-spondent on the matter: "Our statement has done some good." Ickes fanned Pinchot's enthusiasm by reporting that Will Hays, the Indiana Republican state chairman, was interested in the conference. Pinchot replied, "I'm getting keener and keener to have this matter go ahead rapidly." Thus plans were made during December of 1916 and into January of 1917.

Pinchot, like Ickes, was "reaching" now. Pathetically, he informed Ickes that, although Roosevelt wanted no part of a conference, he would not interfere, thus enabling "us to go ahead along the lines we were planning with entirely clear conscience." Roosevelt was now a Republican, little concerned about his party's domestic principles.

The Republican Executive Committee was relatively unimpressed by the Progressives' December 5, 1916, statement. In a January, 1917, meeting, the committee answered the Progressives by electing the extreme conservative John T. Adams, of Iowa, as committee vice-chairman, to balance the more liberal chairman, William R. Wilcox, Hughes's former campaign manager. Needless to say, the committee was lacking in enthusiasm for the "reformation" conference. Clearly, the Progressive talk bored them; and they felt that it bored the people, who were being attracted by the more important events, such as the German government's notification to the State Department that unrestricted submarine warfare would be resumed against neutral shipping.

By February, Pinchot was feeling the cumulative effects of the several obstacles to the conference—Republican organization opposition, Roosevelt's apathy, and the overshadowing international situation. Also, George Perkins was insisting that he should lead any Progressive move to call such a convention. By March, Pinchot was ready to drop the matter. "The whole situation," he wrote to Ickes, "is horribly embarrassed by the fact that the men whom we have been counting on to sign the call among the progressive Republicans in Congress are practically all of them now unavailable." He confessed, "I am very badly puzzled."

Pinchot was saved from the agony of capitulating completely in his fight for doméstic liberalism. The times afforded him relief, demanding that all issues be subordinated to the larger international crisis. Gifford wrote, "The present international complications make it clear that united action of our citizenship is required. Partisan activity, no matter of what purpose or patriotic motive, might be misconstrued at home and abroad." Pinchot was not excusing his withdrawal from the domestic fight; he honestly feared the German onslaught.

The Declaration of War by the President on April 2 added weight to Pinchot's suggestion of "united action." Three weeks later a handful of ardent former Progressives, three of whom had signed the December 5, 1916, statement, joined Pinchot in a declaration of their own: "Believing that our country has entered the great war, right, wisely . . . it is our high duty . . . to take our part in the defense of liberty, democracy and civilization against the attack of militarism." The signers then struck a final blow for progressivism: "To carry forward . . . we believe that . . . certain measures are immediately necessary." Principally, they were universal military service, manpower control, agriculture price supports, a guarantee of the rights of labor, a graduated income tax, excess-profit taxes, and women's rights. Appropriately, a final measure demanded by the Progressives concerned what Pinchot believed to be the progressive movement's principal premise: "The retention and control of all natural resources now held by the Government so that the foundation of national efficiency and industrial strength may not be impaired." To that proposition Pinchot had dedicated two decades—one as scientific conservationist, the other as partisan politician.

*   *   *

The progressive movement had come to an end. Gifford Pinchot had fought the good fight and had made his contribution. Politically, he would come to high office at the state level as Governor of Pennsylvania; but he would not "scrape the stars" as he had during the exciting progressive years of the century's first decades.

During Pinchot's Pennsylvania Governorship he served well and earned the right in 1938 to ask to be considered for the third time for the office. His state administrations were most important as manifestations of the spirit of the earlier progressive era, even though the office of Governor forced him into more provincial and pragmatic considerations than he had been accustomed to in the progressive days. His first administration, 1923–27, marked considerable change in an era of orthodoxy. He reorganized the state government's executive branch by reducing 139 separate agencies to 15 cabinet posts and 3 appointive commissions; by instituting position classification in the Civil Service; and by initiating a sound budgetary system. During his second term, 1931–35, following a mandatory four-year separation from the office, Pinchot continued to carry out his duties in the spirit of liberal Republicanism. Beginning his term at the height of the depression, he allocated 40 per cent of the entire budget to a planned public construction of buildings and roads. When sufficient funds for an adequate relief program were unavailable, he unhesitating sought federal aid. "The fact is," he wrote, "that the only power strong enough and able to act in time, to meet the new problem of the coming winter [1931–32] is the Government of the United States." His second administration also fought for collective bargaining among miners in western Pennsylvania, established the Bureau of Women and Children, and strengthened the

Public Service Commission. Perhaps most remembered by Pennsylvanians was Pinchot's plan for "getting the farmers out of the mud" with the construction of over 12,566 miles of rural roads.

Pinchot's roles as a dynamic and efficient public administrator during his first term as Governor of Pennsylvania, a time of general lassitude, and as an advocate of welfare spending during his second administration, an era of Republican suspicion, marked thorough commitment to the principles of the earlier progressive era. Other leaders in the country—Alfred Smith, the Democratic Governor of New York during the 1920's, and certain western Republican Congressmen of the same period, known as "the Wild Asses of the Desert"—were also committed to such a philosophy. Few former Progressive Party men who had been as dedicated to that earlier movement as Gifford Pinchot, however, lived to seek public office again, much less to espouse the party's ideology when in office.

A half-century has elapsed since Gifford Pinchot and Theodore Roosevelt stood together in the late summer of 1910 before a tumultuous crowd at Osawatomie, Kansas, expounding a high point of that era's liberalism. From the vantage point of the 1960's, Gifford Pinchot's role at Osawatomie, and elsewhere during the first decades of the century, and the progressive movement as a whole can be better appreciated. Historians will disagree about the similarity of that movement to other liberal periods in recent United States history, but few will question the existence of a political bloodline between Bull Moose progressivism and the Populism of the 1890's, the welfare state of the New Deal, and the New Frontier of John F. Kennedy.

Bibliographical Notes

THE GIFFORD AND AMOS PINCHOT Manuscripts, on which this volume is largely based, are located in the Library of Congress. The manuscript collections consist of correspondence, published and unpublished speeches, diaries, magazine and newspaper articles, and cartoons and photographs. Quotations in the text are from the two Pinchot collections unless otherwise indicated.

General historical and political background material not cited specifically in bibliographical notes for each chapter is drawn from the following books:

Bryan, William Jennings. *A Tale of Two Conventions*. New York: Funk & Wagnalls Co., 1912.

Butt, Archie. *Taft and Roosevelt: The Intimate Letters of Archie Butt*. New York: Doubleday & Company, Inc., 1930.

Coyle, David Cushman. *Conservation*. New Brunswick, N.J.: Rutgers University Press, 1957.

Croly, Herbert D. *The Promise of American Life*. New York: Macmillan Co., 1909.

DeWitt, Benjamin P. *The Progressive Movement*. New York: Macmillan Co., 1915.

Doan, Edward N. *The La Follettes and the Wisconsin Idea*. New York: Rinehart & Company, Inc., 1947.

Filler, Louis. *Crusaders for American Liberalism*. New York: Harcourt, Brace & Company, 1939.

Flint, Winslow Allen. *Progressive Movement in Vermont*. Washington, D.C.: American Council on Public Affairs, 1942.

Hicks, John D. *The Populist Revolt*. Minneapolis, Minn.: University of Minnesota Press, 1931.

Link, Arthur S. *Wilson: The New Freedom*. Princeton, N.J.: Princeton University Press, 1956.

Lord, Walter. *The Good Years: From 1900 to the Frist World War.* New York: Harper & Brothers, 1960.

Mayer, George H., and Forster, Walter O. *The United States and the Twentieth Century.* Boston, Mass.: Houghton Mifflin Company, 1958.

Miller, William T. *The Progressive Movement in Missouri.* Columbus, Mo.: University of Missouri Press, 1928.

Mowry, George E. *The California Progressives.* Los Angeles, Calif.: University of California Press, 1951.

Myers, William Starr. *The Republican Party.* New York: Century Company, 1928.

Richberg, Donald. *My Hero: The Autobiography of Donald Richberg.* New York: G. P. Putnam's Sons, 1954.

Ring, Elizabeth. *The Progressive Movement of 1912 and Third Party Movement of 1924 in Maine.* Orono, Me.: University of Maine, 1933.

White, William A. *The Autobiography of William Allen White.* New York: Macmillan Co., 1946.

INTRODUCTION

For information about the youth of Gifford Pinchot, Box 1773 of the Gifford Pinchot Manuscripts is extremely valuable, largely because of annual outlines of Pinchot's activities until he entered Yale University. Pinchot's own *Breaking New Ground* (New York: Harcourt, Brace & Company, 1947) is helpful in understanding Pinchot's Yale days. For general material on Pinchot's ancestry, Editor Helene M. Hooker's introduction to Amos R. E. Pinchot's *The History of the Progressive Party, 1912–1916* (New York: New York University Press, 1958) is helpful. Jules Bertant, in *Paris, 1870–1935* (New York: Appleton-Century Co., Inc., 1936), presents the Paris background. Also consulted was the recent work by M. Nelson McGeary, *Gifford Pinchot: Forester-Politician* (Princeton, N.J.: Princeton University Press, 1960), although its recent date of publication precluded heavy reliance on it.

Breaking New Ground was used extensively in sections on

forestry and conservation activity. For balance the author relies on Andrew Denny Rodgers III, *Bernhard Edward Fernow: A Story of North American Forestry* (Princeton, N.J.: Princeton University Press, 1951). M. Nelson McGeary's book appeared too late for much utilization in the section. Also used for conservation activity were Theodore Roosevelt's *Theodore Roosevelt: An Autobiography* (New York: Charles Scribner's Sons, 1920); *A Century of Conservation, 1849–1947* (Washington, D.C.: Government Printing Office, 1950); and Gifford Pinchot's "How Conservation Began in the U.S.," *Agriculture History*, Vol. XI (1937). Helpful is Henry Steele Commager's *The American Mind* (New Haven, Conn.: Yale University Press, 1950).

For an ideological view of the Progressive movement and its relationship to other periods, the author examined closely Commager's *The American Mind;* Eric Goldman's *Rendezvous with Destiny* (New York: Vintage Books, Inc., 1956); Richard Hofstadter's *The Age of Reform* (New York: Alfred A. Knopf, Inc., 1955); Arthur S. Link's *Woodrow Wilson and the Progressive Era* (New York: Harper & Brothers, 1954); and George E. Mowry's *Theodore Roosevelt and the Progressive Movement* (Madison, Wis.: University of Wisconsin Press, 1946).

CHAPTER I

The significance of Pinchot's role in the writing of the Osawatomie speech is revealed by documents in Boxes 133 and 2078 of the Gifford Pinchot Manuscripts and in Box 8 of the Amos Pinchot Manuscripts. Of less help is the Pinchot Diary of 1910 in Box 3320 of the Gifford Pinchot Manuscripts. Touching upon the Osawatomie address are the following secondary sources: McGeary's *Gifford Pinchot: Forester-Politician;* Mowry's *Theodore Roosevelt and the Progressive Movement;* Russel B. Nye's *Midwestern Progressive Politics* (East Lansing, Mich.: Michigan State University Press, 1959); and Henry F. Pringle's *Theodore Roosevelt* (revised ed.; New York: Harcourt, Brace & Company, 1956). The speech is contained in Theodore Roosevelt, *The Works of*

Theodore Roosevelt (national ed.; 20 vols.; New York: Charles Scribner's Sons, 1926).

The Ballinger-Pinchot affair has, of course, been the subject of two books. Foremost and pro-Pinchot is Alpheus T. Mason's *Bureaucracy Convicts Itself* (New York: Viking Press, Inc., 1941). The first work on the affair was that of Rose M. Stahl, *The Ballinger-Pinchot Controversy* (Northampton, Mass.: Smith College, 1926). For pro-Ballinger accounts the author consulted Henry F. Pringle, *The Life and Times of William Howard Taft* (New York: Farrar and Rinehart, 1939) and Harold L. Ickes' article "Not Guilty: Richard A. Ballinger—An American Dreyfus," *Saturday Evening Post*, Vol. CCXII (May 25, 1940). Alpheus T. Mason, *Brandeis: A Free Man's Life* (New York: Viking Press, Inc., 1946) covers the affair. A competent general history of the period is Oscar T. Barck and Nelson M. Blake, *Since 1900* (3rd ed.; New York: Macmillan Co., 1959).

CHAPTER II

Most helpful in assessing reaction to Pinchot's dismissal are Boxes 120, 121, 130, 131, 133, 134, and 135 of the Gifford Pinchot Manuscripts. Pinchot's Diary of 1910, in Box 3320, is valuable, as is the *Washington Evening Star*. Pinchot's *Breaking New Ground* and, to a lesser degree, McGeary's *Gifford Pinchot: Forester-Politician* and Mowry's *Theodore Roosevelt and the Progressive Movement* touch upon the dismissal.

An understanding of Pinchot's political philosophy in 1910 is best gained through his little book *The Fight for Conservation* (New York: Doubleday & Company, Inc., 1910). A contemporary assessment of this book is found in the *Economic Bulletin*, Vol. III (December, 1910); the *Independent Magazine*, Vol. LXIX (September, 1910); and the *New York Times*, September 10, 1910. Primary sources helpful in understanding Pinchot's thought in the summer of 1910 are from Boxes 127, 129, 132, 133, 135, and 2078 in the Gifford Pinchot Manuscripts and from Box 8 of the Amos Pinchot Manuscripts. A good secondary source is McGeary's *Gifford Pinchot: Forester-Politician*.

The election of 1910 and Pinchot's role in it are best seen from materials in Boxes 111, 126, 133, 135, and 3320 of the Gifford Pinchot Manuscripts and in Box 8 of the Amos Pinchot Manuscripts. Very helpful are Mowry's *Theodore Roosevelt and the Progressive Movement* and, to a lesser degree, McGeary, *Gifford Pinchot: Forester-Politician;* Amos R. E. Pinchot, *The History of the Progressive Party, 1912–1916;* and Pringle, *The Life and Times of William Howard Taft* and *Theodore Roosevelt.* The New York political situation in 1910 is seen in Alden Hatch, *The Wadsworths of the Genesee* (Toronto: Longmans, Green & Co., 1959) and in Ray B. Smith (ed.), *History of the State of New York* (6 vols.; Syracuse, N.Y.: Syracuse Press, Inc., 1922), Vol. IV.

CHAPTER III

Principal primary source materials used for describing the formation of the league are from Boxes 128, 132, 135, 137, 142, 145, 147, and 148 of the Gifford Pinchot Manuscripts. Robert M. La Follette, *La Follette's Autobiography: A Personal Narrative of Political Experiences* (Madison, Wis.: Robert M. La Follette Company, 1913) served as a primary source. Good secondary sources are Belle C. and Fola La Follette, *Robert M. La Follette, 1855–1925* (2 vols.; New York: Macmillan Co., 1953); McGeary, *Gifford Pinchot: Forester-Politician;* Amos Pinchot, *The History of the Progressive Party, 1912–1916;* and Pringle, *The Life and Times of William Howard Taft.*

The material about the La Follette presidential candidacy is drawn from Boxes 139, 143, 146, 148, 149, and 176 of the Gifford Pinchot Manuscripts; from the Pinchot Diary of 1911 and 1912; and from Boxes 9, 10, and 11 of the Amos Pinchot Manuscripts. Useful here are Belle C. and Fola La Follette, *Robert M. La Follette, 1855–1925; La Follette's Autobiography: A Personal Narrative of Political Experiences;* McGeary, *Gifford Pinchot: Forester-Politician;* Mowry, *Theodore Roosevelt and the Progressive Movement;* and Amos Pinchot, *The History of the Progressive Party, 1912–1916.*

For information on the issues of 1910, Boxes 137, 139, 140, 142,

144, and 149 of the Gifford Pinchot Manuscripts were used. Primary source materials are also drawn from Boxes 9, 10, and 11 of the Amos Pinchot Manuscripts. Again used were Pringle, *The Life and Times of William Howard Taft* and *Theodore Roosevelt*. Mowry, *Theodore Roosevelt and the Progressive Movement* and Amos Pinchot, *The History of the Progressive Party, 1912–1916* were consulted.

To cover the Roosevelt candidacy the author drew from Boxes 139, 141, 142, 144, 146, 147, 152, 154, 156, 157, 196, and 2147 of the Gifford Pinchot Manuscripts; from the Gifford Pinchot Diary of 1911 and 1912; and from Boxes 4 and 10 of the Amos Pinchot Manuscripts. The *New York Times* was consulted, as was Elting E. Morison (ed.), *The Letters of Theodore Roosevelt* (8 vols.; Cambridge, Mass.: Harvard University Press, 1954), Vol. VII. The secondary sources used were Barck and Blake, *Since 1900;* Belle C. and Fola La Follette, *Robert M. La Follette, 1855–1925;* McGeary, *Gifford Pinchot: Forester-Politician;* Mowry, *Theodore Roosevelt and the Progressive Movement;* and Pringle, *Theodore Roosevelt.*

CHAPTER IV

Primary source material on the Roosevelt campaign for the 1912 presidential nomination is drawn largely from Boxes 151, 152, 153, 156, and 157 of the Gifford Pinchot Manuscripts and from Boxes 11 and 12 of the Amos Pinchot Manuscripts. Also used were Gifford Pinchot's 1912 Diary; the *New York Times;* and the *Washington Post.* A competent survey of the period is Barck and Blake, *Since 1900.* A more specialized analysis of the Roosevelt campaign for nomination is Mowry, *Theodore Roosevelt and the Progressive Movement.* Helpful are Harold Jacobs Howland, *Theodore Roosevelt and His Times* (New Haven, Conn.: Yale University Press, 1921); McGeary, *Gifford Pinchot: Forester-Politician;* Amos Pinchot, *The History of the Progressive Party, 1912–1916;* and Pringle, *Theodore Roosevelt* and *The Life and Times of William Howard Taft.*

On the formation of the Progressive Party, principal primary sources are the Gifford Pinchot Manuscripts, Boxes 151, 152, 156, 157, and 159, and Gifford Pinchot's 1912 Diary. Helpful, of course, are Oscar K. Davis, *Released for Publication* (New York: Houghton Mifflin Company, 1925); Howland, *Theodore Roosevelt and His Times;* Mowry, *Theodore Roosevelt and the Progressive Movement;* Amos Pinchot, *The History of the Progressive Party, 1912–1916;* and Pringle, *The Life and Times of William Howard Taft* and *Theodore Roosevelt.* John A. Garraty, *Right-Hand Man: The Life of George W. Perkins* (New York: Harper & Brothers, 1960) was consulted, although its recent date of publication precluded heavy reliance on it.

The 1912 campaign is drawn from the Gifford Pinchot Manuscripts, Boxes 150, 152, 2078, and 2147, and from the *Philadelphia North American.* Also used were Garraty, *Right-Hand Man: The Life of George W. Perkins;* Howland, *Theodore Roosevelt and His Times;* Link, *Woodrow Wilson and the Progressive Era, 1910–1917;* McGeary, *Gifford Pinchot: Forester-Politician;* Morison (ed.), *The Letters of Theodore Roosevelt,* Vol. VII; Mowry, *Theodore Roosevelt and the Progressive Movement;* and Pringle, *The Life and Times of William Howard Taft* and *Theodore Roosevelt.*

Gifford Pinchot's relation to the election is drawn principally from Boxes 152, 157, 164, 167, and 2078 of the Gifford Pinchot Manuscripts. Mowry, *Theodore Roosevelt and the Progressive Movement* was used as principal background material. The recent McGeary work, *Gifford Pinchot: Forester-Politician,* was also consulted.

CHAPTER V

For material on the status of the Progressive Party in 1913, the author drew most heavily from Boxes 152, 160, 162, 164, 166, and 2147 of the Gifford Pinchot Manuscripts and from Boxes 14 and 15 of the Amos Pinchot Manuscripts. Gifford Pinchot's 1913 Diary was also used. Principal secondary sources are Garraty,

Right-Hand Man: The Life of George W. Perkins; McGeary, *Gifford Pinchot: Forester-Politician;* Mowry, *Theodore Roosevelt and the Progressive Movement;* Amos Pinchot, *The History of the Progressive Party, 1912–1916;* and Pringle, *Theodore Roosevelt.* In discussing Progressive principles, the author used Boxes 165, 166, and 2147 of the Gifford Pinchot Manuscripts; Gifford Pinchot's 1913 Diary; and the material from Boxes 4, 14, 15, and 24 of the Amos Pinchot Manuscripts. Principal secondary sources used were Mowry, *Theodore Roosevelt and the Progressive Movement* and Amos Pinchot, *The History of the Progressive Party, 1912–1916.*

CHAPTER VI

Primary source material used in describing progressivism in Pennsylvania and Pinchot's relation to it comes largely from Boxes 160, 162, 164, 166, 167, 169, and 413A of the Gifford Pinchot Manuscripts and, to a lesser degree, from Gifford Pinchot's 1914 Diary. Excellent secondary sources are Walter Davenport, *Power and Glory: The Life of Boies Penrose* (New York: G. P. Putnam's Sons, 1931); Donald W. Disbrow, "The Progressive Movement in Philadelphia, 1910–1916" (unpublished Ph.D dissertation, University of Rochester, 1956); George F. Holmes (ed.), *The Story of the Progressive Movement in Pennsylvania* (Philadelphia, Pa.: Council of the Progressive League of Pennsylvania, 1913); and Joseph Lincoln Steffens, *The Shame of the Cities* (New York: McClure, Phillips, 1904). Also examined was William S. Vare, *My Forty Years in Politics* (Philadelphia, Pa.: Roland Swain Co., 1933). Excellent articles are Stanley Coben, "H. Mitchell Palmer and the Reorganization of the Democratic Party in Pennsylvania, 1910–1912," *Pennsylvania Magazine of History and Biography,* Vol. LXXXIV, No. 2 (April, 1960), and M. Nelson McGeary, "Gifford Pinchot's 1914 Campaign," *Pennsylvania Magazine of History and Biography,* Vol. LXXXI, No. 3 (July, 1957). Good general and background sources are Wayland F. Dunaway, *A History of Pennsylvania* (New York: Prentice-

Hall, Inc., 1948); McGeary, *Gifford Pinchot: Forester-Politician;* and Mowry, *Theodore Roosevelt and the Progressive Movement.* For discussion of Pinchot's becoming a United States senatorial candidate in 1914, the primary sources used were Boxes 171, 172, 173, 178, 180, 182, 413, and 413A of the Gifford Pinchot Manuscripts. Other useful primary sources are the *Philadelphia North American;* the *Philadelphia Public Ledger;* Box 15 of the Amos Pinchot Manuscripts; and Gifford Pinchot's 1914 Diary. Also consulted were Davenport, *Power and Glory: The Life of Boies Penrose;* McGeary, *Gifford Pinchot: Forester-Politician;* Amos Pinchot, *The History of the Progressive Party, 1912–1916;* and Vare, *My Forty Years in Politics.* Good background sources are Dunaway, *A History of Pennsylvania* and Mowry, *Theodore Roosevelt and the Progressive Movement.*

CHAPTER VII

For the discussion of issues in the 1914 United States senatorial campaign in Pennsylvania, the author drew largely from the Gifford Pinchot Manuscripts, Boxes 171, 173, 174, 178, 179, 180, 181, and 183. Also important is Gifford Pinchot, *Platform of Gifford Pinchot* (Philadelphia, Pa.: Allied Printing Trades Council, 1914). The *Philadelphia North American* was utilized. Excellent background material is found in Barck and Blake, *Since 1900;* Davenport, *Power and Glory: The Life of Boies Penrose;* McGeary, *Gifford Pinchot: Forester-Politician;* and Mowry, *Theodore Roosevelt and the Progressive Movement.*

In the discussion of the 1914 Pennsylvania senatorial campaign, original sources come mostly from Boxes 171, 172, 173, 174, 175, 179, and 413A of the Gifford Pinchot Manuscripts. Boxes 17 and 18 from the Amos Pinchot Manuscripts were also used. The *New York Tribune* and the *Philadelphia North American* were analyzed. Important secondary sources are Robert D. Bowden, *Boies Penrose, Symbol of an Era* (New York: McLeod, Ltd., 1937); Davenport, *Power and Glory: The Life of Boies Penrose;* Dunaway, *A History of Pennsylvania;* and Vare, *My Forty Years in*

Politics. The following articles were also used: Coben, "H. Mitchell Palmer and the Reorganization of the Democratic Party in Pennsylvania, 1910–1912," *Pennsylvania Magazine of History and Biography,* Vol. LXXXIV, No. 2 (April, 1960), and McGeary, "Gifford Pinchot's 1914 Campaign," *Pennsylvania Magazine of History and Biography,* Vol. LXXXI, No. 3 (July, 1957). Garraty, *Right-Hand Man: The Life of George W. Perkins* was consulted.

The discussion of Pinchot's defeat in 1914 is drawn largely from the Gifford Pinchot Manuscripts, Boxes 171, 174, 176, 179, 183, and 407. Materials in Boxes 17 and 18 of the Amos Pinchot Manuscripts were used. The *Philadelphia North American* was consulted, as were Dunaway, *A History of Pennsylvania* and Mowry, *Theodore Roosevelt and the Progressive Movement.*

CHAPTER VIII

Principal sources examined for understanding the impact of World War I on progressivism in 1915 were Boxes 186, 188, 190, and 2078 of the Gifford Pinchot Manuscripts. Also examined were Box 21 of the Amos Pinchot Manuscripts and the *New York Times.* Principal secondary sources are Barck and Blake, *Since 1900;* Belle C. and Fola La Follette, *Robert M. La Follette, 1855–1925;* Link, *Woodrow Wilson and the Progressive Era;* McGeary, *Gifford Pinchot: Forester-Politician;* Mowry, *Theodore Roosevelt and the Progressive Movement;* and Pringle, *Theodore Roosevelt.*

For information about the national Progressive Party in 1915, Boxes 185, 186, 187, 188, 189, and 190 of the Gifford Pinchot Manuscripts were used. The Amos Pinchot Manuscripts, Boxes 17, 19, 20, and 21, were examined. The *New York Times* and the *Philadelphia North American* were also used. Principal secondary sources used were Claude G. Bowers, *Beveridge and the Progressive Era* (Boston: Houghton Mifflin Company, 1932); Belle C. and Fola La Follette, *Robert M. La Follette, 1855–1925;* McGeary, *Gifford Pinchot: Forester-Politician;* and Mowry, *Theodore Roosevelt and the Progressive Movement.* Garraty, *Right-Hand Man: The Life of George W. Perkins* was also consulted.

The material for the latter part of the chapter, dealing with the Washington Party in 1915, comes largely from Boxes 185, 186, 187, 189, 2078, and 2148 of the Gifford Pinchot Manuscripts. The *Philadelphia Public Ledger* was examined. Principal secondary sources are Disbrow, "The Progressive Movement in Philadelphia, 1910–1916"; Dunaway, *A History of Pennsylvania;* Mowry, *Theodore Roosevelt and the Progressive Movement;* and, to a lesser degree, McGeary, *Gifford Pinchot: Forester-Politician.*

CHAPTER IX

The first half of the chapter, dealing with preconvention progressivism, is drawn primarily from the Gifford Pinchot Manuscripts, Boxes 188, 191, 193, 194, 196, and 198, and from the Amos Pinchot Manuscripts, Box 26. Principal secondary sources used were Barck and Blake, *Since 1900;* McGeary, *Gifford Pinchot: Forester-Politician;* Mowry, *Theodore Roosevelt and the Progressive Movement;* Amos Pinchot, *The History of the Progressive Party, 1912–1916;* and Pringle, *Theodore Roosevelt.* An excellent article is Harold L. Ickes, "Who Killed the Progressive Party?" *American Historical Review,* Vol. XLVI, No. 2 (January, 1941). Garraty, *Right-Hand Man: The Life of George W. Perkins* was consulted.

The second half of this chapter, dealing with the Progressive and Republican conventions, is based on material coming largely from Boxes 192, 193, 194, 196, 198, and 1996 of the Gifford Pinchot Manuscripts. Box 25 of the Amos Pinchot Manuscripts was also used. Another primary source is Morison (ed.), *The Letters of Theodore Roosevelt,* Vol. VII. Important secondary sources examined were Davis, *Released for Publication;* Garraty, *Right-Hand Man: The Life of George W. Perkins;* Howland, *Theodore Roosevelt and His Times;* William Draper Lewis, *The Life of Theodore Roosevelt* (Philadelphia, Pa.: John C. Winston Co., 1919), Link, *Woodrow Wilson and the Progressive Era;* Mowry, *Theodore Roosevelt and the Progressive Movement;* and Amos Pinchot, *The History of the Progressive Party, 1912–1916.*

CHAPTER X

The first half of the chapter, describing Pinchot's campaigning for Charles E. Hughes in 1916, is based on materials coming largely from Boxes 169, 194, 196, 407, 414, and 2148 of the Gifford Pinchot Manuscripts. Boxes 25 and 26 of the Amos Pinchot Manuscripts were also used. Secondary sources used extensively were Barck and Blake, *Since 1900;* Bowers, *Beveridge and the Progressive Era;* Ickes, "Who Killed the Progressive Party?" *American Historical Review,* Vol. XLVI, No. 2 (January, 1941); Link, *Woodrow Wilson and the Progressive Era;* McGeary, *Gifford Pinchot: Forester-Politician;* Mowry, *Theodore Roosevelt and the Progressive Movement;* and Pringle, *Theodore Roosevelt.* Garraty, *Right-Hand Man: The Life of George W. Perkins* was also consulted.

The second half of the chapter, dealing with the final days of the Progressive Party, and the book's conclusion, is based on original sources from Boxes 194, 202, 1947, and 1996 of the Gifford Pinchot Manuscripts. Boxes 25 and 26 of the Amos Pinchot Manuscripts are drawn from. Secondary sources used were Barck and Blake, *Since 1900;* Bowers, *Beveridge and the Progressive Era;* Hofstadter, *The Age of Reform;* Link, *Woodrow Wilson and the Progressive Era;* Mowry, *Theodore Roosevelt and the Progressive Movement;* Pringle, *Theodore Roosevelt;* and, to a lesser degree, Garraty, *Right-Hand Man: The Life of George W. Perkins* and McGeary, *Gifford Pinchot: Forester-Politician.*

Index